D1741074

Portraits of Everyday Literacy for Social Justice

"Utterly compelling, this book enlists us to contemplation, action, and tough realizations surrounding the intertwining of economics and literacy. Susan Jones eloquently reframes long-standing debates in ways sure to engage those who believe literacy to be a fundamental human right."

—Shirley Brice Heath, *Stanford University, USA*

"This book, beautifully written and crafted, is an urgent call to researchers working at the cutting edge of literacy studies to listen to the lived experience of people who experience austerity. Literacy research that values the everyday is needed more than ever in order to address key issues of power, social justice and inequality. The book provides a clear account of everyday literacies of families living on a housing estate in the UK. This book exposes the mechanisms by which so many people have been blamed for policies not of their making, and creates a space where engaged literacy research takes centre stage to articulate and challenge these injustices. A riveting and powerfully articulated 'must read' for all literacy researchers that explores new paradigms for new times to move the field of literacy studies forward."

—Kate Pahl, *Manchester Metropolitan University, UK*

"This is a timely and hugely engaging book; it is a rich ethnographic study with a central focus on the ways in which literacy and inequality are bound together … It is through the sharp lens of literacy that the pages unpick the critical and interconnected challenges it presents in relation to social justice. We enter a community that that has been marginalised in so many ways and where austerity is more than a political discourse—it is biting hard. Importantly, the critical discussion opens up to how we can work towards frameworks that offer resistance and challenge inequality in contemporary Britain and beyond."

—Vicky Duckworth, *Edge Hill University, UK*

Susan Jones

Portraits of Everyday Literacy for Social Justice

Reframing the Debate for Families and Communities

Susan Jones
School of Education
University of Nottingham
Nottingham, UK

ISBN 978-3-319-75944-9   ISBN 978-3-319-75945-6   (eBook)
https://doi.org/10.1007/978-3-319-75945-6

Library of Congress Control Number: 2018935296

Cover illustration: Astronaut Images / Getty

Printed on acid-free paper

This Palgrave Macmillan imprint is published by the registered company Springer International Publishing AG part of Springer Nature.
The registered company address is: Gewerbestrasse 11, 6330 Cham, Switzerland

This book is dedicated to the families who have made it possible.

Preface

This book brings together an increasing focus in public, political, and academic discussion on the impact of socioeconomic policy on everyday lives, exploring these alongside key developments in the field of literacy studies over recent decades. It comes at a time when, as Danny Dorling (2015, p. 1) notes, "[g]rowing income or wealth inequality is recognised as the greatest social threat of our times". Commentators have described contemporary Britain as amongst the most unequal of societies (including Savage 2015; Wilkinson and Pickett 2010), emphasising also that economic inequality is deeply entwined with other factors which affect everyday lives and compound the marginalisation of individuals, families, and communities. The Office for National Statistics (2016) tells us that one in three people living in the UK have experienced poverty in recent times. Not all of these people are in persistent poverty, but many are facing the challenges posed by low pay and precarious incomes and are living at high risk of hardship because of these factors. In 2016, 3.9 million people were believed to be living in persistent poverty in the UK. Those living in a single-person household, both with and without children, those over 65, and those leaving school without formal qualifications are more likely to experience poverty, and to do so for longer periods. The intersection of inequalities is evident in the fact that recent policy reform in the UK has affected women and BME households disproportionately (Hall et al. 2017).

As Jeremy Seabrook (2013) notes, however, "the novelty of these specifics depends upon our readiness to forget the past" (p. 37). Debates about the impact of socioeconomic policy on everyday lives have a long history and are not confined to recent concerns about the consequences of the deeply ideological policies that have been framed by politicians using the seemingly neutral notion of "austerity". The place of literacy has been a consistent theme within these debates.

This book draws upon these long-standing debates, bringing a picture of everyday lives in contemporary Britain, shaped by the politics of "austerity", together with ideas from the field of literacy studies which have centred on broadening our understanding of what it means to be literate. A strong tradition based on ethnographic research in communities has acknowledged the impact of dominant discourses around literacy on lived experience, and this has increased recognition of the rich and complex ways in which we interact with texts as part of everyday lives. Recent paradigms in literacy research have explored literacy as plural and multifaceted: as social, multimodal, digital, material, spatial, and affective. The affordances of literacy according to each of these paradigms, and the history of literacy research represented by them, emphasise the plethora of ways in which literacy is drawn upon to make and share meanings in our everyday lives. It suggests too that literacy can be a helpful lens through which to explore what happens in everyday lives, and the relationship between everyday lives and wider contexts.

Alongside a socio-political context where everyday lives are increasingly *constricted*, therefore, prominent themes in literacy research recognise its central role in the way everyday lives are *constructed* (Jones 2014, 2016). In bringing together these two areas of focus, this book examines the ways in which literacy and inequality are closely linked. Both are regular sources of moral panic, in the UK and across international contexts, and both have formed the basis for social policy across successive governments worldwide. Both are used as measures of nations and as a basis for judging communities, families, and individuals. Often, "low" literacy has been seen as a cause of poverty and quantitative measures of disadvantage are used to make connections between literacy learning and social inclusion (Bynner 2014; McCoy 2013; Centre for Literacy 2012; Kellett and Dar 2007). However, other social and literacy research have argued that some long-standing attitudes towards social inclusion, in reality, serve to further exclude those already marginalised by social and economic challenge, creating further barriers when it comes to literacy learning (e.g. Lister 2004; Duckworth 2014; Hamilton 2014). As will be shown in the portraits of everyday life featured in this book, contemporary neoliberal policy contexts pose acute and interrelated challenges to social justice as viewed through the lens of literacy. Two particular challenges are the increased narrowing of what counts as literacy in educational and social policy and, related to this, the role of literacy in the enactment of policies that have led to the most challenging economic conditions seen in generations. The threat to justice that is experienced by the families featured in this book, and many others like them, as a result of these challenges means there is an immediate need to revisit the links between literacy, inequality, and social justice. This should not be confined to the specifics of the present, however. In bringing together the broad understanding of literacy that has been developed over many decades alongside an articulation of social justice which theoretically frames its complex dimensions, this book aims to disrupt the long and tenacious history of the discourses underpinning these particular policies.

These discourses have fundamentally shaped how everyday lives are viewed, as well as the role of literacy within them. Brian Street (2011, p. 580) identifies a key struggle in the debate on literacy and inequality to be over "the power to name and define". Any discussion of literacy, inequality, and social justice therefore needs to consider not only who gets to say what is unequal but also what we understand by "literacy". This book offers a theoretical analysis of the relationship between *how we see* literacy, and the implications of this for social justice, and for change.

References

Bynner, J. (2014) *The impact of adult literacy and numeracy based on the 1970 British Cohort Study.* London: Centre for Longitudinal Studies

Centre for Literacy (2012) 'Literacy Learning and Poverty Using IALS data on Earnings', *Canadian Literacy and Learning Network*

Dorling, D. (2015) *Inequality and the 1%*. London: Verso

Hall, S., McIntosh, K., Neitzert, E., Pottinger, K.S., Stephenson, M-A., Reed, H. and Taylor, L. (2017) *Intersecting Inequalities: The impact of austerity on Black and Minority Ethnic Women in the UK*, Report by the Women's Budget Group and Runnymede Trust with RECLAIM and Coventry Women's Voices

Hamilton, M. (2014) 'Global, regional and local influences on adult literacy policy in England', *Globalisation, Society and Education,* 12 (1) 110–126

Jones, S. (2014) '"How people read and write and they don't even notice": everyday lives and literacies on a Midlands council estate', *Literacy*, 48 (2) 59–65

Jones, S. (2016) 'Constricting or constructing everyday lives? Literacies and inequality' in Parry, B., Burnett, C. and Merchant, G (eds.) *Literacy, Media and Technology: Past, Present and Future*. London: Bloomsbury, pp. 63–77

Kellett, M. and Dar, A. (2007) *Children researching links between poverty and literacy*. York: Joseph Rowntree Foundation

Lister, R. (2004) *Poverty*. Cambridge: Polity Press

McCoy, E. (2013) 'Lost for words: Poor literacy, the hidden issue in Child Poverty', London: National Literacy Trust

Office for National Statistics (2016) 'Persistent poverty in the UK and EU: 2014', https://www.ons.gov.uk/peoplepopulationandcommunity/personalandhouseholdfinances/incomeandwealth/articles/persistentpovertyintheukandeu/2014 (accessed November 19, 2017)

Savage, M. (2015) *Social Class in the 21st Century*. London: Pelican Books

Seabrook, J. (2013) *Pauperland: Poverty and the Poor in Britain*. London: Hurst

Street, B. (2011) 'Literacy inequalities in theory and practice: The power to name and define', *International Journal of Educational Development*, 31, 580–586

Wilkinson, R. and Pickett, K. (2010) *The Spirit Level: Why Equality is Better for Everyone*. London: Penguin

Acknowledgements

I am hugely grateful to the families with whom I worked on the study that has informed this book for their generosity in allowing me to spend time with them in their homes and for sharing their everyday experiences with me.

The study was funded in part by a Small Research Grant from the British Academy, and I am indebted to their support of the ethnographic research which has informed this book.

Friends and colleagues at the School of Education, University of Nottingham, have provided enormous amounts of moral and practical support, by valuing the research, having faith in me to write the book, and providing feedback and suggestions as it developed. In particular, I would like to acknowledge the unremitting support and guidance of Christine Hall over many years, including her encouragement of me to undertake the research project and to pursue the stories that emerged as a book, as well as her comments on the manuscript.

I was thrilled to be awarded the UKLA/Wiley-Blackwell Research in Literacy Award 2015 for a journal article in *Literacy* that was based on the research featured in this book.[1] I am grateful to the reviewers and to the award panel for their feedback. Elements of Chap. 4, "The Local Library: Literacy and Capital"; Chap. 6, "A Portrait of Family Literacy"; and Chap. 7, "Material Literacies: Writing Home", have grown from this paper, and a chapter published by Bloomsbury in a book edited by Cathy

Burnett, Becky Parry, and Guy Merchant.[2] Cathy and Julia Davies, as editors of *Literacy*, and since as colleagues at UKLA, have been generous in their support. Thanks to Eleanor Christie, Becky Wyde, and their colleagues at Palgrave for their support with the publication of this book and to the reviewers for the insightful comments which have helped to shape it.

And finally, all my love to Jev, Joe, and my family. For everything, every day.

Notes

1. Jones, S. (2014) '"How people read and write and they don't even notice": Everyday lives and literacies on a Midlands council estate', *Literacy*, 48 (2) 59–65.
2. Jones, S. (2016) 'Constricting or constructing everyday lives? Literacies and inequality' in Parry, B., Burnett, C. and Merchant, G (eds.) *Literacy, Media and Technology: Past, Present and Future*. London: Bloomsbury, pp. 63–77.

Contents

List of Figures

1

Everyday Literacy in the Frame

Fig. 1.1 Peggy's framed wedding photograph on her mantelpiece

© The Author(s) 2018

S. Jones, *Portraits of Everyday Literacy for Social Justice*,
https://doi.org/10.1007/978-3-319-75945-6_1

This is my wedding photograph. We were married on the eighteenth of November 1972. This photo is important to me because it was my 25th wedding anniversary and my sister brought me the frame. That's the only wedding photo I've got that I can find at the moment.

  Peggy

Peggy's description of her wedding photograph (Fig. 1.1) comes from a tour she gave me of her new home, a one-bedroom flat in which she lives alone. She moved here after living for 33 years in the three-bedroom house where she had raised her three children.

Upon moving, Peggy was faced with many decisions about what she would take with her and where she would put it. Amongst the items on display in her new flat are framed photographs of her family: her husband, her mother, father, brothers and sister, nephews and nieces, her three children, her grandchildren and newborn great-grandchildren. These form part of what Peggy calls her "special things": the things she has carefully selected to take with her to her new home.

I've been very harsh with myself but there are some things I'll never part with even though I ain't got room to put them in.

In a corner of her living room, Peggy has a cabinet, the top half of which has a glass door through which ornaments are displayed. This is where Peggy keeps her special things. These include items of china, which feature Queen Elizabeth II, bought for her by her mother "because I was born in 1952", the year of the queen's accession to the throne. There is a champagne flute bought for her by her granddaughters on the occasion of her 60th birthday. Sitting in a teacup in this cabinet is a tiny teddy bear, and Peggy reaches for this in order to tell me its story:

This teddy bear here was the last thing my husband ever bought me. He died nine years ago. When I went to see him in hospital, he'd got this teddy bear sticking out his pocket and he says, "I bought it especially for you". So I keep that on show.

Moving and settling into a new house has focused Peggy's mind on what things mean: what they mean *to* her, and what she would like them to mean *about* her. Having her things "on show" is a way for Peggy to curate her life experience, and the feelings of pride, joy, love, and loss that have come with it. Her new flat provides a frame within which we are able to see Peggy's life as she wants to present it.

The move to her new flat was not something Peggy had planned. Six months before her move, during a visit to Peggy's house for our discussions about reading and writing in her everyday life, she explained:

> In April, they'll charge you for the two bedrooms that you're not using – it's called a 'bedroom tax' – and I said to [my daughter], "I can't afford to live here".

The policy referred to by Peggy was part of a raft of reform to welfare services introduced by the government that came to power in the UK in 2010. Officially known as the "under-occupation penalty", the policy was aimed at tenants of social housing "whose accommodation is larger than they need" (Department for Work and Pensions 2013). As of April 1st 2013, the policy cut the housing benefit of those affected by up to 25%. As Moussa Haddad (2012, p. 32) has pointed out, at the time of the policy's announcement, the number of social housing tenants deemed to be "under-occupying" was three times greater than the number of homes available for them to move into, "thus making the penalty essentially punitive". Public discourse quickly saw this policy dubbed "the bedroom tax", and, as Mary O'Hara notes (2015, p. 61), it "quickly became an emblematic symbol of the government's cuts programme, provoking a blend of bafflement and fury" that triggered protests across the UK, "including outside and inside Parliament" (ibid.).

Peggy was one of the many affected by this welfare policy, forced by their circumstances to find somewhere new to live. Our meetings over subsequent weeks included Peggy's updates on this process, and over the course of the next few months, as she prepared to move to her new flat, Peggy shared her feelings about the move.

> I'm a bit unsure about moving because it's the memories in the house […]
> Me and [my husband] and the kids growing up and that.

These are the memories which Peggy worked to capture and display in her new home, in response to the circumstances in which she was placed by government policy.

There is more of Peggy's story in Chap. 7, including how recent paradigms in literacy research can help us to understand the creative and resourceful approaches to meaning making which are part of everyday responses to wider contexts. Peggy's is one of a series of portraits of literacy in the everyday lives of participants who took part in an ethnographic research[1] project which looked at the literacy practices of residents living on a predominantly white working class council housing estate on the edge of a Midlands city. Drawing on the individual portrait presented in each chapter, there is a focus on a different way in which literacy can be viewed. This ranges from the ways in which literacy is imagined within official institutions, including schools and local authority welfare provision, as a measurable and individual skillset, through to the multifaceted ways of understanding literacy that have emerged in more recent years, including the role of the material artefacts in how we make meanings and communicate these to each other, as we have seen in Peggy's experience of moving house.

By looking at the role played by literacy in everyday experiences, and examining insights from across four decades in the field of literacy studies, the book explicitly positions literacy as a helpful lens to explore issues of social justice. This is part of a long-standing agenda within the field of literacy studies which has followed on from the call by Street (1993, p. 2) for "bold theoretical models that recognise the central role of power relations in literacy practices", and work which has explicitly foregrounded the question of power in relation to literacy (Collins and Blot 2003). The particularly acute challenges posed by the specific context of the socio-economic policies of "austerity", and the continued mandating of narrowed models of literacy, mean that there remains an acute need to articulate the multifaceted role of literacy in social justice. The role of literacy in the increasing *constriction* of everyday lives, through a restricted view of what counts as reading and writing in policy, and in the systems through which it is enacted, is seen in examples throughout the book and described in more detail in Chaps. 3 and 4. Alongside this, the lens of literacy can also be useful to illustrate its role in *constructing* everyday lives, as a resource in the often creative, resourceful, and collaborative responses to wider contexts which are part of everyday life. The portraits in Chaps. 5, 6, and 7 offer a direct challenge to the cycle of reductive stereotyping which has been used to justify "austerity" policies and which has echoes across time to Victorian notions of the undeserving poor.

This chapter began with Peggy's description of her most treasured photo frame. The frame is a key concept that runs throughout the book, and I move now to focus on its centrality to the link between literacy and justice. I am drawing here on the work of Nancy Fraser, who sees "the question of the frame as the central question of justice in a globalizing world" (2010, p. 29). The frame is a fundamental element of Fraser's three-dimensional model of justice. This model reminds us of the need to consider the complex intertwining of forces in everyday life. It is therefore a useful framework through which to examine literacy practice as part of that complex intertwining.

Nancy Fraser: A Three-Dimensional Framework for Justice

Fraser's work on justice is based on what she describes as significant "folk paradigms" of fairness (Fraser 2003a, p. 11). The first is that of *socioeconomic injustice*. This, according to Fraser, includes:

> exploitation (having the fruits of one's labour appropriated for the benefit of others); economic marginalisation (being confined to undesirable and poorly paid work or being denied access to income-generating labour altogether), and deprivation (being denied an adequate material standard of living). (1997, p. 13)

This paradigm of justice draws on egalitarian principles where justice involves *redistribution* of resources, goods, or capabilities.

The second dimension is *cultural, or symbolic, injustice*. For Fraser, this includes:

> cultural domination (being subjected to patterns of interpretation and communication that are associated with another culture and are alien and/ or hostile to one's own); nonrecognition (being rendered invisible via the authoritative representational, communicative, and interpretative practices of one's culture); and disrespect (being routinely maligned or disparaged in stereotypic public cultural representations and/or in everyday life interactions). (ibid., p. 14)

The need for *recognition* has been a key focus for those working across many different communities to challenge injustices based on factors such as gender, sexuality, race, or social class.

However, Fraser challenges activists and critical theorists who have historically argued that justice relates specifically and exclusively to either issues of economic inequality, or to cultural identity. She argues that:

> [f]ar from occupying two airtight spheres, economic injustice and cultural injustice are usually interimbricated so as to reinforce one another dialectically. Cultural norms that are unfairly biased against some are institutionalised in the state and the economy; meanwhile, economic disadvantage impedes equal participation in the making of culture, in public spheres and in everyday life. The result is often a vicious circle of cultural and economic subordination. (ibid., p. 15)

That these two dimensions of justice are "co-fundamental and mutually irreducible" (Fraser and Honneth 2003, p. 3) is evident in the ways in which dominant discourses of deficit continue to be used to justify social policy reform, leading to the further marginalisation of those already finding it hardest to get by. The policy that led to Peggy moving home, for instance, is an example of the ways in which a lack of recognition of the lived realities of people's lives has an impact on their economic well-being. Examples throughout this book illustrate this within the everyday lives of research participants and other community members.

Both maldistribution and misrecognition can contribute to what Fraser views as the central issue in relation to justice: "parity of participation". This is vital, she argues, given that "justice requires social arrangements that permit all (adult) members of a society to interact with one another as peers" (Fraser 2003b, p. 36). For this to be possible requires appropriate distribution of material resources so as "to ensure participants independence and 'voice'". Also required are "patterns of cultural value that express equal respect for all participants and ensure equal opportunity for achieving social esteem" (ibid.) Fraser emphasises that she sees both conditions as necessary for parity of participation; "neither alone is sufficient" (ibid.). Hence, justice is based upon "a common normative standard for both of these dimensions, ruling social arrangements and institutions out of bounds when they violate either condition of parity" (Olson 2008, p. 248).

Participation in society can take an economic form, as a worker or an employer, as well as a consumer. Cultural participation "means being an actor in constructing meanings, images, and representations through which we understand our common world" (ibid.). Again, however, dividing up these aspects of justice reduces Fraser's emphasis on participation as being fundamentally about *all* aspects of social life and "the equal autonomy and moral worth of human beings" (Fraser 2003a, p. 232). Neither is this solely about individual freedom and choice. Participation often requires working with others "actively involved in some co-operative endeavour" (Olson 2008, p. 252).

The political nature of participation is emphasised by Fraser. We might think, for example, of instances of injustice which derive from economic issues, such as low wages. Those in receipt of low wages may well also be subject to cultural injustice, which allows the payment of low wages to perpetuate. The marginalisation of migrant workers might be an example here. Both instances of injustice feed into and explain each other, but their interrelated nature works also to compound injustice by leading to unequal participation. Low wages can mean fewer resources through which individuals are able to participate in society. Stigmatisation can lead to the feeling of a lack of political agency, compounding the injustice faced by marginalised groups who can often be excluded from political participation: they might find it hard to see how voting can make a difference to their circumstances, for example.

A paradox exists at the heart of this model of justice, however, which Fraser acknowledges.

> There is an unavoidable circularity in this account: claims for recognition can only be justified under conditions of participatory parity, which conditions include reciprocal recognition. (2003b, p. 44)

Central to "the paradox of enablement" (Olson 2008, p. 261) is the fact that those affected by injustice are amongst the least able to challenge it on its own terms, because of the effect it has on marginalising voice and reducing resources for agency. Solutions to addressing the issues raised by economic and cultural injustice therefore require "dismantling institutionalised obstacles that prevent some people from participating on a par with others as full partners in social interaction" (Fraser 2010, p. 16). To do so requires active attention to a third dimension of justice: the political dimension.

Once again interrelated with the first two dimensions discussed, the political dimension of justice, according to Fraser, "furnishes the stage on which struggles over distribution and recognition are played out" (ibid., p. 17). It "tells us who is included in, and who excluded from, the circle of those entitled to a just distribution and reciprocal recognition" (ibid.). The defining issue of the political element of justice is *representation*. Injustice can involve at least two levels of misrepresentation. The first, "ordinary-political misrepresentation", is tied up with political systems such as the first-past-the-post electoral system, which can deny parity to numerical minorities. The more substantial focus of Fraser's discussion, and the most relevant to the themes of this book, however, concerns "the boundary-setting aspect of the political". This leads to a deeper form of misrepresentation, which she calls "misframing" (p. 19).

Focusing on the Frame

"The question of the frame" is, for Fraser, "a question of justice" (2010, p. 21). It focuses us on the question of "the 'who'" (p. 22) of justice, bringing into relief the ways in which economic, cultural, and representative injustices are the result of political processes which shape lived experiences of social interaction. To be framed by dominant discourse, policy, and political structures is to be either included within or excluded from boundaries that define opportunities to participate in politically authorised social interaction. In relation to the focus of this book, for example, in the field of literacy studies, it has been long argued that some ways of understanding what it means to read and write have been privileged over others. Dominant ways of framing literacy are mandated in education and other policy, leading to people being framed as 'literate' (or not). As such, the setting of the frame "is among the most consequential of political decisions":

> Constituting both members and non-members in a single stroke, this decision effectively excludes the latter from the universe of those entitled to consideration within the community in matters of distribution, recognition, and ordinary-political representation. (ibid., p. 19)

The question of the frame is therefore central to any notion of justice. This is not least because paradigms of justice are themselves framed; they are constructed ideas which are afforded dominance, or otherwise (Fraser 2003b). The notion of framing sits alongside redistribution and recognition as part of a three-dimensional theory of justice. As Fraser has argued:

> no claim for justice can avoid presupposing some notion of representation, implicit or explicit, insofar as none can avoid assuming a frame. Thus, representation is always already inherent in claims for redistribution and recognition. (2010, p. 21)

The "struggle" (ibid.) against maldistribution and misrecognition needs to grasp firmly the question of the frame. This is a challenge taken up by this book.

As well as focusing on the frame, this book also takes up a further challenge posed by Fraser. It locates literacy education and research at the heart of work towards social justice. This involves more than developing knowledge and understanding of the framing of literacy by various forces. As will be shown in upcoming chapters, much research in the field of literacy has acknowledged the limitations of reductive frames which do not recognise the rich variety of communicative resources drawn upon in everyday lives. The challenge lies in the way in which this research has been taken up in practice. For example, it has been acknowledged that mandated pedagogic models of literacy can serve to further marginalise non-dominant voices and reduce the experience of engaging with literacy in schools and colleges to a set of skills which can be measured (e.g. Hamilton 2014; Comber 2016). The injustices which derive from this framing of literacy are both economic and cultural: they reduce equality of opportunity for those failed by a system which actively marginalises them and silences their voices. However, not content simply to treat problems in the form in which they are given within the established frame, Fraser calls on us to make the frame itself the focus of attention and potential reconstruction. This means a "transformative politics of framing" which "aims to change the deep grammar of frame-setting" (2010, p. 23). To truly disrupt such injustices, therefore, an approach is needed which does more than challenge the current frame while leaving intact the workings of the framing process. This approach would lead "to changing not just the boundaries of the 'who' of justice, but also the mode of their construction" (ibid., p. 24). According to Fraser, such an approach moves our focus from the "what" and the "who" to the "how" of justice. Those involved in literacy research and education are in a prime position to take up this challenge. This is what I aim to do in this book.

How This Book Is Framed

Bringing together key paradigms of justice, including economic redistribution and the recognition of diverse cultural resources, Fraser's model of justice is directly relatable to the experience of residents on the estate, who, like many others across the UK and further afield, are finding it hard to make ends meet in an economic climate that has seen the most dramatic cuts to welfare and public spending for several decades. Policies such as the "bedroom tax", which directly affected Peggy, as we have already seen, are justified through pernicious discourse which sees places such as the estate on which she lived regularly represented in the media as deficient, welfare-oriented, low in educational attainment and aspiration.

Such discourse ignores the resilience, resourcefulness, and creativity that is evident in everyday practice.

Fraser's third dimension—the frame—as the central question of justice is the central theme underpinning this book. Attention to the framing of literacy, both as a prominent theme in policy discourse and as a central feature of everyday life, offers insight into its place in both constricting and constructing everyday lives. Using literacy as a lens, each chapter presents a portrait of a different aspect of everyday life on the estate, from public life and the library to the experiences of families and community groups. Each of these aspects of life is linked to a particular way in which literacy can be framed. The impact of framing literacy in this way is considered, including access to resources, both economic and cultural, and the recognition of the richly diverse cultural assets that are drawn upon in the negotiation of everyday life.

By using Nancy Fraser's three-dimensional theory of justice, this book positions literacy research as ultimately political. Literacy has long been associated in policy and practice with economic inequality, and literacy education is frequently framed as being central to addressing issues of unequal distribution. Literacy research has also made a consistent case for the role of a wide range of cultural and symbolic resources in the negotiation of lived experience, and the agency and voice of individuals and communities. The regular struggles over the framing of literacy and its impact on learners' lives also remind us of the fact that it is a site of contestation based on dominant, policy-driven frame-setting. Following a focus on the everyday lives of participant families through the lens of literacy, the book concludes by considering the ways in which the field of literacy is positioned to take up the challenge of transformative justice.

Chapter Outline

Chapter 2—Finding Perspective: Researching Everyday Literacy Practices

This chapter argues that the dynamic complexity of everyday literacy practices is most appropriately observed through ethnographic methods which allow us to observe and describe the connections between the local and the global in everyday practice. The chapter describes the process of research and the ways in which key concepts have been framed within the book. It explains how finding a perspective for the book included consideration of the ethical issues involved in writing it, in telling stories of other people's lives. The chapter introduces the portrait as a way of presenting the experiences of participants within the book, and positioning them in relation to literacy for social justice.

Chapter 3—Literacy on "The Forgotten Estate": What They Haven't Got?

This chapter presents a portrait of the estate as a location for the research that informs the book. Through a focus on the welfare provision and philanthropic investment that is a feature of literacy in the public life of the estate, the chapter explores how this reflects a wider discourse which frames estates, and the communities who live on them, as deficient in skills and knowledge, and in need of state intervention as a result. Drawing on a long history of research in the field of literacy studies which challenges a model of literacy as something people "have" (or not), this instrumental view of its role in everyday lives is examined, along with the implications of this model for social justice.

Chapter 4—The Local Library: Literacy and Capital

This chapter focuses on the library as a community hub upon which many residents depend, yet which has had to respond to wider funding cuts. The role of digital texts in contemporary everyday lives underlines the importance of socially just, publicly funded support for access to text-based resources. Focusing on the place of text in how well people are not only able to get by, but also get on, this chapter explores the framing of literacy as capital. This illustrates the privileging of a narrow model of literacy and its role in everyday lives, and the resulting cost to social justice. The chapter also acknowledges the potential of the library as a public space where the complex experiences of everyday life may be collaboratively navigated.

Chapter 5—Shared Practice in Place: Literacy and the Construction of Community

The portrait in this chapter focuses on Terry and Carol, who have played an integral part in the local church's community activity programme and Bible discussion groups. At these community events, engagement with texts of all kinds suggests a model of literacy which, rather than presupposing a narrow range of skills and the passing on of information, is open to interpretative possibilities. The chapter gives an overview of a social practice paradigm in literacy studies, which presents literacy as socially constructed and locally produced, and as a valuable resource in the negotiation of everyday lives. Such a perspective allows us to see how community is creatively and collaboratively constructed through shared experience, and the place of language and literacy within this process.

Chapter 6—A Portrait of Family Literacy

This chapter focuses on the domain of home, with a portrait of literacy in the everyday lives of one family. The literacy practices of Katie and her dad, Colin, and brother, James, illustrate the contribution of different means of communication to the negotiation of everyday life. The chapter examines how everyday literacy practices reflect the idea of family as a site of active negotiation. It challenges assumptions often seen in social and education policy, where the family is a site of need for specific pedagogic support to develop officially mandated skills. The portrait of Katie and Colin presents both "family" and "literacy" as processes of shared learning and collaboration, as something that people "do" together.

Chapter 7—Material Literacies: Writing Home

In this chapter, we return to Peggy's story and look more closely at the ways in which she responded to having to move to a smaller home in her later life as a result of a welfare policy that did not recognise the complex realities of everyday lives. The perspective of the material in literacy studies allows us to explore the physical, emotional, and artefactual literacy work that is involved in creating a home. This reflects the ways practices around texts of all kinds are key to the negotiation of self and identity, connecting across time and space, linking the local and the global, and opening up interpretation of literacy as part of an ongoing process of the active negotiation and creation of meaning-making spaces.

Chapter 8—Reframing Literacy for Social Justice

In this final chapter, I return to Fraser's (2010) three-dimensional theory of justice and, in light of the portraits presented in the book, reiterate the relevance of this framework to an understanding of literacy for social justice. The lens of literacy is an important means to understand in greater depth both the impact of policy on everyday lives and the complex means by which those lives are negotiated. This includes drawing attention to the discursive frames that shape everyday lives and the literacy practices that are a part of them, and disrupting these frames through research and practice which challenges how they are set. I argue that transformative approaches to literacy for social justice involve seeing it as integral to a wider social change.

Notes

1. This research was partly funded by the British Academy: *New Literacies and Cross-generational learning on a Midlands Council Estate*, Small Research Grant 113219.

References

Collins, J. and Blot, R. (2003) *Literacy and Literacies: Texts, power and identity*. Cambridge: Cambridge University Press
Comber, B. (2016) *Literacy, Place and the Pedagogies of Possibility*. Oxon and New York: Routledge

Department for Work and Pensions (2013) 'Simplifying the welfare system and making sure work pays', https://www.gov.uk/government/policies/simplifying-the-welfare-system-and-making-sure-work-pays/supporting-pages/making-sure-housing-support-is-fair-and-affordable (accessed June 4, 2013)

Fraser, N. (1997) *Justice Interruptus: Critical reflections on the 'postsocialist' condition*. New York: Routledge

Fraser, N. (2003a) 'Distorted beyond all recognition: a rejoinder to Axel Honneth', in Fraser, N. and Honneth, A., *Redistribution or recognition? A political-philosophical exchange*. London: Verso, pp. 198–236

Fraser, N. (2003b) 'Social justice in the age of identity politics', in Fraser, N. and Honneth, A. *Redistribution or recognition? A political-philosophical exchange*. London: Verso, pp. 7–109

Fraser, N. (2010) *Scales of Justice: Reimagining Political Space in a Globalizing World*. New York: Columbia University Press

Fraser, N. and Honneth, A. (2003) 'Introduction: Redistribution or Recognition?', in Fraser, N. and Honneth, A., *Redistribution or recognition? A political-philosophical exchange*. London: Verso

Haddad, M. (2012) *The Perfect Storm: Economic stagnation, the rising cost of living, public spending cuts, and the impact of UK poverty*. Oxford: Oxfam GB

Hamilton, M. (2014) 'Global, regional and local influences on adult literacy policy in England', *Globalisation, Society and Education*, 12 (1) 110–126

Olson, K. (2008) 'Participatory Parity' in Olson, K. (ed.) *Adding Insult to Injury: Nancy Fraser debates her critics*. London: Verso, pp. 246–272

O'Hara, M. (2015) *Austerity Bites: A journey to the sharp end of cuts in the UK*. Bristol: Polity Press

Street, B. (1993) *Cross Cultural approaches to literacy*. Cambridge. Cambridge University Press

2

Finding Perspective: Researching Everyday Literacy Practices

Fig. 2.1 "Research in progress" badge made for me by young people attending a library open day

© The Author(s) 2018
S. Jones, *Portraits of Everyday Literacy for Social Justice*,
https://doi.org/10.1007/978-3-319-75945-6_2

During fieldwork for the study reported in this book, I was in conversation with one participant, Katie, when we were approached by a third party, who asked what the research was about. Katie, who was 13 at the time, explained that the research project was about "how people read and write and they don't even notice".

Katie's comment succinctly captures an idea that is central to this book: that there are different forms and purposes for literacy and different ways in which people engage in practices around reading and writing. Her comment also highlights the fact that some ways of engaging with literacy in everyday life are noticed, and afforded recognition as a result, while others aren't. That some reading and writing practices are not "noticed" could be due to several reasons. It could be that they are so ordinary that they become subsumed in the banality of everyday life and shed the significance accorded to practices which are unusual or new. Equally, it could be that such practices are in fact newer forms of reading and writing that are not yet associated with their more traditional counterparts. There is a suggestion in Katie's comment that she perceived how the everyday literacy practices we were discussing, such as YouTube, X-Box gaming, and cookery magazines, for example, were not always recognised as important and worthy of note. For Katie, these did not seem to belong in the same category as those usually focused upon in institutions such as school, or even education research. However, research in literacy has, in recent decades, highlighted the significance of everyday, vernacular (Barton and Hamilton 1998), or domestic (Duckworth 2014) literacies in the negotiation of complex social contexts and identities. Katie's comment also makes a powerful point about the everyday as a focus of attention. It suggests that there are many important things that can go unnoticed when the richness of everyday experience is not recognised.

This chapter will develop Katie's concise depiction of the research project in which she participated. I outline the context of the project, and the position I have taken in framing the everyday as a site for research and as a focus for discussion of "how people read and write".

What (and Where) Is 'Everyday'?

In common usage, the word "everyday" has many connotations. It is often suggestive of the ordinary, banal, unnoticed, and unnoteworthy. "Everyday value", for example, might be used to describe the staples of a weekly grocery shop; "everyday wear" might include the clothing that we turn to when the occasion doesn't warrant anything particularly special. Everyday practices might also be held in opposition to official or institutional ones, associated with the informal, as opposed to formal, with family rather than work life. For most people, everyday life is, in reality, a combination of these things. It involves negotiating formal and informal contexts, official institutions as well as what constitutes home life, very local circumstances, and the global contexts to which they are connected.

This complexity is inherent in any research of everyday practice, both in terms of its focus and its methods. As Joe Moran has explained (2005, p. 23):

> Everyday needs to be understood as a series of shifting, interconnecting elements that resists the modern notion that sight offers intelligibility.

The relationship between the everyday and dominant social structures has been explored in various ways. Pierre Bourdieu's concept of habitus (1977) refers to practice which is embedded in the established structures of life, structures which we internalise and respond to in a way which can be seen as suggestive of normativity and submission. Michel De Certeau (1984) takes a different perspective, seeing the everyday as a site for resistant practice, which often occurs in the cracks in proprietary power. Framed in this way, everyday meaning making is the site of active and agentive negotiation. However, to characterise everyday practice according to a binary of counter-hegemonic resistance or passive normativity is to limit our understanding of its complexity. Others studying everyday practice have argued that it is the site of creative engagement between individuals and dominant social structures. Paul Willis, for example, argues that everyday culture is a symbolic realm "in part a result, upon conditions, of the creative self-activity of agents, also thereby producing and reproducing themselves" (Willis 2000, p. xvi). Sarah Pink (2012) advocates "seeing practices as possibly resulting in forms of everyday innovation, self-conscious resistance or as maintaining a sense of stability" (p. 19). She notes that, in essence, therefore, the everyday "is where we make our worlds and where our worlds make us" (p. 5).

This framing of the everyday has important implications for undertaking research into everyday literacy practices. It is important to understand the everyday not as a space simply filled with what's left over once the important business of life is done (as is suggested by Lefebvre's (1991) notion of *la vie residuelle*). Neither is the everyday something which research can simply grasp (Moran 2005), or a place to which a researcher can simply go, as we are "'always-already' immersed in it" (Gardiner 2009, p. 385). It is a shifting, dynamic space, as is literally illustrated in Peggy's story, where the focus of the research itself shifted not only thematically, but geographically. Researching everyday lives also includes those episodes which we might not view as common or day-to-day experience, such as the time participants asked me to reschedule a visit we'd arranged because they'd been invited along to a family member's audition for a TV gameshow. This view of the everyday as shifting and contingent needs to be accounted for in any research design, as well as in analysis, theorisation, and in telling of the story of research.

Like several key studies of literacy in everyday contexts (e.g. Heath 1983; Street 1984; Taylor and Dorsey-Gaines 1988; Barton and Hamilton 1998), the research reported in this book acknowledges that the dynamic complexity of the everyday is most appropriately observed through ethnographic methods. Locating research in the sites of everyday life has significant benefits for contesting the dominant framing of ideas. A focus in research on practices within the public domain, at the expense of those associated with everyday experiences, has meant, for example, that female and working class voices have often gone unheard (Stanley and Wise 1993; Pink 2004; McKenzie 2015). However, as Barton and Hamilton (1998) note in relation to literacy, research into everyday practices needs to be aware of how it positions dominant practice so as not to reinforce existing frames:

The normal direction of movement in studies of home literacy is to start with school practices and then to investigate whether and in what ways these are supported in the home. Such a starting-point means that home practices are seen through the lens of school. (p. 189)

Similarly, Willis (2000) warns against research that does not connect everyday lives with urgent issues, or which engages the latter while being "empty of people, feeling and experience". In his view:

well-grounded and illuminating analytic points flow only from bringing concepts into a relationship with the messiness of ordinary life, somehow recorded. (2000, p. xi)

In its focus on everyday life through the lens of literacy, this book aims to do what Willis suggests here by asking not only what a focus on everyday lives can tell us about literacy, but also what a focus on literacy can tell us about everyday lives.

Finding perspective for the research reported in this book means locating it within its wider context. I move next to present the background of the research, offering an account of my own position as a researcher in order to frame the way in which I have come to make meaning from the everyday lives and literacy practices I have observed.

The Background

The genesis of the research presented in this book goes back to October 2008, when the university for which I work commissioned a participatory theatre company to undertake a community arts project based on the history of a council housing estate located a few miles away from its main campus. The project came at a time when the local comprehensive school was about to be demolished and replaced by an Academy, co-sponsored by the University. As part of its commitment to the new school and its community, the arts project aimed not only to establish a relationship in which local people could have a say in the services they were offered but also to provide a basis to challenge the common stereotype which characterised the estate and its residents more broadly within the city, and as part of a wider national discourse: that of deficient, depressed, and powerless people lacking in motivation, aspiration, and skills.

I worked as an ethnographic researcher on this community arts project over a period of two years, as part of a research partnership with the community theatre company (Hall and Thomson 2010; Jones et al. 2013; Thomson et al. 2014). I followed the work of the theatre company as they engaged with residents, exploring their histories of living, learning and working on the estate. Over the course of two years, three participatory theatre productions were researched, produced, and performed as part of this project. The first traced the history of the estate from its origins in the 1930s to its development as part of a post-war inner-city "slum clearance". This show played to packed out audiences in various locations across the estate over five nights. The second performance marked the history of the local comprehensive school on the eve of its closure, and the final production coincided with the opening of the new Academy. Residents took part in a range of ways, from sharing life histories, to providing photographs and appearing in films shown as part of the production, as well as taking their place on the stage. The productions presented the contributions of residents who had moved to live on the estate as newly-weds half a century before alongside those who were about to begin secondary school in the newly built Academy.

During the course of the theatre project, we spoke to residents in their homes, in community centres and social groups, at the health centre and mother and baby groups, on the market, in cafés and the pub, in schools and in the library. We also spoke to local authority employees who worked as part of the broad range of welfare provision associated with the estate. Within the narratives gathered there was a sense of pride in a past where a buoyant community was established through collective solidarity. This contrasted with the estate as a place to live in the present, where dominant discourses of deficit compounded the challenges faced by residents adapting to a post-industrial landscape and bearing the brunt of neoliberal social policy.

While observing the work of the theatre company and talking to residents about their experiences, I noticed the ways in which everyday language and literacy practices were central to their navigation of these contexts. I observed and spoke to participants about the ways in which they used reading and writing in their everyday lives, noticing in particular how the creative and resourceful practices I was witnessing challenged notions of a deficit in skills and participation which dominated the ways in which the estate was framed in public and policy discourse. In contrast to tropes of the council estate as home to isolated older residents or troublesome teenagers, families were learning together across generations, and creatively negotiating their everyday lives.

As the community arts project ended, I secured funding for a further study, working with some of the residents of the council housing estate where the community arts project took place. Two of the families with whom I worked on this second project were also involved in the theatre project; the third family became involved through their connections with the activities of the local church in the community. This project set out to provide an account of how literacy practices, including the use of increasingly accessible digital technologies, were resources for individual and collective negotiation of wider contexts, some of which I've already outlined in brief but will go on to develop in subsequent chapters.

Putting Myself in the Frame

If we understand "everyday" as a contingent and shifting concept, then research in everyday contexts needs to be responsive, with the researcher positioned as a human agent within a dynamic process:

> No camera, no image or sequence of images can show these rhythms. One needs equally attentive eyes and ears, a head, a memory, a heart. (Lefebvre 1996, p. 227, cited in Moran 2005, p. 23)

It's important, therefore, to spend some time here outlining my position as a researcher of language and literacy working with the participants whose stories are shaped and presented in this book. Researchers working in the field of social justice argue for the importance of research which is able to appropriately and ethically reflect the experiences of participants. For some, this means that the researcher is better positioned when they are an "insider" who shares the background and experiences of their research participants. Lisa McKenzie (2015), for example, argues that working class communities have traditionally been ill served by researchers who embody a perspective which is inherently middle class. Vicky Duckworth (2014) also makes a case for research in which participants and researcher share ontological perspectives. In her research into the experience of working class learners in an adult literacy and numeracy class, Duckworth's position is that of a practitioner-researcher who is their tutor at an adult education college, thus placing her "outside" the experiences of her participants in some ways. However, reflection on her own experiences at the intersection of gender and social class, as a woman who has grown up in the same geographic location as her students and has a similar home background to them, offers her insight not only into the experiences of her research participants, but also into the ways in which her research could most ethically "create change and social justice" (p. 103).

Such writing of the self into knowledge (Stanley and Wise 1993) is central to the main theme of this book, that of frame-setting as an issue of social justice. The resources upon which I draw in my own process of frame-setting, which has led to this book, are therefore important to explore briefly here. I came to the study which informs this book as a researcher with an interest in the ways in which language and literacy are used for meaning making across both formal and informal contexts. This interest has often focused on the role of language and literacy in navigating the sites of contestation which are a feature of everyday lives across different communities. As a researcher from the local university, there are many factors that position me as an "outsider" when it comes to the lived experience of residents living on the estate. There are experiences that we share, however, and which have influenced the position I have taken in coming to this research, its undertaking and subsequent sharing.

I grew up in the 1970s and 1980s on a council housing estate in a rural market town in North West Wales, where I lived until I left home aged 18 to go to university. My family all lived within a small radius and had always done so. The wider community was mainly agricultural, but my own family worked in various roles including manual labour, healthcare and civil service, and clerical work. I grew up bilingual: the language spoken at home was Welsh, but in school and in the wider social context, including the media, English was also a commonly spoken language. By the time I was growing up, the Welsh language had been under considerable threat of extinction. For many decades, including the years of my schooling, significant and heavily publicised political activism eventually led to policy being put in place to protect the language in the public sphere. This included the advent of a Welsh language television channel, and, in later years, protected status for the language within education and the legal requirement for all public communication to be bilingual.

The experience of being a bilingual speaker of a minority language means that I grew up acutely aware of the ways in which language, and the wider discourses that surround it, are shaped by political forces. I am also aware of the impact on the identities of those living everyday lives within a contested political sphere. My experience as a bilingual led to my fascination with the ways in which language is used creatively, dynamically, and politically as a resource for meaning making in everyday life.

I was the first of my family to go to university, initially elsewhere in Wales, where I pursued my interest in language and literature before moving to a larger English city to train to become a teacher of English at secondary school level. Once qualified, I worked in schools where significant numbers of learners were themselves members of communities where more than one language was spoken, and where everyday experiences were the site of contested meanings, discourses, and identities. My interest in the everyday use of languages across contexts—be they cultural or linguistic, formal or informal—led me to my doctoral study, which focused on the ways in which two groups of girls in two different bilingual communities drew on the resources of language and literacy to negotiate their everyday lives (Jones 2006a, b, 2007, 2009).

I have now lived in the region where the research featured in this book is located for longer than I have not. Working at the university where I studied for my teaching qualification and subsequent postgraduate qualifications, my teaching has included working with undergraduate and postgraduate students in the field of literacy, including beginning teachers of English and teachers working towards master's and doctoral degrees. In this role, I have continued to observe the ways in which literacy is framed in education policy, how it is enacted in schools across a range of communities, and the impact of this on the experiences of teachers and learners. In my research, I have focused on language and literacy practice in informal contexts, including ethnographic work on the estate which is the focus of this book. My research informs my teaching, including work with beginning teachers on critical and place-based literacy pedagogies (Jones and Chapman 2017; Jones and McIntyre 2014). My teaching also informs my research, including my continued interest in the impact on everyday lives of the dominant framing of literacy in education policy, as experienced by the teachers and pupils with whom I work.

Why is this important? Ruth Behar (1996) focuses on the importance of acknowledging the self in the "business of humans observing other humans in order to write about them" (p. 5). To do so, she argues, involves asking of oneself:

> Who is this woman who is writing about others, making others vulnerable? What does she want from others? What do the others want from her? (p. 20)

The detail that I have shared about myself here goes some way towards answering the first of Behar's questions. The answers to the second two have changed throughout the course of the research, and may be different again in the context of this book. As I have already outlined, my interest in exploring and presenting the everyday literacies of community members with whom I had begun to build relationships over the course of the theatre project was motivated by a desire to counter the discourses of deficit I had also witnessed in relation to the estate and its residents. As a researcher, what I wanted from community members involved in the research, therefore, was their willingness to share their experiences and allow me in to their homes, schools, and community centres to observe their practices and listen to their experiences. I am indebted to the families who welcomed me in to their homes, sharing reflections of their experiences of often acutely challenging circumstances, and to others within the community who gave so willingly of their time to take part in the research.

When it comes to the last of Behar's questions, being a researcher, in particular a researcher of a subject like literacy, places you in the eyes of some groups and individuals as being able to provide something which you are not necessarily in a position to offer. A tension can exist in the relationship with gatekeepers within a field because of two models of the researcher that can predominate: that of "expert" and "critic" (Hammersley and Atkinson 1995). Families welcomed me warmly into their homes and shared their experiences openly, if with some puzzlement and intrigue at times (Jordan 2006). My attempts to gain access to professionals within the community were not always met with such open-mindedness, however. Assumptions about my role, the purpose of my research, and nature of my expertise were evident. As will be outlined in Chap. 3, literacy has a prominent place in the welfare provision of the estate and announcing myself to local authority personnel as a researcher from the university with an interest in literacy saw me invited to attend the meetings of committees, to sit upon advisory boards, and sent action plans to comment upon. While engaging with the activities of the local church in the community, I was also approached for advice on the best ways in which they could support the literacy development of their congregation, including the font size and style and the most appropriate reading age of their newsletter. Observing a participant over the course of one day at school, I felt a keen sense of suspicion of my role in a design technology lesson, which featured a lengthy focus on "literacy", in the form of assessment of the students' spelling of the names of key tools and materials. Teachers had been promised by their deputy head teacher, who was entirely supportive of the research and interested in its aims, that my purpose was to observe a student's literacy practices over the course of a day of her everyday life, and not to evaluate their practice in relation to literacy. However, such is the dominance of literacy on the performative agenda of schools, as will be explored in later chapters, that it seemed to be assumed that I was a representative of this agenda on the look-out for, and ready to pass judgement upon, the teaching of a particular version of reading and writing.

The longitudinal nature of my ethnographic research on the estate meant that during the course of the research, I found myself observing and discussing situations with participants with whom I had built relationships over many years. In some respects, it could be argued that I was in a position of an insider in terms of my knowledge of how their everyday lives were developing over time, and having been given the privileged insight into how they felt about the challenges they faced at a time of increased pressure resulting from wider policy reform. My response to the unfolding circumstances of the lives of participants such as Peggy, forced to move home because of changes to welfare policy, meant that I was drawing on "emotionally sensed knowledge" (Hubbard et al. 2001, p. 121) to make meaning from what I had observed. My personal discontent at the wider context of welfare reform, and the impact it was having on people in the same circumstances as Peggy nationwide, became an unavoidable feature of how I was understanding and responding to the situation Peggy was facing.

Ultimately, however, I am an outsider in the privileged position of being able to write about the lives of others from a position of relative affluence. This carries a risk of compounding the challenge for participants who are rarely in a position to have their thoughts published (Lister 2004). The shape of this book is the result of long deliberation about this tension between my position as an outsider and my response to what I observed as a researcher of everyday literacy practices on the estate.

I now go on to outline how the approach I have taken to conducting and presenting this research is mindful of the issues I have raised here, including its focus on interrogating the relationship between literacy and social justice.

Assembling the Scene

As I will show in the next chapters through a focus on literacy, the everyday lives of those finding it hardest to make ends meet are already heavily framed by what Ruth Lister calls "the hegemony of the measurable" (p. 38). However, taking an ethnographic approach to my study has meant that relationships with individuals, families, and those working within the community were central to the research. In taking an ethnographic approach, the study reflects a tradition in literacy research which, as Barton and Hamilton have noted, recognises that:

methods which take literacy out of its context of use are not appropriate. Instead, methods are needed which enable us to examine in detail the role of literacy in people's contemporary lives and in the histories and traditions of which these are a part. (1998, p. 57)

My approach to the research also grew to reflect the way in which "methodologies themselves construct, and are constructed, in relation to a field site" (Pahl and Allan 2011, p. 191). This involved renegotiation of appropriate research tools through which participants could more effectively share their responses to shifting realities. This included an approach to the use of video, informed by Pink (2007), "using the camera as a tool through which to explore informants' experiences of and engagements with the environment" (p. 245). Data generated from this approach is presented in Peggy's portrait, which was introduced in Chap. 1, and will be explored in more detail in Chap. 7.

A key aspect of my approach to this research was to engage an asset-based model of everyday practices to challenge the deficit discourses which have long been deeply embedded within social policy. The particularly pernicious discourse of deficit which prevailed in policy and in the media at the time of the research made me intensely aware that the way in which the stories of participants was presented needed to become a part of a *reframing*, where the process of research and its reporting supported its underlying aims. As a result, the stories of participants' everyday lives are presented in this book by the means of portraits.

Portraits: Telling Stories of Everyday Lives and Literacy Practices

In presenting portraits of everyday literacies, my approach draws on a tradition in social science of portraiture, developed most notably in recent times by Sarah Lawrence-Lightfoot (Lawrence-Lightfoot and Hoffmann Davis 1997). She explains of her work:

portraits are designed to capture the richness, complexity, and dimensionality of human experiences in social and cultural context, conveying the perspectives of people who are negotiating those experiences. (p. 3)

As both a method of inquiry and documentation, the portrait is both process and product, with each shaping the other. As the central motif of this book, the portrait is an appropriate means through which to explore the issues raised in researching everyday literacies, as a means of presenting research which is closely linked to the aims and ethos of the research itself.

Lawrence-Lightfoot's approach to portraiture in social science builds on a well-established "canvas" upon which writers and researchers have explored the nature of ethnography (p. 8). The blend of art and science, which she argues is the essence of the portrait, reflects the fact that, as James Clifford (1986) has argued, "culture [i]s composed of seriously contested codes and representations [...] the poetic and the political are inseparable". Clifford also emphasises "that science is in, not above, historical and linguistic processes" (p. 2). The history of ethnography is replete with "studies that focus on meaning systems, disputed traditions, or cultural artifacts" (p. 3). The position of ethnography on epistemological boundaries also suggests that the means of conducting and reporting ethnographic research should reflect this hybridity:

> Ethnography is actively situated between powerful systems of meaning [...] Ethnography decodes and recodes, telling the grounds of collective order and diversity, inclusion and exclusion. It describes processes of innovation and structuration, and is itself part of these processes. (p. 3)

Clifford also traces the association between "literariness" and ethnography. He argues that this is "more than a matter of good writing" (p. 4), evoking the literary processes which are involved in ethnography and the way in which it is received by an audience:

> metaphor, figuration, narrative affect the ways cultural phenomena are registered, from the first jotted "observations" to the completed book, to the ways these configurations "make sense" in determined acts of reading. (p. 4)

Clifford Geertz (1973) refers to the role of "thick description" in ethnographic writing, which he describes as the researcher's "own constructions of other people's constructions of what they and their compatriots are up to" (p. 9). This emphasis on the centrality of interpretation in ethnography leads Clifford (1986) to refer to ethnographies as "fictions". Here, he draws on the literal sense of "something made or fashioned" (p. 6), but in so doing also invokes reflection on the nature of truth and its construction within ethnographic texts, which can never be free of "power and history [which] work through them" (p. 7). Ethnographic truths are thus inherently "*partial* – committed and incomplete" (p. 7, emphasis in original). This demands of the ethnographic researcher a "rigorous partiality" (p. 25): a position which again reminds us of the place of ethnographic writing on the boundaries between research paradigms.

Lawrence-Lightfoot's portraiture embraces this position and establishes it as one of dialogue, contestation, and challenge: the means of research therefore represents powerful messages about its subject. Joseph Featherstone (1989) has described Lawrence-Lightfoot's work as "a people's scholarship": "a scholarship in which scientific facts gathered in the field give voice to a people's experience" (p. 376). A key role of the portrait, as described by Lawrence-Lightfoot, is as a:

> counterpoint to the dominant chorus of social scientists whose methods and goals have been greatly influenced by the positivist paradigm, whose focus has largely centred on the identification and documentation of social problems, and whose audiences have been mostly limited to the academy. (Lawrence-Lightfoot and Hoffmann Davis 1997, p. xvi)

This facet of the portrait makes it especially pertinent to my own aims in this book, which include challenging dominant discourses around everyday lives and the literacy practices which are part of them. Like Lawrence-Lightfoot herself, I am drawn to the "intentionally generous" (ibid., p. 9) nature of the portrait. It offers a powerful counter to the kinds of research commissioned and drawn upon by policy makers, which is focused on "pathology and disease rather than on health and resilience" (ibid., p. 8). Such "relentless scrutiny of failure" (ibid., pp. 8–9) leads, according to Lawrence-Lightfoot, to four problems, each of which is recognisable in the context of the research presented in this book. Firstly, our view of the world becomes one which magnifies what is wrong at the cost of recognising promise and potential. This leads to a second problem: that of cynicism and inaction. "Documentation of pathology" (ibid., p. 9) leads to a third issue, which is the blaming of those who are, in fact, most victimised and least powerful in shaping their fate. A focus on failure also results in what Lawrence-Lightfoot terms "facile inquiry", where the emphasis is on the need to "identify a disease and count its victims" rather than to "characterise and document health" (ibid.).

This generosity of approach is a feature of both the process and the product of research. As Lawrence-Lightfoot says:

> the researcher who asks first "what is good here?" is likely to absorb a very different reality than the one who is on a mission to discover the sources of failure. (ibid., p. 9)

It is important to Lawrence-Lightfoot that subjects (or "actors") define this goodness themselves:

> the portraitist's stance is one of acceptance and discernment, generosity and challenge [...] she sees the actors as knowledge bearers, as rich resources, as the best authorities on their own experience. (ibid., p. 141)

The position of the researcher is that of the stranger; she is the one who experiences newness. This openness means the researcher can be faced with surprises, when the realities of the research context force reconsiderations of her assumptions and the re-calibration of hypotheses. This happened in the research presented in this book, in the changing circumstances of the families with whom I worked, and in their responses to these changes. It happened too in my own response to the research, and in the changes in my own understanding of what it means to research everyday practice.

The ethical dilemmas which emerged during the research included the question of how to respond to and to represent the more challenging experiences I'd observed in a way which did not resort to the reinforcement of deficit, or to over-sentimentalised or patronising accounts of "other" lives. I also reflected on what it might mean to ask someone to talk about literacy when they have shared the fact that they have spent a lifetime feeling uncomfortable about reading and writing as a result of their experiences at school. Lawrence-Lightfoot's emphasis on "the good" does not ignore the complex realities of everyday lives, however. Rather, she argues that:

> we begin by asking what is happening here, what is working, and why? But in focusing on what works, on underscoring what is healthy and strong, we inevitably see the dark shadows of compromise, inhibition, and imperfection that distort the success and weaken the achievements. (ibid., p. 142)

In the portraits of everyday literacy presented in this book, my aim is to foreground the role of literacy practices as resources which are drawn upon in all aspects of life for the families involved. This includes their role in the negotiation of challenging circumstances, where, indeed, such a focus illuminates not only the practical and emotional difficulties of navigating welfare policy, for example, but also the tenacity, creativity, and collaboration that is often evident in the process.

This theme is drawn out in the book across a series of portraits, each focused on a different aspect of life in the community of the estate. Lawrence-Lightfoot draws on Eudora Welty's distinction between "listening *to* a story and listening *for* a story" (ibid., p. 12, emphasis in original). Rather than the passivity suggested by the former action, where one does little to give the story shape or form, the latter suggests an active role, where the researcher is central in the creation of a story. The story of the research, and its telling in this book, is one which has involved active identification and shaping of its themes and the selection and positioning of voices within it. In undertaking this work, as the portraitist, I "hope to capture th[e] dialectic of contextual structures and forces defining individual action and perception *and* of actors' invention and shaping the contexts they inhabit" (ibid., p. 58, emphasis in original).

References

Barton, D. and Hamilton, M. (1998) *Local Literacies: Reading and Writing in One Community*. London: Routledge

Behar, R. (1996) *The Vulnerable Observer*. Boston: Beacon Press

Bourdieu, H. (1977) *Outline of a Theory of Practice*. Cambridge: Cambridge University Press

Clifford, J. (1986) 'Introduction: Partial Truths', in Clifford, J. and Marcus, G.E. (eds.) *Writing Culture: The poetics and politics of ethnography*. London: University of California Press, pp. 1–26

De Certeau, M. (1984) *The Practice of Everyday Life*. London: University of California Press

Duckworth, V. (2014) *Learning Trajectories, Violence and Empowerment amongst Adult Basic Skills Learners*. London: Routledge

Featherstone, J. (1989) 'To Make the Spirit Whole', *Harvard Educational Review*, 59 (3) 367–378

Gardiner, M. (2009) 'Book Review: *Everyday Life: Theories and Practices from Surrealism to the Present*, Michael Sheringham', *Space and Culture*, 12, 283–389

Geertz, C. (1973) *The Interpretation of Cultures*. New York: Basic Books

Hall, C. and Thomson, P. (2010) 'Grounded literacies: the power of listening to, telling and performing community stories', *Literacy*, 44 (2) 69–75

Hammersley, M. and Atkinson, P. (1995) *Ethnography: Principles in Practice* (Second Edition). London: Routledge

Heath, S. B. (1983) *Ways with Words*. Cambridge: Cambridge University Press

Hubbard, G., Backett-Milburn, K. and Kemner, D. (2001) 'Working with emotion: issues for the researcher in fieldwork and teamwork', *Social Research Methodology*, 4 (2) 119–137

Jones, S. (2006a) 'One body and two heads: Girls exploring their bicultural identities through text', *English in Education*, 40 (2) 5–21

Jones, S. (2006b). 'A Tale of Two Literacies: Girls growing up biculturally literate in two UK communities', in Hickey, T. (ed.) *Language Learning and Literacy*, Dublin: RAI, pp. 99–113

Jones, S. (2007) 'Land of "My 9": Welsh-English Bilingual Girls Creating Spaces to Explore Identity', *Changing English*, 14 (1) 39–50

Jones, S. (2009) 'Bilingual Identities in Two UK Communities: A Study of the languages and literacies of Welsh and British-Asian Girls', unpublished PhD thesis, University of Nottingham, available at: http://eprints.nottingham.ac.uk/10836/1/Susan_Jones_Bilingual_Identities.pdf

Jones, S., Hall, C., Thomson, P., Barrett, A. & Hanby, J. (2013) 'Representing the 'forgotten estate': participatory theatre, place and community identity', *Discourse: Studies in the Cultural Politics of Education*, 34 (1) 118–131

Jones, S. and Chapman, K. (2017) 'Telling stories: engaging critical literacy through urban legends in an English secondary school', *English Teaching, Practice and Critique*, 16 (1) 85–96

Jones, S. and McIntyre, (2014) 'It's not what it looks like. I'm Santa': connecting community through film', *Changing English*, 21 (4) 322–33

Jordan, A. B. (2006) 'Make yourself at home: the social construction of research roles in family studies', *Qualitative Research*, 6 (2) 169–185

Lawrence-Lightfoot, S. and Hoffmann Davis, J. (1997) *The Art and Science of Portraiture*. San Francisco: Jossey-Bass Books

Lefebvre, H. (1991) *Critique of Everyday Life: Volume 1*. London: Verso

Lefebvre, H. (1996) 'Seen from the window', in *Writings on Cities*, Eleonore Kofman and Elizabeth Lebas (trans and ed.), Oxford: Blackwell, pp. 219–27

Lister, R. (2004) *Poverty*. Cambridge: Polity Press

McKenzie, L. (2015) *Getting By: Estates, class and culture in austerity Britain*. Bristol: Policy Press

Moran, J. (2005) *Reading the Everyday*. Abingdon: Routledge

Pahl, K. and Allan C. (2011) 'I don't know what literacy is: Uncovering hidden literacies in a community library using ecological and participatory methodologies with children', *Journal of Early Childhood Literacy*, 11 (2) 190–213

Pink, S. (2004) *Home Truths: Gender, domestic objects and everyday life*. Oxford: Berg

Pink, S (2007) 'Walking with Video', *Visual Studies*, 22 (3) 240–252

Pink, S. (2012) *Situating Everyday Life*. London: Sage

Stanley, L. and Wise, S. (1993) *Breaking Out Again: Feminist Ontology and Epistemology*. New Edition. London: Routledge

Street, B. (1984) *Literacy in Theory and Practice*. Cambridge: Cambridge University Press

Taylor, D. and Dorsey-Gaines, C. (1988) *Growing Up Literate: Learning from inner-city families*. Portsmouth, NH: Heinemann

Thomson, P. Barrett, A,. Hall, C., Hanby, J., and Jones, S. (2014) 'Arts in the community as a place-making event', in Fleming, M., Bresler, L. and O'Toole, J. (eds.) *The Routledge International Handbook of Arts and Education* London: Routledge

Willis, P. (2000) *The Ethnographic Imagination*. Cambridge: Polity Press

3

Literacy and "The Forgotten Estate": What They Haven't Got?

The starting point for this chapter comes from an encounter with a local government employee, who was based at the children's centre and whose role included some responsibility for overseeing policy approaches to literacy within the community. I had been directed towards this person at the outset of the research project, and in this introductory meeting, I was shown a range of ways in which the local authority and health service staff were thinking about literacy. At the meeting, I explained the aims of my research project, its ethnographic approach and focus on everyday practice, and that my goal was to adopt an asset-based approach to exploring the ways in which participant families used the resources of literacy as part of their everyday lives. The response of the local authority employee was that I should prepare to be disappointed; rather than finding literacy practices as resources in the lives of participants, I was more than likely to discover that literacy was "what they haven't got".

My immediate response was one of surprise. Made in the context of a professional conversation, by someone with a seemingly positive brief to challenge social exclusion, this way of describing people, and the resources with which they navigate their everyday lives, was an unusually frank

© The Author(s) 2018
S. Jones, *Portraits of Everyday Literacy for Social Justice*,
https://doi.org/10.1007/978-3-319-75945-6_3

example of the speaking of deficit by those in official positions. This was someone with first-hand knowledge of the difficulties experienced by people she worked with, and of the challenge of working to alleviate these difficulties for young families in particular. The comment perhaps reflects the frustrations of a job, which, like many public services, has had to respond to cuts in funding and changes to the ideological landscape in which policies are centrally made to be enacted at a local level. However, the comment, and the general description of welfare policy provision on the estate which emerged from the discussion of which it was a part, does echo broader deficit discourses about communities living on the estate and those who share their circumstances across other parts of the UK and beyond. It suggests a narrow way of viewing literacy as something which can be measured and quantified in response to government targets. It also suggests that the dominance of this way of responding to social exclusion has overshadowed other perspectives on everyday lives. Such a narrow view is part of a cyclical process whereby a policy programme that does not recognise complex realities is both premised upon, and reinforced by, perceptions of deficit.

Through the lens of literacy, this chapter locates the everyday experiences described in the book within a wider context of public policy at work on the estate, exploring some of the implications for how we understand the relationship between literacy and social justice.

Literacy Policy on the Estate

Across international contexts, literacy is often featured in policy as a measure of disadvantage, reflecting the ways in which it is "increasingly naturalised as a central feature of the emerging global order" (Hamilton 2012, p. 3). For decades, literacy, in particular, has been a central feature of the wider neoliberal project of social inclusion. This is reflected in the social inclusion policy of the New Labour government elected in 1997, and of its successor Conservative-led governments. Such policies are premised upon the construction of some members of society as "excluded" as a result of a perceived lack of ability to contribute to the wider national project of global economic competition. A key aspect of the society envisaged within this policy context is the notion of a *knowledge economy*. This sees literacy bound up with other aspects of life, such as education, citizenship, poverty, and community regeneration, as part of a wider suite of policy that is premised on an economistic model of development (Hamilton 2012, 2014). The emergence of the knowledge economy in post-industrial society has seen a move away from the work which used to define the lives of residents of this estate, many of whom worked in local mines and factories. It has also meant that individuals and families now face different expectations about the role of literacy in their everyday lives (Brandt 2015).

Adult and family literacy support figures highly within local welfare services on the estate. The local authority has an action plan delivering "literacy awareness training" for public workers such as health visitors, with documentation created to support them to "spot the signs of low level literacy". There is help with form filling at the local housing office. Literacy support for community members is focused heavily on its recipients gaining employment and making an economic contribution to society. Payments to those claiming benefits, including some of the participants in this study, are tied to attendance at computer classes, for example. These cover skills such as word processing CVs and letters of application for jobs.

There is also an emphasis on the role of parents in ensuring that their children develop the resources to make such contributions in the future. This includes a focus on literacy in the family home in the form of reading stories and in supporting homework. For the youngest residents and their families, early intervention schemes supported by the local authority include a philanthropic initiative which funds participation in an international book-gifting scheme, Dolly Parton Imagination Library. This scheme has been adopted across the USA, Canada, and Australia, as well as in the UK, and is commonly, but not entirely, associated with communities made vulnerable by their circumstances, such as those living on a low income, or children who are looked after in local authority care. In the city where the estate is located, the book-gifting scheme operates through the local health service, thus firmly framing literacy within the health agenda. Fronted by the global celebrity Dolly Parton, whose public narrative centres on having grown up in poverty as the child of an "illiterate" father, the scheme provides free age-appropriate books for registered children, delivered to their home once a month between their birth and their fifth birthday. The books are selected by a panel and provided through a contract with one publisher.

Along with Christine Hall, I was involved in small-scale research which explored the operation of this scheme locally (Hall and Jones 2016). In this study, we recognised how the scheme represented the many benefits of book-gifting, and of early reading more widely, which have been widely documented (e.g. Sheffield Hallam University 2012; Bailey et al. 2002). We were able to highlight the many positives of the scheme, not least in the opportunities it affords for social engagement and imaginative interaction around reading in the home. However, we also noted a tendency within the global operation of the scheme towards a problematic model of evaluating reading development:

> despite the obvious difficulty in establishing causal connections in this area of work, where a multitude of factors will influence the child's development and where experimental designs are neither feasible nor ethical, evaluators have emphasised measurement and quantification in their attempts to demonstrate impact. (p. 46)

This belief in unproblematically measuring and reporting the "impact" of an intervention such as book-gifting reflects a broader theme within the model of literacy represented within social policy both as a whole and as it was enacted on the estate. As captured in the words of the local government officer I spoke to, the idea of literacy as "what they haven't got" frames it as a neutral, predefined, and measurable set of skills. It is a thing that people *have*, or, in cases where they do not, they need to be provided with, and the impact of this measured in a quantifiable way. By looking at this model of literacy in more detail, and against a backdrop of the wider framing of everyday lives in communities such as the estate, I now go on to explore some of the issues this raises.

In the Frame: To Have or Have Not?

Literacy is a term fraught with debate, and significantly different discourses about literacy have influenced the ways in which it has been framed in policy and practice over many decades. The term is commonly understood as "shorthand for the social practices and conceptions of reading and writing" (Street 1984, p. 1). This could mean any interaction with reading or writing in a person's day-to-day life. It may also refer to the way of understanding the significance of these interactions. Literacy is a symbolic resource within the wider structuring and regulation of social systems (Barton and Hamilton 1998). As was discussed in Chap. 2, in relation to Katie's summary of everyday literacy practices, some discourses about literacy have been more powerful than others in shaping understanding of what it means to "be literate". This has meant that literacy—or rather its negative, *il*literacy—has been a regular source of moral panic for successive governments, as is evident in the role played by literacy within the wider project of social inclusion.

This dominant view of literacy frames it as "a set of skills to be learned" (Barton and Hamilton 1998, p. 3). As such, an individual is framed as "either/or"—literate or illiterate (Bartlett 2008). Such a view of literacy has been described by Street (1984) as "the autonomous model". Underpinning this model is:

> the assumption that literacy in itself, autonomously, defined independently of cultural context and meaning, will have effects, creating inequality for those who lack it and advantages for those who gain it. (Street 2011, p. 581)

This model objectifies literacy as a neutral collection of measurable skills, to be imparted to the learner with the expectation of some palpable impact. Street points out that this model "assumes a single direction in which literacy development can be traced and associates it with 'progress', 'civilisation', individual liberty and social mobility" (1984, p. 2). These are all ideas which underpin neoliberal policy discourse regarding social inclusion. Mary Hamilton argues that "literate behavior is part of the

Western notion of a line drawn between 'civility' and 'savagery'" (2012, p. 9). In an international development context, literacy is often framed as something which leads to improved outcomes for health and public engagement and "the assumption that without literacy, an adult is unable to function on an equal basis in society" (Robinson-Pant 2010, p. 136).

Because of this view, measures of literacy carry high stakes in national and international comparators of nations and their citizens. Data generated by international measures of literacy, such as the International Adult Literacy Survey (IALS), and more recently the Program for International Assessment of Adult Competencies (PIAAC), are routinely used "as a warrant in policy documents to justify and legitimate the detailed case for policy initiatives" (Hamilton 2014). Within this context, large-scale quantitative research is privileged as a source of evidence to inform policy. This large-scale data comes from assessments which rely upon an assumption, first and foremost, that the sets of skills and practices being tested are in fact measurable. For quantitative measuring to be achievable, what counts as literacy must therefore be reduced to a set of outcomes which can be quantitatively measured.

The dominance of a quantitative, instrumental way of understanding what it means to be literate also has an impact on the ways in which literacy skills are taught across many jurisdictions. A narrowed, instrumental model of literacy which objectifies language has long been part of a hierarchy of practice in education, characterised by the privileging of "schooled" knowledge (Street and Street 1991) over the diverse practices of homes and communities. High-stakes testing is implicated in this narrow conception of schooled literacy, impacting on teachers and learners directly, both through education policy which responds to global measures of competition and through the pressures generated by a performative agenda to teach to the test. The impact of this in both the compulsory and post-compulsory sectors has been widely researched and documented (see, e.g. McIntyre and Jones 2014; Comber 2012; Atkinson 2012). In England, recent iterations of the National Curriculum have seen home and community practices further marginalised, with an emphasis on the teaching and assessment of phonics and grammar in the primary phase and the British literary canon given a central role in the teaching of English in secondary schools (Department for Education 2014).

An instrumental model of literacy, then, frames it as a cognitive skillset benignly acquired by an individual: something we either have, or that we don't. The taking up of this model within policy can be linked to a wider neoliberal discourse of the individual's contribution to society, and of global competition between societies based on a range of measures. The lens of literacy has already allowed us to see how the implementation of policy relies upon the representation of subjects in a particular way. In the case of literacy on the estate, this is as passive and deficient.

At this point, we take a look back at the ways in which the estate itself has, in many respects, been subject to what Ball has described as "the construction of a world of meanings" (2013, p. 17) which have underpinned the last century of social policy in Britain. The next section provides a brief history of the estate, which is one of many large areas of social housing developed by local governments across the UK during the early to the mid-twentieth century. The model of literacy I encountered in my meeting with the local government worker, and that is evident in the examples I observed of the enactment of social policy on the estate, is then located within the wider context of more recent welfare reform, which has directly affected the lives of participants. This bigger picture allows us to explore the idea that a narrow way of looking at literacy is symptomatic of the framing of those facing economic challenge, and is also implicated in exacerbating the difficulties that are faced by those who live on a low income.

A Brief History of the Estate

The beginnings of the estate where the research took place were established in the 1930s, when residents of inadequate inner-city housing were rehomed as part of what was known as the "slum clearance". The first part of the estate was built in crescents of semi-detached, brick homes, modelled on country cottages. This design was influenced by its philanthropic benefactor, who wanted to create the feel of a garden city in the new suburbs which were being created on the outer edges of the city (Matthews 2015). These crescents focused around schools and other community hubs, such as playing fields. With the pressing need to house those bombed out of their inner-city homes in the Second World War, a further 2752 houses were built between 1945 and 1952 (ibid.). These included streets of prefabricated steel- or concrete-structured housing, colloquially known as "prefabs". Built to house the workforce of local mines and manufacturing industries and their families, these semi-detached houses, and surrounding roads, were constructed in part from the labour of former German prisoners of war, who were detained by the British government to contribute to such reconstruction efforts. This housing stock is still home to many on the estate today, and some of those first residents are still represented in the increasingly elderly population of the area. Terry and Carol, whose story is featured in Chap. 5, live in the 50-year-old steel-framed prefab in which Terry's parents lived and in which he was born.

A major motorway was opened in 1959, skirting the edge of the estate. Having initially encapsulated the optimism and aspiration its residents held for their new lives in a modern Britain, in time, the road came to represent the beginning of change in the community, symbolising as it did a new age of mobility, both social and geographic. The modern suburb, designed to offer such a bright future to their parents two decades previously, could not meet the needs of the next generation. Many left the area in the 1960s and 1970s, due to a lack of available housing and limited social and economic opportunity. Some of those who work within the community today, such as the vicar and the Catholic priest, speak of this as a "lost generation" and the impact of this mobility can still be felt in the community. The area has a higher than average population of elderly residents living alone, alongside a much younger demographic of families, moved into the area from other social housing across the city, which, overall, has three times the number of local authority homes compared to England more widely (Office for National Statistics n.d.). Many residents on the estate who struggle to make ends meet are also still experiencing the impact of the closure of the local mines and factories which had supported generations of workers. Residents mourn the loss of local resources and facilities. "It's not like it used to be" is a common theme in conversation with older residents.

One way of providing a picture of the estate in recent times is to look at the official statistics which are generated from sources such as the national census and from neighbourhood surveys. Data from the ONS suggests a higher than average number of residents on this particular estate working in skilled trades, process, plant and machinery operation, and caring and service occupations, compared to the wider city and national figures. The number of residents claiming any kind of working age benefit is nearly twice that of the wider city, and a higher number of people claim incapacity or disability living allowance compared to the city's average. The estate has a higher than average population of elderly residents living alone and of young mothers. The number of people who report to be involved in the unpaid care of family, friends, and neighbours with long-term physical or mental health problems is a third higher than the figures for the wider city. Residents on the estate are predominantly white British, and 96.5% of those aged over three report that they speak English as their main language (ONS 2016).

Despite a significant local authority welfare agenda and a strong presence for this on the estate, including the focus on literacy already mentioned, residents I spoke to described where they lived as "the Forgotten Estate", and this sentiment was reflected in many other comments. It suggests a disconnect between local government priorities for the estate and those of the people who live there. But the residents of this estate are not alone in experiencing the impact of what Fraser (1997) calls a lack of recognition, both in public and policy discourses.

Framing "The Forgotten Estate"

As publicly owned housing, council estates have, since their origins, been subject to public and policy discourse which has shaped the experience of their residents. As can be seen from the brief history of this particular estate outlined above, there has been a shift in the way in which council estates have been framed within this discourse. In her work on council housing estates, Lynsey Hanley (2012) describes how, in the early twentieth century, social housing provision was considered a "national asset" (p. 46). At a time of potential political unrest during the first decades of that century, housing policy was motivated by a desire amongst policy makers to provide for working families. The decades immediately following the Second World War saw the Labour government's housing policy influenced by a "preoccupation [...] with the health and dignity of the working man" (ibid., p. 80). Public housing was designed to be attractive, spacious, light, and comfortable, to "ameliorate the huge inequalities in health and social status that existed in pre-war Britain" (ibid., p. 82). The warmly remembered personal narratives of some of the first residents of the estate, shared in the community theatre project, nostalgically reflect the excitement of moving to a newly built home, often before there was even a road outside or house number to identify it. Many of these older residents recall a sense of hope for the future and collective endeavour in the project of their new community (Jones et al. 2013).

However, as Hanley also outlines, the design of social housing with this specific ideological purpose of reducing inequalities became problematic for those who came to live in them. For some residents, the move to a less densely populated area on the periphery of the city not only meant costly transport to places of work and social centres, but also signalled the loss of a way of life. Despite modern amenities and open space, some of the first residents felt a sense of isolation, and that their familiar communities had been dispersed (Matthews 2015). Another paradox existed in the fact that this new housing had a characteristic design as well as specific location, which made it easier to stigmatise (Hanley 2012). In my own research, I found that even within the estate itself, some residents felt particular kinds of housing were associated with certain people or values. The origins of the estate can still be felt in comments such as this one from a member of the Tenants and Residents' Association, interviewed for the community theatre project:

> We've always felt separate; we've been treated as separate. The other side of [the estate] thought we were posh – brick houses, concrete.

The stigmatisation of council housing estates over recent decades has compounded the challenge for many living on low incomes (Dean and Hastings 2000; Page 2000). It has come at a time when many residents of such estates are bearing the brunt of deindustrialisation and the isolation caused by a lack of public resources. Imogen Tyler (2013, p. 162) argues that recent times have seen the council estate become metonymic shorthand for "new class of problem people". Far from the ideal of post-war socialism, "estates have come to mean more as a cipher for a malingering society than as places where people actually live" (Hanley 2012, p. 146).

Like others across the UK, the council estate featured in this book is framed in public and policy discourse as welfare-oriented and low in educational attainment and aspiration. Some of the time I spent as an ethnographic researcher on the estate coincided with the end of the New Labour government of 1997–2010 and the first months of its successor Conservative-Liberal Democrat coalition. This time also saw an increase in the vilification in popular political discourse of those finding it hardest to get by, many of whom lived in social housing on estates such as the one where my research participants lived (see, e.g. O'Hara 2015; Hills 2015; Baumberg et al. 2012; Garthwaite 2011).

The project of social inclusion had long been on the political agenda, however. From his very first address as prime minister in 1997, in a speech on the Aylesbury Estate, Southwark, Tony Blair publicly proclaimed New Labour's ambition of remodelling a post-industrial society, promising that there would be "no forgotten people in the Britain I want to build" (cited in Tyler 2013, p. 159). New Labour initiatives such as *SureStart* provided a focal point for welfare provision based on early intervention with families, and welfare provision was increasingly tied to developing the skills that would prepare those previously excluded from society to re-integrate into a new knowledge economy. This was the policy I encountered at work in my interactions with local authority personnel and, in particular, in the ways in which they talked about literacy and the provision that was designed around it. As Ball (2013, p. 176) notes, however:

> within this approach exclusion was constructed and addressed as primarily a social problem of community and family inadequacies rather than an economic problem of structural inequality.

Tony Blair's pledge 11 years previously had done little for some of the residents living on "the forgotten estate". And, for many of them, things were about to get worse.

"Austerity" Policy: Are We Really All in This Together?

In 2010, a Conservative-Liberal Democrat coalition came into power in the UK, bringing with it an amplification of a discourse of deficit and undeservedness that was channelled into the justification of a raft of social policy reform. Much of this reform was aimed at what the Chancellor of the Exchequer George Osborne was to call "the unfairness of the something- for-nothing-culture" of the UK welfare system (Hansard 2013). As Clark and Newman have outlined:

> the contemporary politics of austerity combines an economic logic with a particular moral appeal (to shared sacrifice and suffering, to fairness and freedom, to a sense of collective obligation). (2012, p. 309)

Economic measures taken in the name of "austerity" are premised, according to Tyler (2013), on the unshackling of poverty from economic inequality and its framing as a psycho-cultural problem. The message underpinning this is that "we are all in this together" (Osborne 2012). Blame for circumstances brought about by a global financial crisis is attributed to the moral failings of some members of society whose reliance on welfare is deemed to be "unfair". This has led to a new landscape of social class, as described by Mike Savage (2015), where traditional divisions have been realigned and a more disparate class system is dominated by a unifying sentiment of attention directed at the bottom, including a return to levels of stigmatisation which echo the Victorian trope of the deserving and undeserving poor. Alongside this has been the "moralisation of place" (p. 52), linked to communities already marginalised by being the least economically well off, and to where they live, including council housing estates.

Framed as morally imperative, "austerity" policy reform led to the greatest impact on the UK welfare state in half a century. The reform included changes to housing benefit for those deemed to be "over-occupying" their social housing (popularly known as "the bedroom tax", as described in Chap. 1) and changes to the "fitness-to-work" assessment for those in receipt of disability benefits: both policies which affected the circumstances of individuals and families whose stories are featured in this book. The families with whom I worked on the research that informs this book are by no means alone in experiencing the acute challenges which have resulted from this policy reform. For example, The Trussell Trust, a charity which has a network of over 400 food banks across the UK, reported to have provided 1,182,954 three-day emergency food packages to people in crisis during 2016/2017; 436,938 of those who benefitted from these were children. This represents a 6% increase on the previous year and is up from 346,992 in 2012/2013 (Trussell Trust 2017; Garthwaite 2016).

Although the majority of people claim they are in favour of more equal economic distribution (Hills 2015), the media has a significant impact on framing public perceptions. This, argues Dorling (2015, p. 23), is the responsibility of some of the 1% who earn the highest incomes: "they own newspapers and TV channels, and they spread myths to offset the growing consensus among the 99 per cent." Coverage of social and welfare issues is commonly skewed towards "undeservedness" and "lack of reciprocity" (Baumberg et al. 2012). The genre of Factual Welfare Television attracts huge audiences (De Benedictis et al. 2017). Dubbed "poverty porn", programmes such as Benefit Street (Channel 4, 2014) have echoes of Victorian travelogues amongst the urban poor. Mooney and Hancock (2010) describe how the genre "provides fascination and nurtures revulsion among the viewing public and provides a focus for who is to be blamed for a broken society". However, as they go on to note:

> it provides a view of poverty and people experiencing poverty out of context; it offer[s] a vision, and a very partial and flawed understanding of poverty which d[oes] not consider the underlying social and economic factors that work to generate and reproduce poverty over time.

Rather than furthering debate about the structural causes of poverty, these programmes compound the dominant representation of individuals and families in receipt of welfare as a demonised and humiliated other (Tyler 2013), perpetuating media-friendly tropes such as "skivers" versus "strivers", "shirkers" rather than "workers" (Garthwaite 2011).

This kind of framing plays into the "moral vocabularies of justification" for welfare policy reform (Clark and Newman 2012, 304). As Lister notes, "stigmatising labels can produce stigmatising policies" (2004, 114). This divisive discourse was seen in a speech in the House of Commons by then Chancellor of the Exchequer, George Osborne, who referred to "the shiftworker, leaving home in the dark hours of the early morning, who looks up at the closed blinds of their next-door neighbour sleeping off a life on benefits" (Osborne 2012). Within this discourse, which is echoed in other neoliberal contexts (as described, e.g. by Taylor 1996; Sennett 2003), entitlement is a myth and dependence is vilified. As Taylor (1996) has noted in relation to US welfare systems, in such discourse:

> we are encultured into believing that those who live in the margins of society are illiterate, that they have no skills, that they are lazy, indolent, and insolent, that they are criminals, that they have nothing to offer society. (p. 193)

The impact of perpetuating injustice through this discourse is evident in the work of Wilkinson and Pickett (2010, p. 51), who note the way in which "inequality, not surprisingly, is a powerful social divider"; the less economically equal a society, the less trusting its members are of each other.

Wilkinson and Pickett's work emphasises the complex consequences of inequalities. The causes of these inequalities are equally complex. Understanding these, and the role of literacy within them, requires approaches which recognise the complexity of the everyday lives affected. From early housing policy makers, to social inclusion policy, and later reform in the name of "austerity", the estate itself, and the lives of its residents, have been framed in many ways, by different groups of people for different reasons. Much of the process which has shaped this framing has involved disassociating everyday lived experiences from the complex contexts that shape them, reducing them to sets of narrowly defined problems which can be addressed through officially mandated policy approaches. This includes the way in which literacy is framed in the comment I started with from the local authority employee. What, then, are some of the implications of this way of framing literacy within the wider context of social justice?

An Instrumental Model of Literacy: What Gets Forgotten?

Within policy on the estate, literacy is part of a wider approach to addressing issues of maldistribution, and ensuring those deemed to be in need of support are able to develop the right sets of skills to access resources and to make an economic contribution to society. Much of the provision for support with literacy is dominated by what Hamilton and Tett (2012) describe as a discourse of human resource development. Far from being a neutral toolkit for personal development, however, framing literacy within its wider policy context, as seen in the local authority's enactment of social inclusion, illustratives the way in which, as Deborah Brandt (2001) notes, access and reward for literacy are influenced by wider—and often shifting—ideological and economic forces. As Hamilton, Tett, and Crowther have argued, the dominance of this model means that literacy is a potent symbolic cultural resource "deeply and inescapably bound up with producing, reproducing and maintaining unequal arrangements of power" (2012, p. 2). Over-emphasising a narrow, instrumental version of literacy at the cost of a more nuanced view has more far-reaching implications for social justice, not least because of the lack of recognition it represents. This approach to literacy has direct links to the sense expressed by residents of being "forgotten".

Groups targeted for literacy intervention of the kind often seen in social policy are treated homogenously, and policy responses attempt to "speak" for them (Robinson-Pant 2008). The book-gifting scheme, along with other initiatives with literacy as a focus, is an example of what Wainwright and Marandet have termed "supportive power": practices around literacy are supported and encouraged, as long as they "shape subjectivities that fit in with the government's idea of community as a site of empowerment" (2013, p. 519). This framing of subjectivities means an inherent lack of space for diverse voices and experiences to be recognised.

Within an instrumental model, not only is literacy itself objectified, but so too are those who "have" it, or, rather, are deemed not to "have" it. A context has been created which frames as "abject" (Tyler 2013) those yet to develop officially mandated skillsets or subjectivities in relation to reading and writing. Metaphors utilised within this discourse about literacy have historically evoked medical terminology, such as the need for "eradication" (Barton 1994), or the discourse of battle, with illiteracy as an enemy to be vanquished. Those who succeed in this battle are presented through heroic tales of personal transformation, having overcome "gremlins" or similar threatening figures which evoke shame and disgust (Street 1995; Hamilton 2012). Such metaphors leave those seen as yet to battle their demons framed as an "'underclass' needing priority attention from the state" (Hamilton and Pitt 2011, p. 308). In adult education policy, functional skills have been linked to employability, rather than being responsive to learner needs (Hamilton and Tett 2012; Ade-Ojo and Duckworth 2015). "Early intervention" strategies position even the youngest readers as subject to institutional intervention, which assumes need and targets the development of skills and habits that match the subjectivities of the dominant order. The taking up of the philanthropic book-gifting scheme already described is an example of how the development of an officially mandated skillset and subjectivity has become commodified and packaged as a solution to policy "problems". Here, the "problem" is framed within the health agenda, through the alignment of the book-gifting scheme with the local health authority, reflecting Chris Peers' (2011) account of a shift to epidemiological rather than sociological data to inform government policy in early childhood education. The subjectivity promoted by the book-gifting scheme in operation on the estate is that of a reader as someone who will develop, and will carry with them for life, a predefined and measurable set of skills. It could be added that the premise of the book-gifting scheme also suggests that these skills are acquired by virtue of being an individual, a consumer-as-owner of a particular set of print-based books.

Quantitative measures of literacy and its impact are, as we've seen, problematic. This applies both to what is being measured, and to the way it represents skills deemed valuable by policy makers within the societies doing the measuring. The problematic nature of quantitative measuring also applies to the difficulty of being able to represent numerically the wide range of ways in which literacy learning is actually applied in the everyday lives of individuals in diverse contexts (Bartlett 2008; Maddox

2007; Besnier 1993). Some of the consequences of becoming literate which may not necessarily fit the model of social change inferred within a particular policy discourse are also not considered in such views of literacy (Robinson-Pant 2008). An example of this, in an international context, can be seen in Shirin Zubair's work (2001), which reports on how the writing of journals as a private space by women literacy learners in Pakistan was not judged as positive by some men within their communities.

The implications of the entanglement of this narrow model of literacy within policy that so drastically shapes everyday lives are significant. Ball (2006, p. 21) reminds us, however, that imagining the realities of everyday lives to be exactly as they are framed in policy is limiting. Neither can we reduce the impact of such policy to quantitative or instrumental outcomes. Rather,

> policies pose problems to their subjects, problems that must be solved in context. Solutions to the problems posed by policy texts will be localised and should be expected to display *ad hocery* and messiness. Responses indeed must be "creative". (ibid.)

Later chapters will focus on the ways in which the everyday literacy practices of community members are resources through which they creatively navigate the problems that are posed by the policy contexts they experience. Before that, I turn to look more closely at the ways in which models of literacy which fail to notice the realities of people's daily engagement with text lead to structures of support which compound the challenge for those in need of access to text-based resources. This is evident in what has happened at perhaps the most iconic site of literacy within the community: the local library.

References

Ade-Ojo, G. and Duckworth, V. (2015) *Adult Literacy Policy and Practice: From intrinsic values to instrumentalism*. London: Palgrave Macmillan

Atkinson, T. (2012) 'Beyond disempowering counts: Mapping a fruitful future for adult literacies', in Tett, L., Hamilton, M. and Crowther, J. (eds.) *More Powerful Literacies*. Leicester: NIACE, pp. 75–88

Bailey, M., Harrison, C. and Brooks, G. (2002) The 'Boots Books for Babies' project: Impact on library registrations and book loans', *Journal of Early Childhood Literacy*, 2 (1) 45–63

Ball, S. (2006) *Education Policy and Social Class*. London: Routledge

Ball, S. (2013) *The Education Debate* (Second Edition). Bristol: Polity Press

Bartlett, L. (2008) 'Literacy's verb: exploring what literacy is and what literacy does', *International Journal of Educational Development*, 28, 737–753

Barton, D. (1994) *Literacy: An introduction to the ecology of written language*. Oxford: Blackwell

Barton, D. and Hamilton, M. (1998) *Local Literacies: Reading and Writing in One Community*. London: Routledge

Baumberg, B., Bell, K. and Gaffney, D. (2012) *Benefits Stigma in Britain*. University of Kent/Elizabeth Finn Care

Besnier, N. (1993) 'Literacy and Feelings: the encoding of affect in Nukulaelae letters', in Street, B. (ed.) *Cross-cultural Approaches to Literacy*, Cambridge: Cambridge University Press, pp. 62–86

Brandt, D. (2001) *Literacy in American Lives*. Cambridge: Cambridge University Press

Brandt, D. (2015) *The Rise of Writing: Redefining Mass Literacy*. Cambridge: Cambridge University Press

Channel 4 (2014) *Benefits Street*, Love Productions/ Rebel Uncut

Clarke, J. and Newman, J. (2012) 'The alchemy of austerity', *Critical Social Policy*, 32 (2) 299–319

Comber, B. (2012) 'Mandated literacy assessment and the reorganisation of teachers' work: federal policy, local effects', *Critical Studies in Education*, 53 (2) 119–136

Dean, J. and Hastings, A. (2000) *Challenging Images: Housing estates, stigma and regeneration*. Bristol: Policy Press

De Benedictis, S., Allen, K. and Jensen, T. (2017) 'Portraying Poverty: The economics and ethics of factual welfare television', *Cultural Sociology*, 11 (3) 337–358

Department for Education (2014) *National Curriculum for England*.https://www.gov.uk/government/collections/national-curriculum   (accessed November 20, 2017)

Dorling, D. (2015) *Inequality and the 1%*. London: Verso

Fraser, N. (1997) *Justice Interruptus: Critical reflections on the 'postsocialist' condition*. New York: Routledge

Garthwaite, K. (2011) 'The language of shirkers and scroungers?' Talking about illness and disability and coalition welfare reform', *Disability and Society*, 26 (3) 369–372

Garthwaite, K. (2016) *Hunger Pains. Life inside foodbank Britain.* Bristol: Policy Press

Hall, C. and Jones, S. (2016) 'Making Sense in the City: Dolly Parton, early reading and educational policy making', *Literacy,* 50 (1) 40–48

Hamilton, M. (2012) *Literacy and the Politics of Representation.* Oxon: Routledge

Hamilton, M. (2014) 'Global, regional and local influences on adult literacy policy in England', *Globalisation, Society and Education,* 12 (1) 110–126

Hamilton, M. and Pitt, K. (2011) 'Changing Policy Discourses: constructing literacy inequalities', *International Journal of Education Development,* 31, 596–605

Hamilton, M. and Tett, L. (2012) 'More powerful literacies: The policy context', in Tett, L., Hamilton, M. and Crowther, J. (eds.) *More Powerful Literacies.* Leicester: NIACE, pp. 31–58

Hamilton, M., Tett, L. and Crowther, J. (2012) 'More powerful literacies: An introduction' in Tett, L., Hamilton, M. and Crowther, J. (eds.) *More Powerful Literacies.* Leicester: NIACE, pp. 1–12

Hanley, L. (2012) *Estates: An intimate history* (New Edition). London: Granta

Hansard (2013) http://www.publications.parliament.uk/pa/cm201314/cmhansrd/cm130626/debtext/130626-0001.htm#13062665000002 (accessed January 13, 2014)

Hills, J. (2015) *Good Times, Bad Times: The welfare myth of them and us.* Bristol: Polity Press

Jones, S., Hall, C., Thomson, P., Barrett, A. & Hanby, J. (2013) 'Representing the 'forgotten estate': participatory theatre, place and community identity', *Discourse: Studies in the Cultural Politics of Education,* 34 (1) 118–131

Lister, R. (2004) *Poverty.* Cambridge: Polity Press

Maddox, B. (2007) 'What can ethnographic studies tell us about the consequences of literacy?', *Comparative Education,* 43 (2) 253–271

Matthews, C. (2015) *Homes and Places: A history of Nottingham's council houses.* Nottingham: Nottingham City Homes

McIntyre, J. and Jones, S. (2014) 'Possibility in Impossibility? Working with beginning teachers of English in times of change', *English in Education,* 41 (1) 26–40

Mooney, G. and Hancock, L. (2010) '*Poverty Porn* and the *Broken Society*', *Variant,* 39/40 http://www.variant.org.uk/39_40texts/povertp39_40.html (accessed September 28, 2016)

Office for National Statistics (2016) 'Persistent poverty in the UK and EU: 2014', https://www.ons.gov.uk/peoplepopulationandcommunity/personalandhouseholdfinances/incomeandwealth/articles/persistentpovertyintheukandeu/2014 (accessed November 19, 2017)

O'Hara, M. (2015) *Austerity Bites: A journey to the sharp end of cuts in the UK.* Bristol: Polity Press

Osborne, G. (2012) Speech to Conservative Party Conference, http://www. newstatesman.com/blogs/politics/2012/10/george-osbornes-speech-conservative-conference-full-text (accessed March 3, 2017)

Page, D. (2000) *Communities in the balance: the reality of social exclusion on housing estates.* York: Joseph Rowntree Foundation

Peers, C. (2011) 'The Australian Early Development Index: reshaping family-child relationships in early childhood education', *Contemporary Issues in Early Childhood*, 12 (2) 134–147

Robinson-Pant, A. (2008) 'Why Literacy Matters': Exploring a policy perspective on literacies, identities and social change', *Journal of Development Studies*, 44 (6) 779–796

Robinson-Pant, A. (2010) 'Changing discourses: literacy development in Nepal', *Journal of Educational Development*, 30, 136–144

Savage, M. (2015) *Social Class in the 21st Century.* London: Pelican Books

Sennett, R. (2003) *Respect: the formation of character in an age of inequality.* London Allen Lane

Sheffield Hallam University (2012) *Evaluation of Bookstart England: review of resources.* Centre for Education and Inclusion Research

Street, B. (1984) *Literacy in Theory and Practice.* Cambridge: Cambridge University Press

Street, B. (1995) *Social Literacies: Critical approaches to Literacy in Development, Ethnography and Education.* Harlow: Pearson Education

Street, B. (2011) 'Literacy inequalities in theory and practice: The power to name and define', *International Journal of Educational Development*, 31, 580–586

Street, B. and Street, J. (1991) 'The Schooling of Literacy' in Barton, D. and Ivanič, R. (eds.) *Writing in the Community.* London: Sage, pp. 143–166

Taylor, D. (1996) *Toxic Literacies: Exposing the injustice of bureaucratic texts.* Portsmouth, NH: Heinemann

Trussell Trust (2017) https://www.trusselltrust.org/news-and-blog/latest-stats/ (accessed September 28, 2017)

Tyler, I. (2013) *Revolting Subjects: Social abjection and resistance in neoliberal Britain.* London: Zed Books

Wainwright, E. and Marandet, E. (2013) 'Family learning and the socio-spatial practice of 'supportive' power, *British Journal of Sociology of Education*, 34 (4) 504–524

Wilkinson, R. and Pickett, K. (2010) *The Spirit Level: Why Equality is Better for Everyone*. London: Penguin

Zubair, S. (2001) 'Literacies, Gender and Power in Rural Pakistan', in Street, B. V. (ed.) *Literacy and Development: Ethnographic Perspectives*. London: Routledge, pp. 188–204

4

The Local Library: Literacy and Capital

Fig. 4.1 Image taken from the pathway approaching the local library on the estate

© The Author(s) 2018
S. Jones, *Portraits of Everyday Literacy for Social Justice*,
https://doi.org/10.1007/978-3-319-75945-6_4

The local library is one of the most iconic sites for literacy in public life. Many residents of the estate depend on their library, not only for borrowing books, but also as a source of information and a regular place to pop in and chat. This chapter presents a portrait of the work of the library, drawing on observations and interviews with its staff and users, and I have tried to capture their voices in my account of their work and their experiences.

As a public space for the support and development of literacy practices, the library represents some of the wider discourses about literacy and social inclusion discussed in Chap. 3. It has also had to respond to the impact upon its funding of economic measures taken in the name of "austerity", leading to policies which affect the access to information that many of its users depend upon. In many ways, libraries are important institutions in the democratising of the knowledge economy, within which important economic, social, and cultural resources are tied to the accessibility of different kinds of text.

Over the last few decades, there has been a shift away from notions traditionally associated with social class division, such as employment and occupation, towards a focus on the relationship between particular sets of resources and the ways in which social structures are perceived and experienced. This is often discussed through the metaphor of capital (Savage et al. 2005). Later in this chapter, I argue that while we can look at the library as central to redistributing the resources bound up in text-based practice, providing equity of access to texts and the systems which rely upon them, we must also scrutinise what counts as capital and is therefore prioritised in policy related to the work of the public institutions such as the local library. This includes questioning the assumptions made about those who are deemed deficient as a result, and examining the ways in which the politics of "austerity" has compounded the injustices they face.

First, we'll take a look at what happens in the library on the estate.

"Welcome to Your Library"

The library is located at the centre of the estate, just off the main thoroughfare of shops and cafés and the main bus route which links the estate and the wider city. Its central location can be attributed to the philanthropic legacy of the estate's early planners; as is the case on other large estates on the outskirts of the city, the library has been purposely located at the geographical heart of the community. The library is part of a purpose-built community centre, with which it shares a main entrance. Outside, when shuttered closed, the windows of the community centre reveal a colourful message—"Welcome to your library"—advertising the library's facilities, including free computer access (see Fig. 4.1). The building stands alone on land just off the main road, behind a newly renovated medical centre. It is accessible via a footpath which runs alongside the medical centre and the surrounding crescents of houses, towards the north of the estate, and the sixth-form college that is located at the estate's northern edge. This sixth-form college has a strong reputation locally, and its students commute from across the city and its suburbs to attend. The proportion of those attending the college who also live on the estate is, however, very small.

The library is one of the 16 branches run by the City Council as part of a historic statutory duty, enshrined within the Public Libraries and Museums Act 1964, "to provide a comprehensive and efficient library service for all persons desiring to make use thereof" (cited by Sieghart 2014). Like others across the city, this branch is a busy focal point for its community, with weekly tallies of customers typically numbering around 320 adults and 290 children.

The library is run by a team of two librarians and a library group manager, Graham, who has overall responsibility for three libraries in the area. The advantage of such a staffing model, according to Graham, is that

> staff are well known to the customers who come in and there is a rapport built up where if one particular staff member is in on one particular day you tend to find that certain people will only come in on that day because they feel comfortable with that member of staff.

Graham has worked in the library service for nine years, having served as a police officer for 32 years. As well as the two staff librarians, he is supported in his work by a children's librarian for the area, and her counterpart with responsibility for adult library services. Graham describes the work of his team as being very much in response to the needs of their customers, and they are trained specifically to deal with these needs. Many of the adult customers come in to ask staff for help with using the computers, and some children enjoy making use of the library as a safe and welcoming space. Graham says that there are always children waiting for them when they open up on a Saturday morning. They come in to choose their books and then spend the whole day in the library "until we close the door".

> We do have some children who come in [and] they have issues at home and they have issues in their personal lives which, unfortunately, sometimes follows them into the libraries. But our attitude is well at least they come to the libraries. And once we strike up this rapport with them we tend to find that there is a change in the way they see us because some of the kids see us as authority.

The importance of establishing and maintaining this rapport with library users (or "customers" as they are known to staff), especially the younger ones, means that staff are not uniformed. They also have a policy of not staying behind the counters all the time, as the counter can be a barrier. The librarians involve their young customers in their work, especially when it comes to looking after the children's section.

> The children know that their section is for them alone and they look after it and take care of it and if there's a mess they'll tidy it up. And we ask the kids at the end of the night to help us lock down [...] the bunch of keys is hanging up in my office and we decide which kids behave the best in the afternoon or early evening and we ask them to shut the shutters.

On entering the single-storey library space, the counter immediately faces you, upon which are numerous notices and leaflets for local services or upcoming events, displays of featured books and resources, such as the book of the week, or books on local history. There is a colourfully decorated children's area, with bright carpets and furniture, toys, low-level shelving, and book boxes which allow young library users and their parents and carers to see books displayed front on. Next to this area is a dedicated space for teenagers, including two computers specifically identified for their use. A room off the main library space, separated by a glass-panelled wall and door, houses nine public computers and is used for computer classes as well as being available so that individual customers can book a fixed terminal for their own use, either independently or supported by library staff. Around the library, a large collection of books is displayed on shelves and carrels. Titles on display include popular and contemporary fiction and some non-fiction, with displays covering featured themes, such as healthy eating. There are revolving stands which hold public information leaflets such as bus timetables.

The library staff try to ensure their stock remains appealing to their local customers. For this branch, thrillers are most popular, along with romance. Biographies and history books are less popular than in other branches, according to the staff, "but if you do a thriller display or a 'worst crimes in the world' display, they fly off the shelves". Regular customers come to know what day the delivery of new books is due, including the time that the delivery van arrives, and they make sure they are there to greet it. Customers can pay 40 pence to reserve a book, and titles by popular authors, such as Danielle Steele and Clive Cussler, can generate reservation waiting lists of up to 60 names. Staff do their best to order copies from other branches so that customers get their books within four to seven days.

Children and young people are encouraged to take part in the summer reading challenge, which is publicised in local schools, and which involves taking up a challenge to read a certain number of books over the six-week school holiday. The local library is also a vital resource during the school term, and "all the books fly off the shelves" when topics such as the Vikings or the Tudors are covered in local schools. When staff suggest that children go to the central city library or other nearby branches, the young customers will often request that the books are ordered for them to collect at their own library. There is a thriving homework club after school on a Friday, at which printing is free.

The under eighteens and over thirty age groups are the main users of the library, with a large proportion of the latter group being in retirement age and forming the core of the customer base. Many have been visiting the library on the estate since they were children themselves and now bring their own grandchildren. As Graham explains:

You tend to find that if Grandma or Granddad come in they've got a couple of grandkids with them. So they all end up going out with a library card and then you'll find those kids coming back by themselves.

As is the case across the UK, the 18–30 age group is regularly targeted by library staff, who attribute the relative lack of engagement of this age group with the library to a range of factors, including the different demands on their time, and the options they have in terms of accessing resources and information.

The library on the estate, then, is a lively, active community hub. As Graham points out, "libraries are no longer silent places and a lot of people like the buzz that a library offers". For many of the estate's library users, the library is far more than a source of books. Its location means that people will often pop into the library before their meeting at the community centre, or after it. The local children's centre and churches also make use of the library as a venue for events and as a place to engage with residents. I met Terry and Carol, whose experiences feature in Chap. 5, at a community event at the local library, where representatives of various community volunteer groups were invited to an activity morning during the Easter school holidays. At this event, residents were able to find out more about what was going on in their area and try out some of the activities, such as the crafts Terry and Carol arrange at their Messy Church and Stay and Play sessions, held at the local church.

The clubs that meet at the library include leisure groups such as the knitting and crochet group, and a book group which agrees to read a particular book and then meets monthly for members to share their thoughts. Other groups who use the space include Supportnet, which offers support, advice, and companionship to all ages and has members ranging from students in their teens to people in their 90s. The group hosts a weekly drop-in at the library and a ping-pong session every Friday in the adjoining community centre. Parents of young children are encouraged to use the library space by attending Tots Time and Stay and Play sessions. Sessions aimed at enabling and encouraging people to return to work are offered by local enterprises and welfare organisations, and there is a well-attended local councillor surgery held on the first, second, and third Saturday of each month.

As well as the clubs hosted by the library, staff themselves organise author days, art and craft sessions for children, family fun days, and coffee mornings, often with a book-related theme. There is a literacy club, where someone from the local authority is available for help and advice, as well as offering shared reading aloud, group interaction, and socialising. The adult librarian also goes out to local care and residential homes, day centres, and community centres to facilitate reading groups.

For many of the core users of the library, changes to the ways in which we engage with reading and writing in everyday lives have meant considerable shifts in the ways in which they use their library. A key component of the library's service, therefore, is access to computers and support for customers to engage with digital literacy practices.

Computer Access at the Library

Graham explains his customers' interest in accessing support with computer use:

> They want to do it because they know they have to nowadays. It's quite daunting for some people to start pressing buttons and looking at screens because they are not used to it: they are used to writing with pen and paper. But once they get the hang of it, they love it.

Free computer learning sessions are provided across all the city's libraries. These include "One2One" sessions, covering the basics of computing, such as the internet and email, Microsoft Word, downloading, and scanning. Group sessions are also offered, which cover a range of topics including social networking and online shopping. I observed a class that was hosted at the library, which offered an introduction to Facebook. Six adults had booked their place on this two-session course, each for a different reason. Amongst them was Dennis, a grandfather whose young family lived on the other side of the world. He was keen to be able to use Facebook with more confidence so that he could share in his family's experiences through the photographs and messages posted on social media. Dorothy was keen to join groups on Facebook based on her interest in astrology and crystal therapy. Anne was interested in genealogy and, having used online sources to work on her family tree, she wanted to explore the possibility of being able to contact distant family via Facebook.

Members of this class seemed fairly typical of those who come in to the library to use the computers and are amongst the three million people enabled to do so nationally through government campaigns such as *Get Online* (Sieghart 2014). They were aware of the potential of digital technology to enhance aspects of their everyday lives, and felt digital text was overtaking pen and paper in how we communicate with others. They were open to learning the new skills required and excited at the thought of what these skills would open up for them.

For those who are new to using a computer, library staff offer three one-to-one sessions, which start from holding a mouse and clicking. There are follow-ups available if needed. Popular uses of the computers at the library, as outlined by Graham, indicate the central role of digital texts in contemporary life and the importance, for many people, of being able to access these texts as part of the routine of everyday life.

> They'll go on the welfare and benefits site; the direct bus sites. But they'll also use it, funnily enough, just to do Facebook and things like that because they know that that is a way to communicate. "Find My Past" is always popular and researching your family tree and the Central Library does specialised websites on that which we show people how to access. We've got two ladies that come in here regular every week and spend an hour at a time researching family trees and all sorts. A lot of the older generation like to read the newspapers online. [...] They'll look at YouTube to watch the goals from the weekend.

Welfare reforms brought about by the Coalition government have included the introduction of online accounts for benefit claims, which Gordon refers to here. Library computers are often used for online shopping, allowing those who may find it physically difficult to get to shops to access a wider range of goods, also opening up a range of affordable options for those whose ability to shop around is limited. Like others across the UK, the local authority has a policy across all their libraries to block certain sites, including those of payday loan companies. Customers searching for these are redirected to information about alternatives such as local credit unions, Citizens Advice, and other sites with information about managing budgets.

For some library users, the need to be able to access a computer as part of their everyday lives is what brings them to the library in the first instance. Graham explains how coming in to the library to go online can, however, lead them to access the other services on offer:

> Once they are here, they look around and they see books and leaflets and they come to the counter and they want to join. That's how they become part of the library family.

For some members of the community access to computers at the library is a vital resource. For those made vulnerable by a low income, or who are socially isolated, the library offers a welcoming space where important resources are accessible, along with the support of staff and other community members. As a publicly funded service, however, the library has seen the impact of recent social policy which has led to changes in the services that can be offered.

The Library in Times of "Austerity"

Sieghart (2014, p. 21) points out that "the 21st century librarian will need to be more of a community impresario with digital and commercial expertise who can champion their communities' needs and generate new business and audiences for the library". Graham embodies this role.

A key aspect of Graham's role in recent times has been the negotiation of substantial change brought about by cuts to public spending. Across the city, the library service has also been part of a wider policy to integrate housing, health, and welfare services. This has seen the advent of Joint Service Centres in other parts of the city. These are newly built facilities where libraries, many of which were built up to a century ago and are costly to maintain, have been relocated to the same buildings as the local doctor and pharmacist, along with support with welfare and housing needs, and community resources such as youth clubs.

The principle of the Joint Service Centre is not only to respond to reduced local authority budgets but is also part of the discourse of the "one-stop shop" (Nichols et al. 2012, p. 5) involving the amalgamation of public and welfare services. This sees aspects of life such as health, housing, and leisure combined within a holistic service provided by the government. Graham outlines the logic behind this:

> You can go into that building and you can get a library book and go on the computer; you can sort your benefits out; you can sort your welfare out and your housing issues and you can go upstairs and see your doctor; go to the pharmacy and get a prescription; book the community centre for a room or a squash court and out you go – all done. Instead of here, there and everywhere.

Despite this logic, however, library staff across the city have observed an impact on library use: "with it goes your identity". Joint Service Centres, as well as funding cuts, have led to the closure of many local branch libraries. The consolidation of library services into the newer buildings addresses some issues, not least the running and maintenance costs of smaller branches, but it has left some people with difficult journeys on public transport in order to get to their new library.

Graham's colleagues across the city have noted another impact on libraries as a result of this policy. He describes one Joint Service Centre he knows in particular:

> To get to your health and your benefits and your housing and your pharmacy and your youth club, you have to go through the library and people just literally just walk straight through like it doesn't exist […] a lot of the staff there will recognise people that used to come into the library on a regular basis but they don't use it at all any more because they don't feel it's a part of the community any more. They'll go straight through the library to get to the benefits or to the doctors' upstairs.

Seen through the lens of literacy, there is a particular kind of framing in operation here whereby people's access to print and digital text is a problem to be addressed, along with their health and welfare issues.

The quest for efficiency in public services which is represented by the Joint Service Centres is also reflected in changes to the way in which people are expected to use the library. The introduction of automated issue and return services is an example of how the library service is being viewed as anonymously consumer-driven, along the lines of supermarkets and banks. RFID (Radio Frequency Identification) machines have been introduced to libraries across the city, which automatically issue books for customers and accept them through a letter box when they are returned. The rapport and sense of community which comes from being "in the library family" is affected not only because of the impact on the number of staff required, but also in the experience of library users, some of whom refuse to use the machines, only to be directed towards them by staff who are themselves encouraged to ask customers to use them.

Those who rely on the library for access to computers have also felt the impact of cuts to public spending enforced by government in recent years. Graham described the charging policy introduced for the use of computers at the library:

The first hour is free and it's a pound an hour after that.

Non-members are charged £2 for 30 minutes. The immediate impact of this on some of the most vulnerable library users is made clear when Graham describes the process involved in engaging with services which are increasingly online:

On a Monday, all the terminals are full because that's when you get your free hour and then it tends to tail off again until the end of the week when it picks up again as people realise that they need to do this or do that. Certainly things like benefit and welfare claims because they have to come back to check the reply.

The association of library services with health and welfare is an indicator of the ways in which engaging with information has been naturalised in policy as an essential aspect of everyday life. However, charges for computer use also suggest a lack of coherence in the enactment of policy, and a lack of recognition of the impact of official systems that rely on accessing information digitally.

The library on the estate works hard to provide services which respond to the interests and needs of the people who use it. This is not limited to support with access to economic resources, but also reflects other forms of resource that are drawn upon in everyday life, which are often considered as different forms of capital. A focus on the role of the publicly funded library within this metaphor offers a useful perspective on the link between literacy and social justice.

In the Frame: Literacy and Capital

For centuries, public libraries have provided what has come to be regarded by many as an invaluable service at a local level, as well as one in which national values, identities, and aspirations are enshrined. In 1850, William Ewart, MP for Dumfries in Scotland, secured the passing of a bill through the British parliament "which established the right of every town to a free public library" (Manguel 2006, p. 96). In the USA, Carnegie libraries were established in the late nineteenth century by philanthropic industrialist Andrew Carnegie. Despite being monuments to their ruthless industrialist founder, Carnegie libraries are lauded as "a fruitful cultural instrument that helped awaken thousands of intellectual lives" (ibid., p. 102). As Rayward and Jenkins have stated (2007, p. 361), libraries "are both physical spaces of intellectual work and highly symbolic places" which act as "important components of social and institutional memory". They go on to argue that:

> information infrastructure – the organizational arrangements, technologies, and practices by means of which information is routinely generated, disseminated, and used within a society – is a basic and all pervasive social "glue". Both social continuity and social change are dependent on and are supported by this infrastructure. (p. 362)

Although writing primarily about times of radical social change, such as war and revolution, Rayward and Jenkins nonetheless highlight here the place of libraries as a repository of social values, as well as their relationship to how we organise and publicly share knowledge and information.

The universality of the library service, as depicted in Sieghart's 2014 Independent Library Report for England, suggests that libraries are freely available for the benefit of all. Sieghart found that in "in England, over a third of the population visits their local library. In the poorest areas, that figure rises to nearly a half" (p. 5). This accords with attitudes to local library use by residents on the estate. As Graham, the library manager, pointed out, as well as being a source of reading material and information, the library is also a space which represents public sharing, be this in print or digital form, or through personal interaction. Pahl and Allan (2011) found that participants in their study of a public library in Rotherham saw it as an accessible, safe, and welcoming meeting point for friends. As a public space in societies which are becoming increasingly private, the library offers neutral ground for social interaction with strangers of differing ages, classes, ethnicities, genders, and religions. Catherine Compton-Lilly (2017, p. 25) sees the public library as "a space of possibilities" which supports the realisation of aspirations across generations. As is the case for many of the estate's residents, a regular trip to the library can offer consistency and routine, and thus can become imbued with a deep sense of attachment (Leckie and Hopkins 2002). For those whose home circumstances are difficult, such as the mothers and children living in a homeless shelter who were featured in the work of MacGillivray et al. (2010), the library is a quiet place offering respite from stress, and the opportunity to engage in one's interests without distraction or judgement.

The experience of many library users, and the values of library staff, suggests that public libraries represent an underlying ideology that is "inherently democratic, neutral, educational, and inclusive" (Leckie and Hopkins 2002, p. 333). However, the symbolic relationship between the library as a public institution and other government departments with local, regional, and national priorities means that the work of the library in the community can also reflect ideologies related to literacy such as those discussed in Chap. 3, where officially mandated literacy skills are tied to the subjectivities valued by those in power. This, in turn, shapes access to and support for literacy practices at a local level, and challenges the inherent neutrality, democracy, and inclusivity of publicly funded support for literacy. As we saw in Chap. 3, one of the key ideological forces behind this model of literacy is the belief in a particular role for literacy in social inclusion, premised upon the idea of certain groups of people being deficient in the "right" kind of assets to get by in life, while those with these assets are better placed to accumulate more. This means they can do more than just get by, but also get on.

The metaphor of capital emphasises the value of a resource as a source of power or influence for those in possession of it. The metaphor also has associations with economic notions of investment and accumulation, as well as the exploitation that can be a part of those processes. Capital incorporates the idea of volume. It is something of which there can be more, or less; there can be more for some people and less for others. This is partly because individuals and groups within society can accrue capital, leading to "the storing and accentuation of advantage" (Savage et al. 2005, p. 42). As Savage (2015) describes, in twenty-first-century Britain, to understand the differences and inequalities traditionally attributed to social class, one must look to the ways in which these divisions have been historically forged through processes which support the uneven accumulation of capital across society.

Libraries are important institutions in the redistribution of the assets bestowed by access to texts. Because of the association with what is deemed valuable by society, these assets are also central to the ongoing accrual of capital. One way in which this can be seen is in the access to computers provided by the library. This has links to economic resources, for example, through welfare, or through the ability to shop around online. The use of computers isn't purely tied to accessing economic resources, however, and, in addition to its economic form (which is perhaps the most obviously associated with inequalities), capital has been conceived and explored in other forms. For example, social and economic policy may be premised on a notion of *human capital*, which reflects the value of a person to an organisation or national interest. Part of the objective of providing computer classes is to develop this human capital to enhance people's contribution to the economy.

Cultural capital relates to one's cultural "tastes" (Bourdieu 1984), some of which may be more socially approved than others. These can "carry a cachet that is cultivated and reinforced by influential people and institutions. And, when such forms are legitimate, they can generate resources and advantages" (Savage 2015, p. 95). Cultural capital is not purely linked to economic status; Bourdieu (1984) cites examples of rich industrialists who may not be widely considered to demonstrate much "taste" in their choice of home furnishings, and despite the wealth on display, the huge extravagance of their homes may be considered vulgar in some circles. Savage (2015) explains that when first described by Bourdieu, the notion of cultural capital provoked concern over elitism. However, cultural practice has since diversified and there has been a focus on increasing accessibility across a range of cultural forms, as illustrated by the diverse and rapidly evolving literacy practices which are part of contemporary everyday lives. Based on a recent study of social class in the twenty-first century, Savage claims that cultural capital should now be understood to include self-assuredness in "maneuvering between choices on the menu" (p. 115). In contemporary everyday life, therefore, it becomes increasingly beneficial to have confidence in navigating the eclectic cultural forms which exist in the varied social contexts in which we find ourselves, and through the broad range of media with which we may engage. At the library, reading groups can be seen to support the development of cultural capital, as can classes in using Facebook. The latter also supports people to make and maintain connections with each other through the online practices which have become such important aspect of everyday life for many of us.

The networks of friends and colleagues to which we have access, based on our social standing, may be considered *social capital.* Put simply by John Field (2008, p. 1): "relationships matter". One of the most well-known accounts of social capital is presented by Robert Putnam (2000), whose depiction of shifts in American society towards more social isolation articulates a view that working together for a communal goal has benefits not least for wider society but also for individual health and well-being. This agenda was taken up in social policy on both sides of the Atlantic. Former US President Bill Clinton is known to have taken a particular interest in Putnam's depiction of American society at the end of the twentieth century, and Putnam's ideas of social capital and community can be seen to have informed the recent social policy discourse of the Conservative government in the UK, which was discussed in Chap. 3. Savage (2015) presents social capital as another significant factor in the experience of social class in the twenty-first century, arguing that it "also has an exclusive character which benefits those in the most advantaged situations" (p. 129).

For Bourdieu, different kinds of capital, such as cultural and social capital, work in different ways to gain advantage in various areas of life, or "fields" (Bourdieu 1984). We can take education as an example here. A middle-class family might have the experience and understanding of the higher education system to enable them to support their children to gain access to and succeed within it. They may be part of social networks which have enabled their children to gain support from others with their education, or have been able to broaden their children's educational experience with trips to the theatre or to historical places of interest which feature in the school curriculum. However, as Savage et al. (2005, p. 44) point out, "some advantages, by virtue of those advantages, can translate into other fields". Parents' stock of economic, social, and cultural capital to benefit their children educationally will have the knock-on effect on those children being advantaged when they enter the field of work. This includes knowledge and experience of valued cultural practice and discourse, as well as the social networks which can afford flexibility in finding employment in competitive fields. The debate over the lack of diversity within professional arenas such as journalism and politics often centres on this issue. Those entering these professions can often do so because of their links to particular educational institutions or by virtue of them having the means to gain experience working in unpaid roles while being supported by their families. As Savage (2015, p. 46) notes, therefore, "some resources permit groups the ongoing capacity to enhance themselves (which is denied to those without access to them)". The connection between different forms of capital is also central to understanding its links to inequalities. Capital exerts what Bourdieu (1984) has called *symbolic power*. The efforts of well-resourced and well-connected parents act like an inheritance, meaning that capital accrued is passed on, reinforcing existing balances of power. Tacit acceptance of social arrangements like this results in *symbolic violence* being perpetrated upon those who are subjected to such systems of dominance.

The overlapping nature of different forms of capital, the advantages or disadvantages which result from this, and the impact on the lived experience of individuals and communities have been the focus of much discussion in relation to literacy and inequality. One of the most significant contributions in this area in recent times has been that of Neuman and Celano, who have looked at the implications of provision of opportunities for literacy practice and the development of capital. The significance of their reading of literacy and inequalities is particularly evident if we consider the ways in which different forms of capital support each other. They argue that "paradoxically, it is often the nonmaterial resources like social and cultural capital that carry the greatest potential for inequality" (2012, p. 4). In their research, based in public libraries in Philadelphia, Neuman and Celano present a survey of the "ecology" of literacy across different communities in the city. Like other cities across the globe, it is a place where a "new political geography divorces the interests of the rich from the welfare of the poor, creating a more polarized society" (2012, p. 121). They examine the social environment of literacy and the opportunities for reading and writing which exist in differing neighbourhoods, arguing that these settings for literacy are important sources in developing understanding of the inequalities which exist in the academic outcomes of children from different communities. "The environment", they say, "affects what activity settings are likely to be possible, the task demands, the scripts for conduct, the purposes or motives of the participants, and the cultural meaning of the interactions" (Neuman and Celano 2001, p. 11). As such, the environment for literacy has a direct impact on the capital available to individuals, families, and communities.

Through quantitative analysis of the resources available in communities where residents were either of low or middle income, as well as observation of the use of these resources in public libraries, Neuman and Celano (2006) build their case for "leveling the playing field" for children and young people from different socioeconomic backgrounds. They argue that the differential outcomes in children's educational attainment can be directly linked to the varying stocks of capital in their families and communities. A low-income household, for example, will have less economic capacity to buy books and other resources for learning. Observations in parts of the city which were home to the communities they studied also revealed that the occurrence of print in the local environment was also varied. The number of signs displayed was greater in the more well-off suburbs, and they were in a better state of repair. In the less well-off areas, the number of places selling reading materials was smaller, and the range available was narrower (Neuman and Celano 2001, 2006, 2012). One implication of this, the authors argue, is that reduced access to print results in the curtailing of opportunities for interaction with family members around reading and writing. This, they suggest, limits encounters with vocabulary outside everyday experience and the decontextualised language which is widely understood to be important in the cognitive process of learning to read.

A key argument for Neuman and Celano is that an imbalance in resources for literacy learning, and in the opportunities to engage with them alongside other people, has a direct impact on the experience of learning to read. They cite Stanovich's (1986) model of The Matthew Effect which, using an allusion to the New Testament, argues that those who are rich in reading skills get richer, while the poor get poorer. Neuman and Celano warn that a lack of opportunity to develop key reading skills at a young age sets up children from less well-off homes and communities to start their schooling on "a negative spiral of cumulative disadvantage" (2006, p. 180). Being behind at school results in a "knowledge gap", not least as "students who are likely to read a lot, know a lot; those who are reluctant readers are likely to read less, and know less" (2012, p. 5).

Here we have a model of literacy as a source of *information capital*. This form of capital is of particular value in a knowledge economy:

> Today, the prosperity of companies and nations has come to demand high-level human and information capital – knowledge workers – who can mobilise their skills and talents to promote innovation and greater productivity. As the newest form of human capital, information is seen as having an intrinsic value in and of itself; further, sharing information can be a means of sharing power. (p. 4)

Two aspects of information capital work together to confer advantage on those who possess it. The first is that exposure to print leads to word knowledge. This enhances the development of knowledge through reading, and greater knowledge facilitates quicker, and more extensive, reading.

The second is the development of confidence in "the intellectually disciplined process of actively and skillfully conceptualizing, applying, and/or evaluating information gathered from multiple texts in new digital environments" (p. 19).

Neuman and Celano argue that a knowledge gap compounds the detrimental effect of social inequalities on social mobility and educational opportunity, meaning "students who live in concentrated poverty will not have a fighting chance" (p. 7). Theirs is a model which directly promotes literacy as central to the acquisition of capital; it challenges unequal processes of accumulation which lead to equally unbalanced benefits for those with, or without, the capital which is valued. "Leveling the playing field" involves creating equal access to material resources. In fact, they argue that any policy strategy to redress the imbalance of resources should target *more* of them at the less well-off communities, as well as more opportunities to engage with these resources in ways which are deemed valuable to literacy development, including encountering reading being modelled by "scaffolding adults" (p. 6).

Libraries are a central resource in Neuman and Celano's campaign to "level the playing field". Their ecological study of neighbourhoods in Philadelphia found that as institutions, libraries serve as a crucial hub. They note too that:

> committed to social justice and free and equal access for all, the library has been one of the few institutions that have historically focused on breaking down social, economic, and educational barriers. (ibid., p. 16)

More importantly, for Neuman and Celano, the library provides information. When information is viewed as capital, the library is therefore "a critical pathway for social and economic mobility" (p. 16).

Viewing literacy as information capital foregrounds some of its direct links to inequalities. We have seen in the portrait presented at the beginning of this chapter that one of the most valuable functions of the local library to many of the estate's residents is as a place where they can access and engage with information. Neuman and Celano make direct links between information capital and human capital, with knowledge an essential component of each. Having knowledge enhances an individual's capacity to engage with society and also to affect change within it: "the expert is someone who not only knows everything about a game but who can anticipate the next play" (p. 105). Supporting the development of information capital is therefore aimed at increasing the agency of all young people as they enter a world where they will need "the Four C's" "to compete in global society: critical thinking, communications, collaboration and creativity" (p. 105).

The emphasis throughout the work of Neuman and Celano is therefore on redressing imbalance in access and accumulation of information capital so as to maximise human capital. Their case for supporting literacy development to increase the agency of individuals and their communities is in many ways a powerful one. It is an argument which places literacy at the heart of the debate regarding the inequalities which are ingrained by many different factors into lived experience across different communities.

However, a closer look at how literacy is framed within a model of social inclusion premised on capital allows us to dig a little deeper into some of the implications of this for social justice.

Literacy and Capital: Gains and Losses

The use of the term "capital" suggests that the possession of these advantages is supported by wider structures in society:

> in order for a resource to become a form of capital, it needs to be shown that there are systemic processes allowing the garnering of such resources by those who possess it. (Savage et al. 2005, p. 45)

These "systematic processes" include those which are involved in the definition of what counts as valuable literacy, for example, why it is deemed of value, and to whom (see Chap. 3). So, whose knowledge and practice is valued in the public systems which support literacy and its role in the development of different forms of capital?

Let's start with the youngest library users. Recent years have seen an increase in focus on this group in libraries, with dedicated areas designed for their use and activities organised for them, as can be seen in the library on the estate. As was discussed in Chap. 3, such "early intervention" is a feature of neoliberal social policy. This aims to build a child's human capital, in particular, their capacity to succeed in school, and therefore to go on to be a useful member of society in later life. Early intervention policy is often premised upon an economistic argument (e.g. Field 2010), based on the idea of the savings to be made on public spending in the future when individuals are targeted early on to develop the knowledge, skills, and dispositions required for dominant cultural and social systems. Writing in an Australian context about a national measurement of learners in the early years, Peers (2011, p. 135) challenges such a framing of young children as human capital:

It lays down rules about how we should think about the child. It also introduces notions of an economically defined citizenship in relation to the child, by making us think about causes of economic success or failure (in a child's future life as an employee) decades before they might ever take effect.

This focus on the youngest of users means that, as Sue Nichols (2011) observes, libraries are no longer places of stillness and quiet; rather they are the focus of much energy directed at engaging these customers and their families. Nichols and her colleagues have examined the space of the library from the perspective of young children and their carers, and their work demonstrates that attending to the library as an activity space for younger users, and as a locus of activity around early and family literacy, reveals important issues of power, difference, and values (Nichols et al. 2012).

The way in which the library is physically organised reveals a lot about and how it is intended to be used, and how the accessing and sharing of information and knowledge is imagined. Helen Smith (2018) describes a public library in a small town in the East Midlands of England, showing how its librarians had designated a particular, closed-off space within the library as a "children's area". This, they told her, made it "part of the library but, if you like, a separate part of the library". This space was demarcated by shallow book boxes and small furniture, rugs, toys, and educational posters. Books for older children had their own space on shelving behind the fiction shelves, and young adult books were shelved with the adult fiction. In her analysis of what "counts" as literacy in this library, Smith notes the prominence of fiction, and of reading scheme books. Both were presented so that they were within the easiest reach of adults choosing books to read with their children. Activities organised to promote literacy within the library were heavily modelled on the pedagogies young readers would encounter at school, with young children encouraged to sit still in a group and listen to the library assistant reading to them from the front. They took turns and put up their hands to answer questions, and dutifully completed craft-based activities which had been modelled for them by the adult leading the session. Although some of the activities put on at the library to engage children and their families during the school holidays suggested some acknowledgement of popular culture and reference to family films, the emphasis was on supporting the literacy development of the youngest readers, and preparing them for success in school. Staff working at the library reported their perceptions of their role, and how they felt it was their responsibility to support the literacy development of young children, but also to model the behaviours which were valued in parents and carers, namely, how to choose the "right" books and how to engage with their children to ensure they were learning. Smith's work echoes the findings of Nichols and her colleagues (2012), who report a perception of the library as "the grandparents of the community, responsible for passing on cultural traditions which have been threatened by cultural diversity and globalisation" (p. 153).

The messages about literacy in the library on the estate include its importance to success in school, which also involves certain physical and social behaviours which are modelled by librarians in their family literacy sessions. However laudable such an aim is for a public institution, the way in which key actors are positioned within such messages about literacy must also be recognised. It has been noted that a model of literacy as capital to be accrued by children, who are themselves human capital, positions the parent or carer as a resource for the child's development (Peers 2011, p. 138). Family literacy activities promote particular kinds of engagement around texts, some of which can frame families as deficit when their own experiences diverge from those being modelled by this public institution. Family literacy programmes, despite their attempts to diminish disadvantage, can serve to augment it when parents whose literacy practices differ from those promoted may not feel the pleasure of the encounter but rather perceive it as punishment (Janes and Kermani 2001). Ward and Wason-Ellam (2005, p. 97) found in their study of community libraries in Canada that some librarians were sensitive to this aspect of their role and had noticed that "the literacy 'label' tended to discourage some people from participating in some library programs". Their research also highlights the other barriers to accessing the resources held within the public library. This includes physical access, which can be difficult for those on a low income with young children, who may find themselves having to trek across town on public transport to find a well-resourced library (Nichols et al. 2012; MacGillivray et al. 2010), incurring financial cost, and having to expend the considerable time and physical exertion it can take to get anywhere with very small children without a car. Although the resources found once they arrive at the library will come free of charge, they still require "knowledge of the service, and a positive expectation of the outcome" (Nichols et al. 2012, p. 15). Branding lack of engagement with reading as a deficit on the part of the parent therefore runs the risk of ignoring a range of factors which are a feature of everyday life on a low income.

As was discussed earlier in this chapter in relation to different types of capital, a library represents an opportunity to access and share knowledge and to accrue the capital needed to get on. As well as the children's section, another key aspect of the work of the library on the estate is in providing access to computers. As Ward and Wason-Ellam note, "public libraries reflect the society that sustains them, providing insight into the currently acceptable interactions with literacy" (2005, p. 92). Being able to use a computer is currently enshrined within the enactment of public policy, and classes such as those held at the library are popular not least because of the way in which welfare systems are now digitally accessed. In reality, however, as Graham the library manager outlined, those who have no choice but to use the library to access the welfare system are disadvantaged in at least two ways. Firstly, there is the impact on economic resources. To be able to access benefits, claimants have to endure a lengthy and complex process of form filling, which can be time-consuming, even for the most confident computer user. To be told the outcome of this, the user then has to return, and, as Graham has described, be charged for the privilege of accessing this information.

Secondly, the time it takes to engage with information in this way also adds to the challenge. Neuman and Celano (2012) describe the ways in which students from less well-off backgrounds rely on the computers at their community library to complete their homework. The same is true for many of the young people who come to the library on the estate. However, having to think ahead in order to book a slot on the computer, having to wait for others to finish before taking their turn at an allotted time, and having to complete tasks under time constraints necessarily affect the ways in which library customers can use a computer. This is another factor which contributes to the reality of managing life on a low income: it is very time-consuming (Lister 2004; Toynbee 2003).

Having to rely on public resources like this can limit access to information. In the case of those claiming benefits, it compounds the ways in which they are already framed through the "fundamental asymmetry" of a bureaucratic system as suppliers of information (Sarangi and Slembrouck 1996, p. 45). In the face-to-face and telephone encounters described by Sarangi and Slembrouck two decades ago, service users, unlike the civil servants with whom they are dealing, were not entitled to demand information themselves. Nowadays, interacting with a faceless system on a shared computer and under time constraints, a person claiming benefits still has little opportunity to ask for information, accentuating the imbalance of power in their relationship with the system.

Much of the focus on a so-called digital divide between those with access to computers and those without is on providing this access in public spaces such as libraries (Viseu et al. 2006). This policy was often based upon a belief that public access would be a temporary step towards people's private ownership of the means to access. Viseu et al. outline some of the issues which differentiate public and private access to computers. These include location, with public access necessitating a trip; the nature of the physical space in which it takes place, and the number of people who use the terminals. Some of the features identified in relation to public access are reminders of the ways in which such access is premised upon assumptions about its value and about the role of digital interactions in everyday lives. The use of the computers in a public space can be limited by what is deemed "worthy" usage (p. 636). Time is an additional factor, meaning that interactions are often short and ephemeral. There is usually no capacity to store data on a public computer, adding to the transitory nature of a person's engagement with it. The capacity for being "private-in-private" is limited when one has no choice but to use a public computer to interact with, for example, online banking or benefit claims. Those who use shared computers also face a challenge in creating and maintaining a stable digital identity (p. 649), often reliant on free commercial email services which are regular targets for spam and hackers. In an age where everyday life is so reliant upon digital interaction, choices are even more limited for those without their own access to a computer. Assumptions about people's access to computers can mean that their daily lives become shaped by the need to access and share information which is demanded of them, in order to be able to make ends meet.

There are benefits from using a computer in a public space, including the facility of support from others. This was a significant factor for those in Viseu et al.'s study who were choosing to access computers in public places, rather than in private. For some of the other users in the community space where computers were used, being able to offer this technical support provided an important means of feeling valuable, and valued. This points to the fact that physical access is not the only factor in the isolation of those who do not own their own computer. It also emphasises the limitations of a model of literacy support which is based solely on redistribution.

Eubanks (2012) has explored the relationship between policies based on redistribution and their impact on the lived experiences of women in marginalised communities in the USA. She argues that a view of social justice which frames access to computers as a purely redistributive issue fails to acknowledge the realities of people's experience of technology. Within such an approach, she argues:

> marginalized communities – and the people who live within them – are seen only as products of lack and destitution, not as vast reservoirs of assets, resources, networks, expertise, strength, hope, passion, and innovation. (p. 8)

In the lives of working class women with whom she works in a YWCA community learning centre, Eubanks argues that their experience is "marked not by technology lack or deficiency but by technological *ubiquity*" (p. 9). A wider definition of the place of IT in people's lives allows recognition of the number of people who work in the field involved in data entry and processing, for example. She also highlights the role of working class women in supporting the careers of those considered to be involved in "high-tech" work, working as cleaners and in childcare, for example. This allows us to see how assumptions about the wholesale good of technology can be unpacked. As such,

> seeing high-tech equity only as broadly shared access to existing technological products ignores other social values, neglects decision-making processes, sees citizens only as consumers, and ignores the operation of institutions and social structure. (p. 26)

Eubanks points out that, unlike the deficit which is assumed in redistributive models, many of those who seek public use of IT will already have extensive experience of computers, not least because of the computerisation of welfare systems. This, according to Eubanks, is "not very different from invasive home visits by caseworkers, extensive care records or evaluations in workhouses by 'overseers of the poor'" (p. 82). The digitisation of welfare systems has facilitated an intensification of surveillance and discipline, contributing to the system becoming increasingly opaque, unpredictable, and arbitrary. Eubanks states:

> Welfare admin tech are political [...] they provide a form of hidden legislation, an emerging technological constitution that shapes manageable subjects for neoliberal governance and can play a significant role in reproducing power asymmetries. (p. 83)

As Eubanks (2012, p. 23) warns, therefore: "working toward an information age that protects human rights and acknowledges human dignity is far more important than strategies centred on access and technology distribution allow". The policy of charging for computer use at the library does little in this regard. Rather, it emphasises, as Clarke and Newman

(2012, p. 306) describe, "the ways in which new landscapes of inequality get mapped on to existing ones". As Sieghart (2014) points out in the Independent Library Report for England, libraries support the work of many government departments, given the increasing requirement for engaging with public services online, from vote registration, vehicle tax renewals, driving test bookings, and passport applications. At a time when the demands upon them to access online services is only increasing, this is another example of the punitive impact of cuts in public spending on the least able to absorb it.

What Is at Stake for Literacy and Social Justice?

The metaphor of capital has been usefully employed across a range of sociological discussions which focus on inequalities, and it underpins much of the policy which is in place to address these inequalities and their impact. It is useful because there is, embodied within the metaphor, an acknowledgement of the power of certain resources in allowing us not only to get by, but also to get on in life. The recognition of different forms of capital emphasises that this involves more than just having economic capacity, and that the different assets that are afforded by cultural and socially valued practices and connections intertwine to confer advantage.

A critical view of capital also allows us to acknowledge its role in the power structures of society, and in the inequalities which exist between those who "have" certain capital and those who do not. The lens of literacy makes visible some of these inequalities. While the notion of capital offers a means through which inequalities may be challenged, it also allows us to see the ways in which public approaches to literacy can actually compound some of these inequalities. As we have seen in the portrait of the library on the estate, some of what it offers as a public institution reflects this.

Approaches which address the unequal distribution of resources are important. The implications of unequal access to information, for example, are seen in the work of Neuman and Celano, already discussed. Sieghart's Independent Library Report for England (2014) emphasises that:

> The library does more than simply loan books. It underpins every community. Is it not just a place for self-improvement, but the supplier of an infrastructure for life and learning. (p. 5)

The library also offers the chance to exercise agency and choice as a consumer of reading material, as well as experience of owning books otherwise only available through commercial consumption (Nichols et al. 2012), a fundamental principle of book-gifting schemes also. This means that those without the disposable income to buy books, magazines, and audiobooks, and to fund computer facilities, are not excluded from the social, cultural, and economic benefits these bring. The library provides many users with the opportunity to read, seek, and share knowledge as a means to feel less marginalised (MacGillivray et al. 2010). The recent closure of large numbers of libraries as a result of the cuts which have come with economic cuts made under the guise of "austerity" is obviously a threat to their users' abilities to enjoy these benefits.

Within the libraries that remain, however, models of support for literacy which go no further than redistribution can do little to address the complex causes and implications of inequalities. Approaches which reflect the instrumental model of literacy explored in Chap. 3, where literacy is a neutral, definable skillset asset to be acquired, risk compounding the marginalisation of those already positioned in deficit. Assuming these skills are, in themselves, capital ignores the question of what is valued as capital, and who gets to decide. As we have seen in previous chapters, economic resources are a fundamental part of the experience of inequality, but economic capital is not in itself enough to define these inequalities, or indeed to define one's position in society (Savage 2015). Fraser's multiple dimensions of justice emphasise that redistribution alone is insufficient (2010). Over-reliance in public policy on the pursuit of narrowly defined sets of practices frames knowledge as the most important thing in a knowledge economy, and not the person with that knowledge, or, indeed, the multiple knowledges that they may represent. The privileging of certain practices within public systems, such as the enshrining of welfare access within digital systems, or of school-based learning for the youngest of users, means that those who rely on the library for support are framed according to deficit, with little recognition of their diverse experiences.

However, the enactment of policies around literacy within the public space of the library also shows that this framing does not go unchallenged, reminding us that the library as a public space should reflect what the public wants, not just what the policy context thinks is good for us. Smith's (2018) study of a local library in the East Midlands of England explores the ways in which parents and their small children engaged with the opportunities offered by the library. These structured events framed these library users according to their potential as future school pupils, or, in the case of parents, as custodians of this human capital. In small and creative ways, however, both children and adults disrupted the discourse which aimed to shape their use of the library, instead finding their own ways to make use of the space to explore and share experiences.

Such a way of looking at what the library represents for its users emphasises its role as more than just a provider of narrowly framed and officially mandated services. This also reminds us of the reason that many people have used and loved their libraries across time:

> The power of readers lies not in their ability to gather information, in their ordering and cataloguing capability, but in their gift to interpret, associate and transform their reading […] knowledge lies not in the accumulation of texts or information, nor in the object of the book itself, but in the experience rescued from the page and transformed again into experience, in the word reflected both in the outside world and in the reader's own being. (Manguel 2006, p. 91)

The power of people to make their own meanings, and to share their own experiences in different ways, drawing on a range of textual resources, offers a direct challenge to discourses which frame them as deficient. It also disrupts the notion that any approach to social justice can be based on one dimension of these experiences. In the next chapter, I explore what happens in a local community group when they come together to share their experiences through texts.

References

Bourdieu, H. (1984) *Distinction*. London: Routledge

Clarke, J. and Newman, J. (2012) 'The alchemy of austerity', *Critical Social Policy*, 32 (2) 299–319

Compton-Lilly, C. (2017) *Reading Students' Lives: Literacy learning across time*. New York: Routledge

Field, F. (2010) *The Foundation Years: preventing poor children becoming poor adults*. London HM Government

Field, J. (2008) *Social Capital*. Second edition. Abingdon: Routledge

Fraser, N. (2010) *Scales of Justice: Reimagining Political Space in a Globalizing World*. New York: Columbia University Press

Janes, H. and Kermani, H. (2001) 'Caregivers' story reading to young children in family literacy programs: pleasure or punishment?', *Journal of Adolescent and Adult Literacy*, 44 (5) 458–466

Leckie, G. J. and Hopkins, J. (2002) 'The public place of central libraries: findings from Toronto and Vancouver', *Library Quarterly*, 72 (3) 326–372

Lister, R. (2004) *Poverty*. Cambridge: Polity Press

MacGillivray, L., Ardell, A. and Curwen, M. (2010) 'Libraries, churches, and schools: the literate lives of mothers and children in a homeless shelter', *Urban Education*, 45 (2) 221–245

Manguel, A. (2006) *The Library at Night*. New Haven: Yale University Press

Neuman, S. and Celano, D. (2001) 'Access to print in low-income and middle-income communities: An ecological study of four neighbourhoods', *Reading Research Quarterly*, 35 (1) 8–26

Neuman, S. and Celano, D. (2006) 'The knowledge gap: implications of leveling the playing field for low-income and middle-income children', *Reading Research Quarterly*, 41 (2) 176–201

Neuman, S. and Celano, D. (2012) *Giving Our Children a Fighting Chance: Poverty, literacy and the development of information capital*. New York: Teachers College Press

Nichols, S. (2011) 'Young children's literacy in the activity space of the library', *Journal of Early Childhood Literacy*, 11 (2) 164–189

Nichols, S., Rowsell, J., Nixon, H. and Rainbird, S. (2012) *Resourcing Early Learners: New Networks, New Actors*. London: Routledge

Pahl, K. and Allan C. (2011) 'I don't know what literacy is: Uncovering hidden literacies in a community library using ecological and participatory methodologies with children', *Journal of Early Childhood Literacy*, 11 (2) 190–213

Peers, C. (2011) 'The Australian Early Development Index: reshaping family-child relationships in early childhood education', *Contemporary Issues in Early Childhood*, 12 (2) 134–147

Putnam, R. (2000) *Bowling Alone: The collapse and revival of American community*. New York: Simon and Schuster

Rayward, W. B. and Jenkins, C. (2007) 'Libraries in Times of War, Revolution, and Social Change', *Library Trends*, 55 (3) 361–369

Sarangi, S. and Slembrouck, S. (1996) *Language, Bureaucracy and Social Control*. Harlow: Longman

Savage, M. (2015) *Social Class in the 21st Century*. London: Pelican Books

Savage, M., Warde, A. and Devine, F. (2005) 'Capitals, assets, and resources: some critical issues', *The British Journal of Sociology*, 56 (1) 31–47

Sieghart, W. (2014) *Independent Library Report*. Department for Culture, Media and Sport

Smith, H. (2018) 'Cooking the books: what counts as literacy for young children in a public library?', *Literacy*, 52 (1) 31–38

Stanovich, K. (1986) 'Matthew Effects in Reading: Some consequences of individual differences in the acquisition of literacy', *Reading Research Quarterly*, 21 (4) 360–406

Toynbee, P. (2003) *Hard Work: Life in Low-Pay Britain*. London: Bloomsbury

Viseu, A., Clement, A; Aspinall, J. and Kennedy, T. (2006) 'The interplay of public and private spaces in internet access', *Information, Communication and Society*, 9 (5) 633–656

Ward, A. and Wason-Ellam, L. (2005) 'Reading beyond school: Literacies in a neighbourhood library', *Canadian Journal of Education*, 28 (1/2) 92–108

5

Shared Practice in Place: Literacy and the Construction of Community

Fig. 5.1 A chain of wishes displayed within the local church

© The Author(s) 2018
S. Jones, *Portraits of Everyday Literacy for Social Justice*,
https://doi.org/10.1007/978-3-319-75945-6_5

Previous chapters have focused on the ways in which the everyday experiences of residents on the estate, and the place where they live, are framed by a discourse of deficit. This includes the privileging of an instrumental model of literacy within the public sector, and the role of this model of literacy within the systems that enact social policy. As we have seen, this model does not always recognise the realities of everyday lives, or how they are negotiated. In this chapter, the focus turns to Terry and Carol, and their friends and family, who are involved in community activities based at St Joseph's, their local church. Based on interviews and observation of their work in the community, their portrait offers much to challenge the narrow framing of communities such as those who live on the estate.

Terry and Carol

Terry and Carol live on the estate with their three teenage sons, in the prefabricated steel-framed home in which Terry was born half a century ago. As Terry says:

> I've lived here all my life – 49 years – and I've never moved. Lived there all my life. Born there. Born in the front room. Not many people can say that, can they?

Terry worked as a security guard until five years ago, when he experienced life-threatening health problems which have meant that he has been unable to work since. Carol, his wife, cares for Terry and their sons. However, she herself experiences health problems which can mean that sometimes the children have to take care of both parents.

Terry and Carol have long been involved with volunteering in their local community, including many years as volunteer leaders in the Scouting movement. I met them during an open day at the local library. They had a table there to promote their church's community activity programme, with which they had been involved for over three years. They agreed to take part in the research project and share this work.

St Joseph's is located just off the main thoroughfare which runs through the centre of the estate, close to amenities such as the parade of shops, pub, medical centre, and library. This thoroughfare is the main bus route through the estate, which makes the church easily accessible on foot or by public transport. Built in the 1950s, at the time of the largest expansion of the estate, the church is surrounded by streets of the prefabricated houses and bungalows that were a feature of this phase of the estate's development. There is a church hall nearby, with a detached house in between that serves as the vicarage.

Terry and Carol live down the road, within walking distance of the church. They were married at St Joseph's, and they and their children were baptised there. However, Terry admits that he "was one of those who when they were brought up you had to drag them to church". The couple felt an acute need in the area for activities to engage young people and this is what led them to set up an activity club at the church hall. This is held after school on a Wednesday, and on a Sunday afternoon. Soon after it was set up, the club expanded to involve the parents and carers of the children attending. As Terry explains,

> I originally wanted to open a youth club, but then it became more and more like a drop-in because we had more and more adults that wanted to stay, so it became a drop-in where the adults can come with their children and they can stay for a cup of tea.

The drop-in play session on a Sunday is followed by a family church service. This was also instigated by Terry and Carol, as was a monthly Messy Church session, where up to 50 local residents—parents, carers, and children—spend a Saturday afternoon at the church hall engaged in craft and play activities before an informal session of music and story. The Messy Church session ends with a shared hot meal for all attending, prepared in the hall's kitchen by Carol and her friends.

Preparation for the drop-in youth club and Messy Church is a large part of the weekly routine for Terry and Carol:

> It's sorting out crafts and things like that. Make sure we've got the games out and make sure we've got enough tea, coffee, sugar, juice. On Wednesday we get bread in so we can make toast for them for when they come in after school.

They prepare different activities each week, sourcing materials for these themselves. Drop-in sessions include games and puzzles, colouring competitions, making collages from magazines and catalogues, and cake decorating. The work is collated and displayed in the room as the group have their snack and drink. Terry is always thinking of new activities for the club's members:

> Last couple of times, I've made badges out of milk bottle tops with cardboard in and them get them to write on the cardboard and glue a pin on the back and make a badge. We're quite inventive when it comes to it.

The groups convened by Terry and Carol have proved to be very popular with all ages:

> Over Christmas we stopped doing the Wednesday one, because the hall was being used, and they missed it because there was nowhere to go. We encourage the mums and dads, whoever's bringing the kids, to stay if they want to and have a cup of tea. No other place does that around here. If they want to stay, they can have a cup of tea and watch their kids play.

The facility for parents and carers to come and stay with their children as they play is an important aspect of the group for Terry and Carol. It allows children who may have caring responsibilities at home to play with other children; it encourages adults to stay while their children play "so they can have a natter with other adults".

At other points during the week, the couple are involved in other social groups, including a group for carers, which meets for informal networking and support. The carers' group has regular input from local charities and support services. Working together to run the group, and to collectively share and navigate everyday experiences, provides valuable support in itself for those who may otherwise be isolated by their circumstances. Carol says,

> It's like our own little family. If anyone has got a problem, you know you can turn to one of them for help. I mean, we go and help Sally do carers' group and she will come and help us with youth club.

The carers' group has a similar aim to the family drop-in session in providing a space for being with others, and, as Carol describes, it provides "a bit of time for people to get to know each other".

The family service, which takes place on a Sunday after the stay and play session, and during Messy Church, which happens monthly on a Saturday, adapts the traditional format of a Christian religious service to suit the different ages and tastes of those present. Both feature a combination of ways to share and engage with words and ideas. The services involve listening to the spoken word, through text read aloud as well as through stories told by those leading the service and by members of the congregation. The whole group is invited to join in with singing songs, which are accompanied by pre-recorded music played through a small public address system. The lyrics of these upbeat songs are projected in lively and colourful font across a screen which is erected for the purpose. They are accompanied by large physical actions in which regular attendees partake with great energy, while those who are new (like I was) can quickly join in.

During the Sunday family service, members of the congregation are invited to respond to the themes raised in the service, or to current issues and affairs, by drawing, colouring, and writing. This work is then displayed collectively within the church. One week, the congregation wrote wishes on strips of yellow paper, which were then joined in a chain and displayed (Fig. 5.1). These wishes might relate to personal circumstances, or to immediate family and friends, as well as extending more widely, such as to refer to the victims of recent terrorist atrocities in other countries.

In one service where the theme had been the Christian metaphor of the flock, members of the group decorated or wrote messages on small paper images of sheep. They were then invited to come to the front of the church and place their own sheep alongside the others (Fig. 5.2). Amongst the flock of paper sheep were ones coloured in brightly, or which featured shapes and signs drawn in pen, and others which bore written messages. These ranged from thoughts relating to personal circumstances ("I pray that D- will be nice to me") and to family ("I pray for my granddad") to thoughts for wider communities ("Everyone who is ill"; "people in Boston").

Fig. 5.2   Decorated sheep displayed on the steps at the front of the church

Alongside their work in leading drop-in sessions, Terry and Carol attend discussion groups facilitated by the minister, Reverend David, where passages from the Bible are explored. Terry enjoys this opportunity to read and discuss what he describes as "stories":

> It's just little short stories. I can't read a big book because I lose interest but little short stories I can read.

Their engagement with the text in the discussion group is also supported by play, and the opportunity to engage physically with others, as Carol explains:

> It's not just sitting down and reading the Bible. If somebody told me that I'd have to go there and sit and read it I wouldn't bother. [David] plays

games with it and then you start taking it in that way. [...] He'll do it as a play. It sticks in my mind more if it's done as a play or as a game.

The way in which Terry and Carol describe their reading also suggests a model of literacy which, rather than presupposing a predefined set of skills and the passing on of information, is open to interpretative possibilities. Terry describes the stories they've shared at the discussion group:

The favourite one we've done is Moses and the Ten Commandments and where he actually goes to the Pharaoh and the ten things that he has to do before the Pharaoh will release his people and one is turn a stick into a snake. I mean there is no way that I would grab a stick if it were to turn back into a snake!

I probably like it more because we analysed it and why he would do such a thing and why would he do this and that and it just sticks in your mind more. When you start analysing it sometimes we can just talk and talk and talk about it.

As Terry explores what he would do in the position of Moses, he is able to place himself inside an authoritative text and be part of the meaning he makes of it. The focus of the discussion is not merely on what has happened, but on why.

Reverend David, who facilitates the reading groups, is a minister with responsibility for working with children, young people, and their families in the area. He sees the role of the church as "to respond daily, weekly, monthly to the needs" of the community.

We had a big tragedy just before Christmas so I made sure [my assembly at the local school] was to do with how people were feeling and giving an opportunity for people to actually recognise their thoughts and feelings and the chance to talk them through with somebody.

In his view, what the church offers has to be "related to passions or an experience which [people] will treasure or even ones that have made them feel uncomfortable". As such, for Reverend David, the work of the church emerges from dialogue with the community and remains responsive, enabling its members to come together around common experiences.

The support offered to individuals within this community uses resources which emerge from within it. These are not reliant upon the dominant models of practice which may not have served some members of the community well. It is interesting to note that the approach taken in the church community groups recognises the limitations of a narrow model of what it means to be someone who reads, including the impact of this on people's confidence. As Reverend David notes, "if we get new people then handing them a book is not the biggest welcome in the world".

The reading groups facilitated by Reverend David are attended by people ranging from teenagers to those in middle age. There is specific attention in the groups to openness of interpretation and this is supported by a particular approach to the reading, described here by Reverend David:

> We don't have the same version of the Bible, on purpose. What's amazing is the discussion will go something like this: I'll say "what have you noticed about this?" and they will always pick up "well it didn't say that word in my one". And they have quite a banter and they like that. I will say to them, "if you don't like how it is put there how would you say it?"

Rather than arriving at predefined goals, reading in this instance is about emphasising the openness of meaning. Group members explore their personal responses to the text, their own interpretations of it, and how they "would say it". This shared practice of negotiating meanings is a powerful representation of how literacy can be viewed as a *social* practice. This has been a prominent approach in literacy research for over four decades. The next part of the chapter looks at some of the key ideas to have shaped our understanding of literacy as a social practice, and the possibilities this opens up for exploring the links between literacy and social justice.

In the Frame: A Social Practice Model of Literacy

For over four decades, literacy research has highlighted how we engage with text and language in multiple ways across the different aspects of our lives, and for multiple reasons. These interactions are shaped by the social, cultural, and political contexts in which they take place. As we have seen in previous chapters, not all of these ways of engaging with text carry the same value in society.

In contrast to the "autonomous" model of literacy (discussed in Chap. 3), which objectifies (and reifies) a supposedly neutral set of skills, an "ideological" model acknowledges that literacy "is an active process of meaning making and contest over definition, including its own definition" (Street 2011, p. 581). Ethnographic accounts of literacy have offered insight into some of the rich "contextual worlds" (Taylor and Dorsey-Gaines 1988, p. 200) in which literacy takes place. This includes the range of ways in which people engage with literacy across social, cultural, and linguistic contexts, across generations and community spaces (e.g. Saxena 1994; Zubair 2001; the authors within Pahl and Rowsell 2006 and Gregory et al. 2004; Nabi et al. 2009). Each of these accounts of literacy in everyday lives has challenged a model of literacy that divorces it from the contexts in which it takes place.

As a seminal example of such research, Shirley Brice Heath's study (1983) of literacy within the communities of the Piedmont Carolinas emphasises the social and cultural context for the "literacy events" she observes. Heath defines literacy events as "any action sequence, involving one or more persons, in which the production and/or comprehension of print plays a role" (p. 386). Her study emphasises the role played by collaborative, intergenerational practice and oral tradition in these interactions around text. Heath's account also makes clear that literacy events of this kind are not always recognised within officially mandated accounts of what it means to read and write. The children of working class communities, such as those which Heath refers to as Roadville and Trackton, are disadvantaged by the lack of recognition afforded to their rich linguistic repertoire when they start school, and are judged as being behind before they've even begun.

At a similar time to Heath's study, Street (1984) also described a rich variety in role and purpose for reading and writing in his study of study of literacy in Iran. He observed Iranian boys in contexts ranging from an Islamic school, to a marketplace, to a state school. Practices around literacy were distinct within each of these contexts. "Literacy practices", for Street, incorporate individual literacy events, but also encompass the wider ideological contexts within which they take place. As the young

Iranians he observed moved across contexts, they engaged in very different kinds of practice related to reading, writing, and talk. Street identifies
three distinct kinds of literacy practice within these contexts: the
"Maktab" literacy of the Islamic school, the "commercial literacy" of fruit
selling in the marketplace, and the literacy of the state school, which, in
the 1970s, encouraged its citizens to learn English as members of an
outward-looking nation state.

Research such as that conducted by Heath and Street, and the social
practice model of literacy which has emerged from it, emphasises two
things in particular. The first is that literacy is not a single, universal
practice. As David Barton (1994, p. 38) explains, "a literacy is a stable,
coherent, identifiable configuration of practices" associated with a specific context. Hence, literacy should in fact be understood as a plural
concept: as different literac*ies*. As is demonstrated in earlier chapters,
there are some literacies which are valorised over others; these dominant
literacies are ones which provide "avenues to acquiring social goods"
(Lankshear 1997, p. 69). Like all literacy practices, these dominant
practices need to be understood in their social, cultural, and historic
context.

The second point emphasised by a social practice model of literacy is
that literacy practices are understood as being "situated" (Barton et al.
2000). Rather than merely focusing on the texts and practices of formal
educational contexts, literacy is therefore recognised to include the locally
produced "texts of everyday life, the texts of personal life" (Barton and
Hamilton 2000, p. 9). In the context of this chapter, for example, these
texts would include song lyrics and the products of craft activities, as well
as Bible stories and support materials produced by carers' charities.
Elsewhere in this book, examples of such texts include YouTube videos,
knitting patterns, and recipes from magazines.

Ethnographic studies have highlighted the diverse role of literacy in
everyday lives, including within homes and families (e.g. Heath 1983;
Taylor and Dorsey-Gaines 1988; Minns 1990; Purcell-Gates 1995;
Taylor 1998; Pahl 2002). Recognising the importance of the multiplicity
of ways in which reading and writing are part of everyday life for individuals, Barton and Hamilton (2000, p. 13) have also called for attention
to the social meanings taken on by literacy "as a community resource,

realised in social relationships rather than as the property of individuals".

It has also been argued that, rather than being solely situated within a specific context or domain, literacy crosses domains and can be used by individuals and groups to navigate complex and potentially conflicting social, cultural, and linguistic territory. For example, in my own previous research, I observed groups of young bilingual girls from two UK communities—one a group of British-Asian girls who lived in a Midlands city, another a group of Welsh-English bilinguals living in North West Wales. As a means to explore their developing identities, the girls in both communities made creative use of a range of different reading and practices associated with the often divergent cultural and political contexts of their everyday lives (Jones 2006a, b). In some instances, literacy practices, emerging from contested linguistic, cultural, and political domains, became central tools to explore and demonstrate emergent bilingual and bicultural identities (Jones 2007). For these girls, the particular affordances of digital text supported their navigation of wider contexts while allowing the negotiation of complex identities and the language and literacy practices associated with them.

The digital and visual practices afforded by increasingly significant and accessible technologies are changing the ways in which we work together to share and make meaning from experiences. Visual and digital texts are central to how families, such as Katie and Colin's, featured in Chap. 6, come together, with technology such as Skype being a vital resource for communicating with extended family living at a distance. Such practices open up interpretation of literacy practices beyond consideration of "readily apparent material settings" (Sheehy and Leander 2004, p. 3) such as the classroom or bedroom, and allow us to see literacy as part of an ongoing process of the active negotiation and creation of meaning-making spaces, many of which are often liminal and immaterial.

Moje (2004) traces the ways in which literacy practices "shape and are shaped by" the ways in which Latino/a youth navigate material space as they walk around their city. Pahl (2007) describes the way in which time acts as a lens through which layers of meaning may be made, interpreted from the texts of everyday life, such as a child's drawing. Recent work in literacy with roots in material anthropology (Pahl 2015; Pahl and Rowsell 2010; Jones 2014) also invites us to reflect upon the ways in which we understand literacy as an individual and collaborative meaning-making practice. The materially situated negotiation of meanings in everyday life through "stuff" (Miller 2010) is presented in Chap. 7, in Peggy's story.

Fundamentally, seeing literacy as a social practice means framing it as "a relational and positional concept, not an individual possession" (Hamilton 2012, p. 11). Lesley Bartlett questions the way in which instrumental models of literacy seek to define an outcome or a result for literacy: what it promotes, or confers, or affects. Rather than focusing on literacy's "verb", Bartlett argues that we should see literacy itself as the verb: reading and writing are things that people *do* (2008, p. 750).

The portrait of Terry and Carol illustrates how literacy practices rely on interpersonal engagement: meanings are negotiated through being shared with others. This foregrounding of active engagement in the process of making meaning challenges the deficit discourse of communities which was outlined in Chap. 3, as well as the narrow model of literacy which emerges from such discourse, and is a feature of the enactment of policies which are based upon it. For Terry, Carol, and their friends and family, literacy practice is central to much of what happens when they come together to share experiences and to create new ones. Literacy is part of an active process not only of making meanings but of constructing communities through shared practice in place. In the next part of the chapter, I examine what this shift in focus—from seeing literacy as an individual skill to seeing it as a situated, collective practice—means for reframing both literacy and community.

Literacy and Community

The latter years of the twentieth century saw theories relating to place and space increasingly used to describe social practice. Research in literacy has been richly informed by this "spatial turn" (Soja 2004). The research which informs this book is perhaps quite obviously linked to "place" in the sense of a specific geographic location: an estate on the edge of a city in the Midlands of England. Studies of everyday literacy practice have long been associated with specific geographic locations: Heath's (1983) study of communities located in the Piedmont Carolinas and Barton and Hamilton's (1998) study of Lancaster, England, are two notable examples. These studies are specific in their detailed accounts of what happens in these particular towns and communities and this is one way of making a link between literacy and a "place". Looking at literacy practice through a focus on a particular place also reminds us of the need to attend to the inextricable relationship between any social practice and the context in which it is situated. Next, I explore how the notion of place has been understood in cultural and social studies, and how this has informed our understanding of literacy.

Place

Place has been described succinctly by Tim Cresswell (2004), a cultural geographer, as a "meaningful location" (p. 5) which is the result of a "rich and complicated interplay of people and environment" (p. 11). A location, such as the estate, acquires a sense of place, for those who know it, as a result of their engagement with it at a cultural and symbolic level. A sense of place, particularly in relation to where we live, is often the result of time spent there (Lippard 1997), and this sense is made up of "layers of sedimented meaning derived from memory, sentiment, tradition and identification with a spatial location" (Corcoran 2002, p. 48). The subjective, and indeed emotional, work of place-making is suggested by Tuan (1977, p. 8), who argues that "what begins as undifferentiated space becomes a place as we get to know it better and endow it with value".

Places need to be understood beyond notions of borders and margins, as both "a product and process of socially dynamic relations" (Sheehy and Leander 2004, p. 1). My focus in this chapter is on the ways in which a group of people work together in a place. I'm interested too in what this collaboration suggests about how we might develop our understanding of that place, in particular as a kind of place which has been subject to very prominent negative representations, as we saw in Chap. 3. These deficit constructions of the estate as a place do not always recognise the kind of collaboration seen in the portrait of Terry and Carol's work with the church. We've seen in Chaps. 3 and 4 that the lived experience of inequality and poverty can shape a place in terms of the physical resources within it. It can also affect a place at a symbolic level. The relationships between people and places, and the impact of this on inequalities, are emphasised when we observe the imbalance of power between large cities, and particular areas within them, which are a focal point for political and economic decisions, and other areas (Massey 2005; Comber 2016). Changes in the lived experience of residents on the estate, such as deindustrialisation and the increasing mobility of its population symbolised by the building of the nearby motorway, have impacted on the experiences of those living within it. These factors can affect "the symbolic qualities" of a place (Relph 1976, p. 66), emphasising the relationship between place and power. The moralisation of place described by Savage (2015) has meant that the values endowed on places such as the estate by popular political discourse, and by those who may not actually know the lived realities of life in that place, result in the caricature of a whole residential area of a city as defined by dysfunctional families and individual failures. Often already geographically segregated by their location on the edges of a city, places like the estate are further marginalised by such discourses (Shields 1991).

Place always involves a coming together of people in a particular time and space. These people bring with them experiences from other times and other places, which result in any one interaction being, in fact, a constellation of specific, local, and contemporary realities which include a past from which they emerge, a present in which they are negotiated, and a future which they will impact upon. The "operations" involved in the dynamic process of making meaning are described by de Certeau (1984, p. 118). Everyday experiences involve changing the relationship between what he terms "place" and "space". Place, he argues, is an "instantaneous configuration of positions", held still, as it were, and illustrated by the metaphor of a *map*. "Space", on the other hand, is "composed of intersections of mobile elements […] actuated by the ensemble of movements deployed within it" (p. 117). Rather than a map, this can be imagined as a *tour*, actively taking in elements from across time and space in order to configure a meaningful experience in the present. For de Certeau, a place suggests the order of the world: something that can be *identified* and understood through *seeing*. The dynamic nature of space, however, depends on the active insertion of subjects into relationships with this order; rather than being observed, it is actualised through movement and operation. Crucial to the process of making meaning is a constant oscillation between places and spaces.

It is this aspect of shared negotiation that confers upon place what Edward Soja calls "a significant practical and political dimension" (2004, p. x). He argues:

> [i]f our spaces and places, our human geographies, are socially constructed, it logically follows that they are not immutable or naturally given. This means that they can be socially changed, made into something better than they were through collective action (ibid.)

Doreen Massey also argues for the transformational quality of place, based on an inherent quality which she calls "throwntogetherness" (2005, p. 151). Because place happens when people come together, it is always the result of a "simultaneity of stories-so-far" (p. 12). It is always in the process of being made (p. 51) and—crucially—always holds the potential for the new.

One of the ways in which a place can be constructed is through what Julian Rappaport (2000) calls "community narratives". These are the stories which are told about a community, and by a community about itself. Dominant cultural narratives are "communicated in shorthand" (p. 5), such as through the stereotypes outlined in previous chapters. As Rappaport notes, community narratives are "resources which empower or impede" (p. 6). Viewing place in the way suggested by Massey challenges the possibility of any narrative *about* a place being fixed, or indeed owned by any group or individual. Rather, the ways in which people work together create new possibilities not only for themselves but also for the way in which their community is framed by others.

Community

As was outlined in Chap. 3, estates such as the one where Terry and Carol live have across many years been the subject of attention within policy, whether it be the philanthropic intentions of the first developers in pre-war housing in the area, or the government departments responsible for the post-war reallocation of social housing to areas such as the estate, and the policy dream of establishing these new communities populated by a workforce which contributes to a shared vision of regeneration and hope for the future. Latter years have also seen the notion of community being focused upon places such as the estate, but not always with the optimism of previous decades.

Raymond Williams has claimed of the term "community" that "unlike all other terms of social organisation (*state, nation, society, etc*), it seems never to be used unfavourably, and never to be given any positive opposing or distinguishing term" (1988, p. 76, italics in original). The word has become a familiar tag in political speeches and public life. We hear such terms as "community care", "community policing", or "community cohesion" without necessarily leaping to assume a connection between this and a context of social, cultural, economic, and political upheaval across the last half a century (Studdert 2005), or to see its use as a "rhetorical antidote to neo-liberalism and its atomisation of the individual" (Studdert 2016, p. 623). However, debate about the nature of community has characterised academic and policy discourse over many years. Whereas this book is not the place to outline these historic sociological debates in depth, it is helpful to highlight one or two dominant ideas that have framed the way "community" is understood in public and policy discourse, in particular as they affect the everyday lived experiences of Terry, Carol, and other residents of the estate. It's also helpful to explore how a different way of understanding community, and the work of Terry and Carol, and their community groups, can contribute to reframing how we see literacy practice.

Field (2008, p. 9) notes that "lamentation over the decline of community has become a leitmotif of contemporary journalism". Models of community which have shaped policy can often be seen as "underpinned, in one way or another, by a narrative of loss which [...] uses the past as a yardstick to indict the present for some perceived deficiency" (Studdert 2005, p. 31). One such model is premised upon the idea of social capital, which, as was outlined in Chap. 4, has shaped policy in relation to community across neoliberal jurisdictions. Focused on the links that exist between people, and the resources which we are able to draw upon as a result of these connections, social capital has been described using metaphors such as glue and oil (Studdert 2005; Putnam 2000), suggesting its role in bonding people together while also easing social interaction. Social capital is linked to other forms of capital, including cultural and economic: the connections we have to others, and our capacity to generate such connections, particularly to those who may not live in direct proximity to us, can depend on our education and our income (Savage 2015). Conversely, a lack of "connectedness" to people and places away from where we live is seen as one of the defining features of "social exclusion" (Lister 2004; Page 2000). Putnam's (2000) account of social capital in American communities depicts an economistic view where individualistic values have had a detrimental impact on the productivity of society. His ideas have influenced neoliberal politics since the mid-1990s. The resulting policies have a restorative aim, based on the notion of community as having been lost, or having failed in some way as a result of individual moral dereliction. A social capital model also suggests that "social problems are solvable through non-economic solutions and the moral health of society is prior to, and causative of, economic problems" (Studdert 2005, p. 38). This takes us back to the way in which whole communities have been routinely disparaged by the deficit discourse which was described in Chap. 3. Everyday lives become the focus of attention and intervention, and the development of social capital becomes the top-down aim of government, rather than a goal grounded in lived realities within communities.

Although also concerned about a "loss" of aspects of social life which support community, Richard Sennett (2012) argues for the importance of co-operation in contemporary society. He defines co-operation as "an exchange in which the participants benefit from the encounter" (p. 5). He offers the metaphor of the conversation as an illustration of the kind of co-operation which he sees as vital to community, identifying specifically two forms of conversation: dialectic and dialogic. It's helpful at this point to further elucidate Sennett's metaphor, as it moves us conceptually from a view of community as externally defined by policy and popular discourse, and in need of external intervention, to a model which centres on the co-operation which takes place within community.

Derived from classical philosophy, the dialectic and the dialogic are have long been central to debate about the nature of human interaction and our understanding of the world around us. Classical models of the dialectic, such as those attributed to Socrates, arrive at an understanding through a process based on oppositions: the dialectic is the result of discussion of thesis and antithesis, with the aim of arriving at a synthesis. The process of arriving at a synthesis also presupposes the "essence or logos of a thing" (Nikulin 2010, p. 24). To define a synthesis is to negate the different voices and positions embodied within the process of that definition, and, in seeking this essence, the dialectic also presupposes its object to *be* reducible to an essence. The dialogic, on the other hand, according to Sennett (2012, p. 19), "does not resolve itself by finding common ground". As Rupert Wegerif (2013, p. 3) notes, the dialogic "assumes that there is always more than one voice": the development and co-existence of multiple meanings is inherent within the spaces created by the interaction of different perspectives. The dialogic is therefore bound by the notions of "unfinalisability", of "allosensus", rather than consensus (Nikulin 2010).

When applied to community, the dialogic model of the conversation depicts a space where openness of possibility is not only *allowed* but is a definitive feature. This challenges the reductive discourses generated by dominant policy and popular media, taking us closer to a model of community where meanings are collaboratively negotiated as a result of the "simultaneity of stories-so-far" which constitute social practice in place (Massey 2005, p. 12).

David Studdert's conceptualisation of community takes this further to argue that community is not merely a "mechanistic and idealist" state towards which policy can take us, something which is to be built through health or policing or education (2016, p. 623). Rather, Studdert suggests:

> [i]t is more fruitful to understand community as a verb: communing: being-ness produced as an outcome of ongoing action in common (ibid.)

Studdert (2005, p. 3) argues that every community is constituted by features including:

- Hybridity
- Action, not thought, as creative of community
- Communality as something constructed by some form of conscious or unconscious agreement
- Community as something more than the individual

Drawing on the work of sociologist Hannah Arendt, Studdert argues that community is not reducible to pre-emptive value. Rather it is the result of plurality: "the soil of our conditioned being-ness" (2016, p. 624). When we interact with others, we bring together our experiences from the "web" of worlds that we have experienced outside the immediate context of our social interaction. This acting together in public "creates linkages, relationships, and commonality"; it creates a public space which then itself works its way into the wider "web" from which our individual experiences are taken. Community is not only somewhere which facilitates this interaction across time and space; it is itself constituted by this interaction, by means of a "temporary unity of all perspectives" (p. 637) which exists in the time and space in which the interaction takes place.

This way of viewing community suggests an ontological shift which sees it "as a condition of being, rather than deploying the more traditional tropes of 'lost', 'saved' or 'to come'" (Wills 2016, p. 640). It moves us away from a view of community as pathologised, to be rescued by experts or brought into the service of the state (ibid.; Rappaport 2000). This shift in ontology has powerful potential to disrupt the deficit models which arise through dominant narratives about communities such as the estate. Alongside the understanding of place outlined earlier in this chapter, this has significant implications for our understanding of literacy. That community is always relational, existing within a particular space and time, means "respecting the community that already exists and allowing local people the space and resources to start where they are" (Wills 2016, p. 646). Communities and their members are not merely passive recipients of intervention and the received wisdom of policy makers. This way of understanding community sees it as defined by collaboration, cooperation, and action. Places are constituted by the collective action of people within them, by a coming together of lived experiences, which results in meaning existing in flux, always being created. This challenges the possibility of stereotypes about place, and what a place means. Linked to this, Sennett's metaphor of the dialogic opens up space for multiple possibilities and voices. Studdert's assertion that community *is* plurality also disrupts the possibility of any one meaning being held still. For an understanding of literacy in particular, these are powerful ideas.

I turn now to explore the ways in which the concepts of place and community have been discussed in literacy research, to consider both what looking at literacy from the perspective of community adds to our understanding of literacy, and what the lens of literacy adds to our understanding of community. In relation to both, there is much to challenge the narrow models which have dominated understanding of both in public and policy discourse.

Reframing Literacy and Community

Earlier chapters have presented the estate as somewhere which is shaped in some ways by particular models of literacy. A focus on the community interaction in which Terry and Carol are involved also emphasises how a place shapes the literacy practices which happen within it (Comber 2016). As explained earlier, prominent ethnographies of literacy have done much to connect literacy practices with the places in which they happen. The New Literacy Studies paradigm foregrounds this relational context, as Barton and Hamilton (1998, p. 23) have reminded us:

> Literacy practices are located in time and space. Reading and writing are things which people do, either alone or with other people, but always in a social context – always in a place and at a time.

Research and practice within the area of critical literacies highlights the potential of place-based approaches to illuminate issues of power in pedagogic contexts. Freire's emphasis on literacy as both "reading the word and reading the world" (Freire and Macedo 1987) highlights the centrality of the relationship between the world around us and the ways in which we come to understand it through engaging with the written and spoken word. Drawing upon community resources and funds of knowledge is a feature of critical literacies (Moll et al. 1992; Comber 2016), where place is used as a focal point for critical engagement with the possibilities of language and literacy. A community's knowledge and resources are drawn upon for classroom work, and students are positioned as researchers of language in ways which acknowledge the breadth of experience that relationally constitutes place (e.g. Baker-Bell 2013; Jones and Chapman 2017).

A model of place as both the process and product of dynamic relations has also influenced our understanding of the links between literacy and place. A spatialised view of literacy foregrounds a direct link between literacy practice and the realisation of place as dynamically constituted through practice (Sheehy and Leander 2004). Building on Studdert's model of community as being-ness resulting from actions in common (2016, p. 623), the next part of this chapter explores the way in which literacy practice can be seen as central to the collective negotiation of community.

Literacy Practice in Community Groups

In their study of literacy in Lancaster, Barton and Hamilton (1998) found that all of the participants they interviewed were in some way connected to at least one local organisation, be that a residents' association, sports or leisure club, or a Scouting group. Barton and Hamilton's focus on their participants' involvement in such groups revealed the significant role of literacy practices in the organisation of groups, as well as how they structure, and are structured by, the collective goals of those involved. They found that members of all sorts of community organisations were involved in activities such as gathering and distributing information in the local community, or engaging with local press and other influential people, drawing on material resources and skills to generate and engage with texts such as letters, petitions, posters, and leaflets. Literacy practices were observed to be central to communication both within the group, including record-keeping and other administrative tasks, and between the group and the outside world. The production of texts in groups also reflected a range of discourses which are brought into the group by its members from their lives outside the group. The sharing of knowledge and skills relied heavily on an oral tradition. There was a valuing of people's varying individual areas of expertise, and a resourcefulness in drawing upon these in order to get things done for the group as a whole.

Barton and Hamilton use the examples of literacy practices in local groups to argue for the role of literacy in democratic practice. They note that "literacy practices are not necessarily democratic in their own right. Neither can they, on their own, promote democracy" (p. 228). Some literacy practices can be used to structure organisations in ways which exclude those who do not have the literacies required of them to participate, but Barton and Hamilton emphasise that in the groups they observed, "it was not the literacy in itself which was democratic; rather it was the practice" (p. 229). They argue that looking at literacy practices in community groups demonstrates "the validity of regarding literacy as a communal resource, rather than simply a set of skills located in individuals" (p. 230). For the work of the group to be done, a set of resources has to come together and, where "no individual had all these resources, […] it was in combination that they were effective" (ibid.).

This view of literacy practices in groups echoes the model of place and community outlined already, illustrative as it is of the shared work of negotiating meaning making for a common goal in a particular time and space. The work of Terry and Carol in their community is focused on the local church. As a locus of shared literacy practice, places of worship and practices around religious text have been the focus of much research that emphasises the potential of literacy as a collaborative resource.

Literacy in Faith Communities

Critiques of the role of religion in society have often emphasised text as a source of power to which congregation members have little or no access. Religiously conservative times and societies have seen access to the interpretation of text as a symbolic resource limited by barriers of language and literacy. Eric Rackley (2014) describes a history in the USA of "religious infused literacy instruction", where the three Rs of education—reading, writing, and arithmetic—were "superseded by the first R – religion"

(p. 417). Rappaport (2000) cites Biblical narratives as a source of "tales of terror", with traditional means of reading and sharing such texts serving the ideological ends of the ruling classes. Such "tales" can be reclaimed, however, and communities which have been the traditional subjects of punitive readings, such as the LGBTQ+ community and those with mental health issues, are shown by Rappaport to have reclaimed stories and, through collective acts of interpretation, to have turned them into "tales of joy". Echoing this shift to viewing religious texts as sources in the agentive interpretation and negotiation of everyday life, the young people in another US study, who are from Methodist and Latter Day Saints churches, were motivated to engage with religious texts not only to learn about their religious traditions and how to apply these in their daily lives but also as a source of comfort and strength to endure life's challenges (Rackley 2016).

Literacy research across faith communities has shown the diverse role of engagement with religious texts in informal learning and community contexts. The education provided at Sunday schools was, at one time, one of the few sources of formal literacy teaching experienced by some less affluent groups in Christian societies (Nichols et al. 2012). Across diverse contemporary faith communities, learning is focused on a range of ways in which community is negotiated and maintained, including language acquisition and cultural socialisation (see, e.g. the authors in Lytra et al. 2016; Rosowsky 2017; Kenner and Ruby 2012; Volk 2008). Like St Joseph's, the church Terry and Carol attend, practice in many churches reflects an expression of the Christian mission not through direct instruction but through service to community. Nichols et al. (2012) describe the work of churches serving different communities in the USA and Australia, and note their alignment with wider educational discourses. This sees churches making the most of their material, economic, and symbolic infrastructure within the community to provide services to families as part of a "children's ministry". This is echoed in the role played by Reverend David at St Joseph's, and in the church's support of Terry and Carol's goal of providing much needed space for families to meet and play together.

The spaces of community supported by the church are valued for many reasons, including the opportunities they represent for "being-ness produced as an outcome of ongoing action in common" (Studdert 2016, p. 623). In their research with mothers and children living in a homeless shelter, MacGillivray et al. (2010) outline the way in which the church represents a safe space to be, physically as well as emotionally. For these families living in precarious circumstances, the church offered continuity and stability amidst continual change. Children who were living in homeless shelters were able to quickly bond with their peers at the church they frequented, and church-related literacies offered powerful ways of connecting to others who were hopeful about the future and who positioned themselves positively as learners. Engagement with adults as "intimate strangers" in such community organisations leads to important learning for young people (Heath 2013, p. 47). Like those who attend the groups facilitated by Terry, Carol, and Reverend David, the youths described by Heath engage in interactions devoted to "artistic and scientific pursuits centred on building a sense of inclusion through instrumental guidance, critique, and humor" (p. 50). For Heath, "community youth organisations widen children's sense of where language, curiosity, and imagination can take them" (p. 66).

Jonathan Eakle (2007), in a study of a Christian faith-based school, draws comparisons between narrow views of literacy and essentialist views of meaning in religious texts. Emphasising the multimodality that is central in religious contexts, through oral and aural practice as well as in visual display, Eakle argues that the openness of possibility explored in the engagement with religious texts he has observed constitutes "literacies of authorship" where "movement, collisions, and exchanges of content in everyday life […] pass among individuals, collectives, and texts as links in chains of power relations" (p. 476). This is suggestive of the shifting, relational spaces in which engagements with text occur, and which themselves constitute the work of community.

Faith communities are amongst many groups where collaborative engagement with literacy practices in all their forms supports the construction of community. This role for such groups emphasises what Jane Wills (2016, p. 649) notes in relation to the participants in her research: "they understood community to be about social relationships rather than the four walls of a church". Terry's reflections on the practices in the reading group underline the fact that it represents more than an engagement with Christian faith. Such practices also reflect the ways in which a range of other communities come together to share reading.

Sharing Reading as Community

The success of "mass reading events" (Fuller and Rehberg Sedo 2013), led by celebrities such as Oprah Winfrey, or Richard and Judy in the UK, is testament to the power of feeling we're all reading the same text, and sharing our responses with others. Book groups have long fulfilled this social function of reading for their many members, who come together in community spaces, or in each other's homes, over a cup of tea or a glass of wine, to share their views about a text they've all agreed to read beforehand. More recently, the proliferation of online book groups has provided a space for readers to interact over their reading from further afield. These are often focused on specific genres, or on choices influenced or curated by celebrities or vloggers.

The growing popularity of "shared reading" has also emphasised the social qualities of reading. Unlike in a more conventional book group, in a shared reading experience, people join together to listen to a story or a poem being read aloud, reading along with a copy of the text if they want to. Shared reading is an integral part of the work of Liverpool-based charity *The Reader*, which promotes the benefits of reading for wellbeing across different communities. Shared reading groups meet in a range of venues including libraries, health centres, care homes, and schools. People join for a range of reasons, not least because of the impact the experience can have on health and wellbeing. The research reports that regular involvement in shared reading can increase confidence and self-esteem, as well as physical wellbeing (Dowrick et al. 2012; Longden et al. 2015). Engaging with literary texts allows readers to see their own predicaments from different perspectives (Berthould and Elderkin 2013, p. 2), to know that they're not alone in the world, and that their experiences are shared with others. This could be either within the world of the story they are reading, or within the community which they are a part of while they read. This sharing of the experience of reading, and the co-operative work of interpretation, has been noted by Sam Duncan (2012, pp. 87–88) in her work with adult reading circles, to be a key motivation for attending. She notes that "members do not come to their circles simply to express their already formulated conclusions about the book (or about life): members come in order to formulate ideas communally".

My colleague, Kevin Harvey, and I have written about our involvement with a shared reading group in a different part of the city to the estate where Terry and Carol live, and what happened on one occasion when we read Kafka's short story *Metamorphosis*, where the protagonist, Gregor, wakes up one morning having transformed into a giant insect (Jones and Harvey 2016). Renowned for its ambiguity, the story made for rich discussion. Whether it was trying to decide the exact type of insect Gregor had become, or why his family responded to him in the way they did, the members of the group drew on a range of resources to collectively arrive at a reading that made sense to them. The group brought together experiences from their childhoods and their current relationships with their own families. They speculated on how they themselves would respond to finding a family member in the same predicament as Gregor.

The experiences shared in the group reading came through what de Certeau (1984) describes as an oscillation across different times and places. Members worked together, listening to and responding to the experiences of others, sharing their own, and placing themselves in the world of the story, in same way as Terry did with the story of Moses and the snake. Asking each other "what they would do" is an example of the power of the subjunctive, which, according to Sennett (2012, p. 23), opens up "an indeterminate mutual space, the space in which strangers dwell with one another".

In lots of ways, the interpretation of this group of what might be considered "ordinary readers" echoed the concerns of many noted critics across the years, including Nabokov (1980), who similarly puzzled over the kind of insect Kafka was describing, famously sketching how he pictured this in his own copy of the story. However, the reading of Kafka's story that took place in that church hall on one Wednesday afternoon was also a unique one, made by the group through active collaboration which resulted in a locally specific interpretation (Swann and Allington 2009). Such collaborative reading, either in the shared reading group described here, or in the Bible discussion group attended by Terry and Carol, shows how reading can be something that brings us together through the active sharing of our experiences, as well as being an experience that defines us as a group in common. It is a particularly powerful illustration of a "simultaneity of stories-so-far", as described by Massey (2005, p. 12), and the active "being-ness" articulated by Studdert (2016) which is central to the work of coming together around a text to negotiate meanings.

This is not to suggest that individual subjectivities are surrendered to the meaning established by the group. Drawing on the research of Elizabeth Long into women-only reading groups in the USA (Long 2003), Duncan (2012, p. 87) describes the appeal of reading groups as "places of potential (if temporary) loss of self (in identification with actions and characters) and, simultaneously, places for exploration of personal and social identity". In her survey of reading group practices, Hartley (2001, p. 132) recognises that empathy is "the core reading-group value". Research into the discourse of reading groups has also emphasised the careful cultural and linguistic patterns which are often evident as a social means of encouraging and managing diverse opinions (Peplow et al. 2016).

However, as Long (2003) points out in her exploration of reading through history, despite its prominence in the Western cultural imagination, reading is an inherently communal act. It engages individuals in a "social infrastructure" (p. 8) involving the authority of another, be they authors, texts, or teachers. Shared reading positions the reader is an agentive participant in this infrastructure, as the goal is to collaboratively construct meanings with the resources which are brought to the group by its individual members. Each participant contributes to the process of reading, working together to make meanings which emerge from dialogue. Dmitri Nikulin's (2010) analysis of dialogue provides a helpful reminder of the central importance of this to social justice:

[t]hat dialogue is about the person means that no-one is (to be) obliterated and no-one is (to be) reduced to a common and anonymous denominator. (p. 80)

Constructing Meanings: Constructing Communities

The examples of shared literacy practice presented in this chapter illustrate a concept which is fundamental to a model of literacy as social practice. As Hamilton reminds us, when we consider this way of looking at literacy,

> [a] different syntax is needed to signal a different ontology. Thus you can 'have' literacy as an individual skill or 'be literate' but you can't 'have' or 'be' a literacy practice as it is a relational idea. (2012, p. 11)

This encourages us to move from the sense suggested by reading as a *noun*, of one fixed meaning, which is echoed in the instrumental models of literacy outlined in previous chapters, where narrow ideas about what it means to read and write have been shown to constrict the lived experience of residents on the estate. Rather, as has been argued by Bartlett (2008), we need to think of reading, as well as other forms of literacy, as the more dynamic *verb*. In the case of Terry and Carol, this suggests communities operating together to create meanings that emerge from the unique combination of their experiences. This opens up new possibilities for meaning. As Theodore Zeldin notes:

> when minds meet, they don't just exchange facts: they transform them, reshape them, draw different implications from them, engage in new trains of thought. Conversation doesn't just reshuffle the cards: it creates new cards. (1998, p. 14)

The lens of literacy has allowed us to see processes and practices which are not always accounted for in dominant discourses of everyday practice. The work of Terry and Carol in the community directly challenges notions of deficit and passivity. Rather than being examples of a group of people in need of intervention according to an instrumental model of literacy, or a community lacking in the resources needed to live fulfilled lives, the practices shared here demonstrate the rich and varied role of language in the negotiation of everyday experience. A focus on literacy allows us to see how a community is constructed through its shared experience.

Crucial to this way of viewing both literacy and community is a model of literacy which goes beyond information sharing—a process described by Sennett as "an exercise in definition and precision". Rather, interaction is based on communication, "which mines the realm of suggestion and connotation" (Sennett 2012, p. 28). These are interactions around text which emphasise not just what but what if.

In the next chapter, we move from the wider community of the church and church hall to the family home of Katie and Colin to look at another example of shared literacy practice.

References

Baker-Bell, A. (2013) '"I Never Really Knew the History behind African American Language": Critical Language Pedagogy in an Advanced Placement English Language Arts Class,' *Equity & Excellence in Education*, 46 (3) 355–370

Bartlett, L. (2008) 'Literacy's verb: exploring what literacy is and what literacy does', *International Journal of Educational Development*, 28, 737–753

Barton, D. (1994) *Literacy: An introduction to the ecology of written language.* Oxford: Blackwell

Barton, D. and Hamilton, M. (1998) *Local Literacies: Reading and Writing in One Community.* London: Routledge

Barton, D. and Hamilton, M. (2000) 'Literacy Practices' in Barton, D., Hamilton, M. and Ivanič, R. (eds.) *Situated Literacies: reading and writing in context.* London: Routledge, pp. 7–15

Barton, D., Hamilton, M. and Ivanič, R. (eds.) (2000) *Situated Literacies: reading and writing in context.* London: Routledge

Berthould, E. and Elderkin, S. (2013) *The Novel Cure.* London: Canongate.

Comber, B. (2016) *Literacy, Place and the Pedagogies of Possibility.* Oxon and New York: Routledge

Corcoran, M. (2002) 'Place attachment and community sentiment in marginalized neighbourhoods: A European case study', *Canadian Journal of Urban Research*, 11 (1) 47–67

Cresswell, T. (2004) *Place: a short introduction.* Oxford: Blackwell

De Certeau, M. (1984) *The Practice of Everyday Life.* London: University of California Press

Dowrick, C., Billington, J., Robinson, J., Hamer, A. and Williams, C. (2012) 'Get into Reading as an intervention for common mental health problems: exploring catalysts for change', *Medical Humanities*, 38, 15–20.

Duncan, S. (2012) *Reading Circles, Novels and Adult Reading Development*. London: Bloomsbury

Eakle, J. (2007) 'Literacy Spaces of a Christian Faith-Based School', *Reading Research Quarterly*, 42 (4) 472–510

Field, J. (2008) *Social Capital*. Second edition. Abingdon: Routledge

Freire, P. and Macedo, D. (1987) *Literacy: Reading the Word and the World*. New York: Bergin and Garvey

Fuller, D. and Rehberg Sedo, D. (2013) *Reading Beyond the Book: The Social Practices of Contemporary Literary Culture*. Abingdon: Routledge

Gregory, E., Long, S. and Volk, D. (2004) *Many Pathways to Literacy: Young children learning with siblings, grandparents and communities*. London: RoutledgeFalmer

Hamilton, M. (2012) *Literacy and the Politics of Representation*. Oxon: Routledge

Hartley, J. (2001) *Reading Groups*. Oxford: Oxford University Press

Heath, S. B. (1983) *Ways with Words*. Cambridge: Cambridge University Press

Heath, S. B. (2013) *Words at Work and Play*. Cambridge: Cambridge University Press

Jones, S. (2006a) 'One body and two heads: Girls exploring their bicultural identities through text', *English in Education*, 40 (2) 5–21

Jones, S. (2006b). 'A Tale of Two Literacies: Girls growing up biculturally literate in two UK communities', in Hickey, T. (ed.) *Language Learning and Literacy*, Dublin: RAI, pp. 99–113

Jones, S. (2007) 'Land of "My 9": Welsh-English Bilingual Girls Creating Spaces to Explore Identity', *Changing English*, 14 (1) 39–50

Jones, S. (2014) '"How people read and write and they don't even notice": everyday lives and literacies on a Midlands council estate', *Literacy*, 48 (2) 59–65

Jones, S. and Chapman, K. (2017) 'Telling stories: engaging critical literacy through urban legends in an English secondary school', *English Teaching, Practice and Critique*, 16 (1) 85–96

Jones, S. and Harvey, K. (2016) 'He should have put them in the freezer': creating and connecting through shared reading', *Journal of Arts and Communities*, 7 (3) 153–166

Kenner, C. and Ruby, M. (2012) *Interconnecting Worlds: Teacher Partnerships for Bilingual Learning*. Stoke-on-Trent: Trentham Books

Lankshear, C. (1997) *Changing Literacies*. Milton Keynes: Open University Press

Lippard, L. (1997) *The Lure of the Local*. New York: The New Press

Lister, R. (2004) *Poverty*. Cambridge: Polity Press

Long, E. (2003) *Book Groups: Women and the Uses of Reading in Everyday Life*. Chicago: University of Chicago Press

Longden, E., Davis, P., Billington, J., Lampropoulou, S., Farrington, G., Magee, F., Walsh, E., and Corcoran, R. (2015) 'Shared Reading: assessing the intrinsic value of a literature-based health intervention', *Medical Humanities*, 41 (2) 113–20

Lytra, V., Volk, D. and Gregory, E. (eds.) (2016) *Navigating Languages, Literacies and Identities: Religion in Young Lives*. New York and Abingdon: Routledge

MacGillivray, L., Ardell, A. and Curwen, M. (2010) 'Libraries, churches, and schools: the literate lives of mothers and children in a homeless shelter', *Urban Education*, 45 (2) 221–245

Massey, D. (2005) *For Space*. London: Sage

Miller, D. (2010) *Stuff*. Cambridge: Polity Press

Minns, H. (1990) *Read it to me now! Learning at home and school*. Buckingham: Open University Press

Moje, E. (2004) 'Powerful Spaces: Tracing the Out-of-School Literacy Spaces of Latino/a Youth', in Leander, K. and Sheehy, M. (eds.) *Spatializing Literacy Research and Practice*. New York: Peter Lang, pp. 15–38

Moll, L.C., Amanti, C., Neff, D. and Gonzalez, N. (1992) 'Funds of Knowledge for teaching: using a qualitative approach to connect homes and classrooms', *Theory into Practice*, XXXI (2) 132–141

Nabi, R., Rogers, A. and Street, B. (2009) *Hidden Literacies: Ethnographic studies of literacy and numeracy practices in Pakistan*. Bury St Edmunds: Uppingham Press

Nabokov, V. (1980) *Lectures on Literature*. New York, USA: Harcourt Brace

Nichols, S., Rowsell, J., Nixon, H. and Rainbird, S. (2012) *Resourcing Early Learners: New Networks, New Actors*. London: Routledge

Nikulin, D. (2010) *Dialectic and Dialogue*. Stanford: Stanford University Press

Page, D. (2000) *Communities in the balance: the reality of social exclusion on housing estates*. York: Joseph Rowntree Foundation

Pahl, K. (2002) 'Ephemera, mess and miscellaneous piles: Text and practices in families', *Journal of Early Childhood Literacy*, 2 (2) 145–166

Pahl, K. (2007) 'Timescales and ethnography: understanding a child's meaning making across three sites, a home, a classroom, and a family literacy class', *Ethnography and Education*, 2 (2) 175–190

Pahl, K. (2015) *Materialising Literacies in Communities: the uses of literacy revisited*. London: Bloomsbury

Pahl, K. and Rowsell, J. (eds.) (2006) *Travel Notes from the New Literacy Studies: Instances of Practice*. Clevedon: Multilingual Matters

Pahl, K. and Rowsell, J. (2010) *Artifactual Literacies: Every object tells a story*. New York: Teachers College Press

Peplow, D., Swann, J, Trimarco, P, and Whiteley, S. (2016) *The Discourse of Reading Groups: Integrating Cognitive and Sociocultural Perspectives*. Abingdon: Routledge

Purcell-Gates, V. (1995) *Other People's Words: the cycle of low literacy*. Cambridge, MA: Harvard University Press

Putnam, R. (2000) *Bowling Alone: The collapse and revival of American community*. New York: Simon and Schuster

Rackley, E. (2014) 'Scripture-Based Discourses of Latter-Day Saint and Methodist Youths', *Reading Research Quarterly*, 49 (4) 417–435

Rackley, E. (2016) 'Religious Youth's Motivations for Reading Complex, Religious Texts', *Teachers College Record*, 118 (11) 1–50

Rappaport, J. (2000) 'Community Narratives: Tales of Terror and Joy', *American Journal of Community Psychology*, 28 (1) 1–24

Relph, E. (1976) *Place and placelessness*. London: Pion

Savage, M. (2015) *Social Class in the 21st Century*. London: Pelican Books

Saxena, M. (1994) 'Literacies among Punjabis in Southall' in Barton, D. and Ivanič, R. (eds.) *Worlds of Literacy*. Clevedon: Multilingual Matters, pp. 195–214

Sennett, R. (2012) *Together: the rituals, pleasures and politics of co-operation*. London: Penguin

Sheehy, M. and Leander, K. (2004) 'Introduction' in Leander, K. and Sheehy, M. (eds.) *Spatializing Literacy Research and Practice*. New York: Peter Lang, pp. 1–14

Shields, R. (1991) *Places on the Margins: Alternative geographies of modernity*. London: Routledge

Soja, E. (2004) 'Preface', in Leander, K. and Sheehy, M. (eds.) *Spatializing Literacy Research*. New York: Peter Lang, pp. ix–xv

Street, B. (1984) *Literacy in Theory and Practice*. Cambridge: Cambridge University Press

Street, B. (2011) 'Literacy inequalities in theory and practice: The power to name and define', *International Journal of Educational Development*, 31, 580–586

Studdert, D. (2005) *Conceptualising Community: Beyond the state and the individual*. Basingstoke: Palgrave Macmillan

Studdert, D. (2016) 'Sociality and a proposed analytic for investigating communal being-ness', *The Sociological Review*, 64, 622–638

Swann, J. and Allington, D. (2009) 'Reading groups and the language of literary texts: a case study in social reading', *Language and Literature*, 18 (3) 247–264

Taylor, D. and Dorsey-Gaines, C. (1988) *Growing Up Literate: Learning from inner-city families*. Portsmouth, NH: Heinemann

Taylor, D. (1998) *Family Literacy: Young children learn to read and write* (Second edition) Portsmouth, NH: Heinemann

Tuan, Y-F. (1977) *Space and Place: The perspective of experience*. Minneapolis, MN: University of Minnesota Press

Volk, D. (2008) 'Julializ and Bible Readings in the United States', in Gregory, E. (ed.) *Learning to Read in a New Language: Making sense of Words and Worlds*. London: Sage. pp. 30–34

Wegerif, R. (2013) *Dialogic: Education for the Internet Age*. Oxon: Routledge

Williams, R. (1988) *Keywords: a vocabulary of culture and society*. London: HarperCollins

Wills, J. (2016) '(Re)Locating community in relationships: questions for public policy', *The Sociological Review*, 64, 639–656

Zeldin, T. (1998) *Conversation: how talk can change your life*. London: The Harvill Press

Zubair, S. (2001) 'Literacies, Gender and Power in Rural Pakistan', in Street, B. V. (ed.) *Literacy and Development: Ethnographic Perspectives*. London: Routledge, pp. 188–204

6

A Portrait of Family Literacy

The portrait in this chapter draws upon interviews with one family, and observation of the ways in which a range of texts feature in their everyday lives. A social practice model of literacy, as discussed in Chap. 5, encourages us to consider literacy practices within the wider contexts in which they are located, including where and how we read and write, the kinds of texts with which we engage, who is reading and writing, and who else they read and write with. For Katie and Colin, literacy is something which they *do*, and which they do *together*. Although both Colin and Katie engage in reading and writing on their own, and with other people outside the home, I have chosen to focus here on how literacy is part of what they do together as a family. By attending to their interactions around the texts of their everyday lives, and to the wider social, cultural, and political contexts in which these interactions take place, I explore not only how a family *does* literacy but also, in turn, how literacy shapes family.

© The Author(s) 2018
S. Jones, *Portraits of Everyday Literacy for Social Justice*,
https://doi.org/10.1007/978-3-319-75945-6_6

Katie and Colin

Katie is 13 years old and lives with her brother James, who is 20, and her dad, Colin, who is in his late 40s. Colin has cared for his two children since the sudden death of his wife a decade ago. The family live in a semi-detached house on one of the main roads which form the outer edge of the estate. Katie attends the recently built Academy, which was co-sponsored by the university, while James attends a residential college for students beyond the age of compulsory schooling who have profound and multiple disabilities. Most of the time, it is just Katie and her dad at home, but James' needs still impact their everyday lives in many ways. This includes the physical modification which has been necessary around their home, as well as the ongoing need for the family to access various resources to meet the requirements of his care.

I first met Katie and Colin when Katie came to audition for a role in the first of the plays which were to be performed as part of the community theatre project described in Chap. 2. She was nine years old then and had seen a poster in the waiting room at her local doctor's surgery calling for participants. She had an interest in drama, and came along to hear more about the project, ending up being cast in a major role as the daughter of the central family who were the focus of the play. Colin came along with Katie to that first read-through of the play, and although he would wholeheartedly support his daughter's participation, he was adamant that he would not be performing himself. Once she was cast, Colin brought Katie along to every rehearsal and collected her at the end, having had to be at home in the meantime to care for his son. Colin often brought James in to the rehearsal room when he came to meet Katie, and would always stay to chat as long as he could. He was able to secure respite care for James so that he could see Katie perform in the play, and carried on supporting her participation when she went on to take part in the other two plays in the trilogy.

Over the course of the theatre project, Colin and Katie were both aware of my work as a researcher, and both had been interviewed about their involvement in the plays. When it came to the new project on everyday literacy practices, I turned to the family to ask whether they would be interested in taking part, approaching Colin in the first instance. He immediately said that he would be pleased for Katie to participate but that he himself would be "no use" to the project, as he didn't do any reading or writing. When I went on to talk about the kinds of things I'd be discussing with Katie in terms of her reading and writing, Colin was surprised that practices such as social media and reading newspapers and magazines would be relevant, and he became interested in what I would find out by talking to his daughter. During my visits to their home, Colin would leave Katie and me to talk in the living room, having made us a cup of tea. However, he would regularly drop in while Katie and I were talking, and offer thoughts that had occurred to him since I'd last visited, or having been called by Katie to share an anecdote or to confirm details of a story she was telling. In this way, I became more and more aware of the ways in which practices around text were an integral part of the family's everyday interaction with each other and with the wider world.

When I first visited Katie and Colin at home, Colin was in the process of re-decorating the living room. I was struck by a painting which hung over the fireplace to adorn the space while the work was being undertaken. This was a striking image of a character with a yellow rectangular body and a bright red, round head bearing a curly moustache and black hat. The figure was waving a Spanish flag, and next to it, in green paint, were the words "El Lollypop", and a heart shape. I got the sense that this painting had been given pride of place in the room, and in response to my smile when I saw it, Colin explained that his daughter had painted it for him for Father's Day. I didn't pick up the reference alluded to in the painting, and Colin told me that it represented his favourite film, *Forever Young, Forever Free*. Made in South Africa in 1975, this is a film about a friendship between a young boy who lives in a Lesotho village and a white orphan who finds himself living in a Catholic mission there. In her painting, Katie interpreted the film's alternative title, *E'Lollipop*, as the more Spanish sounding "El Lollypop", which then became the figure depicted in Spanish national colours, waving the country's flag. In painting this as a gift for Father's Day, based on her dad's favourite film, Katie was also playing with the word "Pop" as a pet name for her father.

Shared practice around language and literacy is a feature of everyday family life for Katie and Colin in many ways. On a typical visit to their home, I would listen to Katie describing her engagement with fan fiction based on contemporary rock bands, and her father playfully comparing these to his own favourites as a younger man. The pair also told me about how they would look forward to flicking through the magazines Colin brings home from his healthy eating group, and deciding what they would cook together.

> Katie: We, like, sit and read the magazine together to get recipes and stuff [...] we've got a recipe [for a visiting friend] 'cos we were reading through the magazine together. It's sort of like a sticky ginger thing with chicken.

Such scenes would be quite typical in many households, as would be the place of different forms of text at the heart of such interactions. Over the course of my visits to their home, I learnt that Katie and her dad have had to work closely together to navigate everyday experiences over many years. I saw how that work continues as new technologies emerge as part of family life, and new demands are made on families in their circumstances.

Colin suddenly found himself a widower when Katie was four years old. Before this, he worked in a range of jobs, including painting and decorating and working in a warehouse for a large retail company. He particularly enjoyed driving as part of his working day, and would often undertake journeys which took him far from home, where he saw new parts of the country. This often meant being away for long hours, sometimes overnight. He worked six days a week, and, as he says, "I would come home from work and kiss the kids goodnight and that were it". On Sundays, he would go with a group of friends from work on fishing trips, where he would enjoy "sitting there in the quiet and waiting". For Colin, fishing is "a mental sport, because you are always thinking strategically about how to catch the fish". Having been encouraged by his workmates to take it up, Colin decided that "if I'm going to catch a fish, I want to catch the best". He described how he "would go and get the videos and the books and read up on it", watch fishing programmes on Discovery Channel, and do research on the internet.

The sudden death of his wife brought a huge change to Colin's life, and he had to give up work to care for his children. Because of James' special needs, the level of challenge was particularly acute.

> I had to learn what James was saying because he doesn't speak; he uses the machine or he syllabolises, and I'm sitting there and I'm thinking 'what the hell are you talking about?' because I didn't have a clue. Katie would say 'he wants a cup of tea' and I'm going 'why don't he say that?' Now I can understand him but because I hadn't been with him I didn't have a clue what the hell he was talking about. She taught me a lot about how to look after him.

Explicit attention to the communication of meaning has been a central part of everyday life for Katie and her dad. James makes use of speech-generating devices, including a Lightwriter and, more recently, an iPad. With the latter device, he is also able to watch music videos and to Skype and use FaceTime with his father and sister when he is away from home at the residential college. Even though James spends most of term time away from home, the family's routine is still focused on ensuring that the right resources are accessed to provide for his care. Although this is a routine aspect of life, it is not without its challenges for Colin, who told me that he doesn't feel confident as a writer. This, he said, is because he "messed about too much at school and didn't study".

Colin was brought up in a children's home "basically from when I was born until fifteen", when he moved into a bedsit on his own and worked as an apprentice painter and decorator for the council in his home city. Because of the precarious nature of employment in strike-ridden 1970s public service, he moved to the city where he now lives, and found lodgings and more work painting and decorating. Apart from his fishing books, Colin says that he hasn't read a book since he was in the children's home, where there was a single bookshelf from which the young residents could choose their reading material. One of the books that sticks in his mind from this time is *The Ragged-Trousered Philanthropists* by Robert Tressell (1914), which he'd wanted to read:

> because I'd always known from an early age that I wanted to be a painter. When I was in the kids' home, one of the painters came in and I was telling

him that I wanted to be a painter and all this and he said to me 'you want to read this book' and I think he were taking the mickey but I got the kids' home to get the book.

Even though he didn't get past the first couple of chapters as a 12-year-old, Colin says, "I probably will when I'm seventy". He is immensely proud of his daughter's prolific reading habit.

> You want to see her little bookcase – it's jammed. You go into her bedroom and constantly there will be a book on the bed and on the floor. She loves to read and I'm pleased about that.

Katie's taste for reading fiction is something Colin recognises that she shares with her late mother. Katie has a Kindle, and, with her father's permission, she downloads e-books onto this for reading. However, she prefers what she calls "actual" or "normal" books. She will often use the free sample function on her Kindle in order to decide whether or not to buy a physical copy of the book to finish reading it. Amongst her favourites are bestselling true-life dramas, such as those written by Casey Watson, or crime novels such as Martina Cole's. Towards the end of the research project, she was particularly fond of the John Green novel *The Fault in Our Stars* (Green 2013), a love story about teenage cancer patients, and had read that several times. This taste for adult themes and titles reflects a shift Katie describes in her reading habits, away from children's authors such as Jacqueline Wilson, whom she described as being "a bit twee".

Asked to complete the sentence, "reading is…", Katie's response was "something I do daily".

> In bed, on the bus, in parks, on trains, in school, during lesson when I shouldn't. They can't tell me off in English though because I am still doing English. I read a book under the table in Maths.

Katie differentiates between the reading and writing which is part of the school curriculum, where "we are told what to read and write", and the ways in which she engages with text in her own time. One example of

Katie's writing outside school is an ongoing collection of stories she has co-authored with her cousin, Aiden, which they have called "The Chronicle of Mr Happy Magical No-Name Unicorn (formerly known as Mike)". Although one continuous story, Katie thinks that if it were broken down into short stories, there would be about 27 of them. These stories have been jointly composed by the cousins over a period of three years, either when they have met on family occasions or in communication in between these face-to-face visits.

> If any of us have an idea we'll write it down and then we'll tell each other as much as we can remember about it and decide whether it is going to go into the book or not.

Despite the seemingly upbeat fantastical setting, the adventures Mr Happy Magical No-name Unicorn (formerly known as Mike) often have an element of the banality of the everyday world about them. As is seen in the description Katie gave me of one story, below, this is coupled with more than a tinge of the violence that is a feature of the video game narratives which she also enjoys.

> Mr Happy Magical No Name Unicorn (Formerly Known as Mike) he got bored and so he, like, went to the library and he held up the librarian and he said 'give me tokens to use the computer or I'll blow your brains out'.

As Katie points out about the Chronicles, "I don't really think it had an audience. It was just, like, to make us laugh".

At school, English and drama are Katie's favourite subjects. She dislikes writing. She is left-handed and finds it tricky to keep her writing neat without her hand smudging the ink. She has a keen interest in learning: she has taught herself to play the guitar, for example, and is "in the top set for everything" at school. However, in our conversations about school, Katie would often be less than enthusiastic about the formal routines and expectations of the classroom, especially when the relevance of what she was being taught was less than obvious to her. She enjoys the feeling of being knowledgeable, and is often keen to share general knowledge trivia in conversation, or to apply her knowledge in other playful ways. For example, "knowing that the Olympics in 1900 happened in Paris" came in handy at school during a game of "Would I Lie to You?" (where a player presents a story about themselves, and others try to work out whether or not it is true by questioning the teller). Katie's story involved her "great great grandad [who] was a gold medallist in the hundred metres sprint in the Paris 1900 Olympics".

Katie is a member of the science club, which meets after school, and also the school library book club, which meets at Friday lunchtimes. At the time I was observing Katie at school, the group were discussing the shortlist for the Brilliant Book Award. This involved the group undertaking tasks such as reading the opening paragraphs of books and guessing which title they are from. They were provided with booklets into which they wrote a record of the books they had read, and any notes on particular favourites. The group I observed was run with a tone that was recognisably pedagogic, and an expectation about reading being based on hard copies of fiction texts. A suite of computers lined the edge of the library, each bearing a sign that read: "the library computers are to be used for homework and Accelerated Reader[1] Quizzes only". Katie makes regular use of the school library. For a time, when there was an issue with checking out books on the system, which is based on fingerprint recognition, and Katie's "finger didn't work", she would hide the books she was reading in the library at lunchtimes, so that others could not take them out.

Katie's reading is important to her, and is also viewed positively by Colin. He links it to his aspirations for his daughter:

> For me, with her, all I want is her to grow up and have a job where she's not dependent on a bloke [...] that's why I keep saying that she's got to read and she's got to do her homework and everything in that way. [...]

> I want her to be as intelligent as she can be but I still want her to have fun and enjoy herself [...] I want her to grow up the same as her mother and to be able to do what she wanted.

Like many young people of her age, however, her reading and writing practices move with Katie in and out of the school gates. In my observations of Katie at school, and when we talked about school during my visits to her home, there were many examples of the ways in which literacy and learning disrupted boundaries between school and home as physical and symbolic spaces. One of these examples was Katie learning to play guitar. She has lessons at school, and attends guitar club on Wednesdays, as well as an after-school club. She has learnt songs by one of her favourite artists, Taylor Swift, and other classic rock guitar tracks such as "Smoke on the Water" by Deep Purple. In between her school lessons and clubs, Katie teaches herself new songs by watching YouTube tutorials on her phone, or by playing along to music videos. She demonstrated this to me on one of my visits to her home. Katie feels this is a good way to learn "because with a guitar teacher in person you can't really say 'stop, can you say that again', because they'll get annoyed with you but with YouTube you can rewind and play it again".

Another example of practices moving across the boundaries of home and school is also based on Katie's viewing of YouTube. She and a friend watch videos of gamers who garner huge followings by posting videos of themselves playing computer games and commenting on the gameplay. One particular contributor had, at the time of the research, built a significant reputation for playing the online game *Happy Wheels*. In this game, various characters drive different wheeled vehicles around a two-dimensional course, trying to dodge barbaric obstacles before meeting a ludicrously grizzly end. Particularly taken by a phrase used by this gamer as a function of the game, Katie and her friend began running up to people they knew in school shouting "Chairmode activate!" Those on the receiving end of this greeting were often bemused by this physical enactment of a phrase taken from a computer game commentary, if not annoyed (often an objective Katie deliberately sought). For Katie and her friend, however, its performance bore significance in bringing them together in a physical space, through a physical act, which represented something they had both observed separately within a digital sphere.

Katie enjoys playing computer games as well as watching others do so. Having done her homework, and with her dad's permission, she enjoys playing open world role play games on her X-Box, where she chooses an avatar and wanders around a fantasy world:

You can choose the way that the story ends and stuff by the way that you live life and you and become more skillful and stronger.

Being in control of her destiny within the game is appealing to Katie:

I love being able to, like, take control of actually what is happening and stuff. I don't like doing it in real life though because I get scared that I'm going to make a muck up, but on this you actually can't. [...] I can take risks but it doesn't really matter.

Colin also plays games occasionally, although he prefers tactical shooting games. He plays these on the easiest level to start with, so that "tells me what I'm going to be doing", before playing again at the harder level, and doing it "the proper way". Colin enjoys the strategy involved in such games, and has this as his main focus, "rather than killing everybody".

Colin's experience of computer gaming goes back to the early days of home computing, and an old Amiga which he used for gaming. However, he feels that using computers for other means is not something which has come naturally to him. The family got their first personal computer 15 years ago, and the children have made lots of use of this, and subsequent digital technology, in the home. Colin described to me how James "loves his iPad", and, like his sister, "he's very quick at learning and he can work a computer no problem". Colin describes his response to computers as partly relating to the difference in his experience with them compared to that of his children.

They're not scared of them whereas my generation are because we are thinking that if it breaks it is going to cost a fortune but they are just thinking 'I can do it' [...] I'm scared of them and they're not; that's the be all and end all.

Colin says he is "not a technological person":

If you put me in the garage now and asked me to build you a bird's nest or something, then, yeah, I can get the machine out and do it. I can do that and, as I say, I'm more use with my hands than my head.

However, as with many families, the computer has come to play a central part in everyday life. Although he prefers to use the computer "for people to get in touch with me rather than me them", Colin now makes use of his laptop to communicate with the many agencies involved in James' care. This can involve writing emails to update staff at the residential school on James' weekend home visit, or completing complex forms in order to access financial support for his care needs. Aside from the filling in boxes with information, some of these forms also involve longer passages of writing detailing the exact nature of James' needs and the demands of his care. When Colin does this writing, he says

> it's all written in one go; it goes from food, to incontinence aids, to food. There are capitals here there and everywhere, there are no full stops, there's no punctuation. It's written as I would talk.

Colin says that he will quite often "get totally stuck in writing", feeling less than confident with the technical aspects and extremely aware of expectations that this form of writing be judged to be accurate. The family pool resources for such tasks, however, with Katie reading through what her dad has written, checking spelling and punctuation.

> I'll say to her, 'I'll write this out, but tell me if it's OK' and so I'll write it on a jotter and then she'll go over it and change things and correct my spelling mistakes and put the punctuation in.

As Katie says,

> We help each other out like that [...] say I'm stuck on a maths problem he'll help me out with that and then, in return, if he's typing a letter or something I'll help with his spelling and stuff.

Colin moderates Katie's support depending on the audience.

> She uses, like, speech marks and things like that but I know the people I'm sending it to would know that it wasn't my work. If I write to my sister on email and Katie will check it I'll say not to change it. She can put full stops and capitals but that's it.

Colin wants his sister to "read it as I wrote it", but it is still important to him that the spelling is correct.

> Because I don't want to look dumb. If I'm being honest, I don't want to look thick. I managed to fight my way through life and I've been through fifteen years without looking too thick and I still don't want to.

Katie has also helped her father when it comes to sending text messages, but as mobile phone technology has advanced, he is also able to utilise the speech to text function on his phone to compose longer texts. This has given him confidence in being able to communicate with friends and family with the ease facilitated by SMS communication. In a shift to what we might expect from different generations' use of mobile phones, Colin comments on Katie's assistance with texting:

> Before I used to ask Katie to text for me but now I do it myself. But she even puts speech marks and punctuation on the text. I said to her that's going a bit overboard.

Katie has introduced Skype into family life. Initially using the app on her iPod to Skype her brother when he was at his residential college, Katie has since introduced her father to video chat. He now communicates regularly with his sister in Germany and his younger brother, who also works abroad.

> Me and our kid will talk for two or three hours. We wouldn't be just talking to each other because I would be doing something else and so would he but we would be talking to each other while we were doing other things.

Through social media, Katie also communicates with others who share her interests, both locally and further afield. Although lots of the focus of discussion on social media is on her favourite band, Green Day, their members and their music, the range of topics described by Katie also includes: "Unicorns, teddy bears, rainbows, ASDF[2] movies, zombies, Beowulf." Like many social media users, Katie uses this digital space to curate an identity, and as a space where she can engage with others with shared interests. To Colin, Katie's online persona is a reflection of his daughter's personality, as he suggested by advising me: "if you really want to know what she's like, check out her Twitter account".

Like many others of her age, however, Katie's engagement with social media and the digital world becomes very much part of the immediately local, day-to-day family life. On some of my visits, Katie explained that she had not been online recently, as her father had confiscated her devices—a regular occurrence, as she described:

> Basically if I keep my room clean I'll be fine and I can have loads of stuff but if it's dirty and my dad tells me to clean it then I'll still keep it but if I don't clean it up in a week then it gets taken off me. That usually happens every month or something.

> It starts off and he'll take my phone off me and then he'll take my iPod and then he'll take my laptop and he'll keep, like, increasing it.

This is another way, then, in which literacy operates within family life for Katie and Colin, where the connections between wider audiences and contexts and the operational work of family are evident. For Katie and Colin, engagement with texts of all kinds is threaded through their everyday life, across generations and formal and informal contexts for learning, across audiences and purposes, times and spaces. From father and daughter working together to access the support they need to look after James, to the ways in which Katie navigates the mandated literacy demands of secondary school, to the social spaces the family are able to explore digitally, literacy is part of everyday life. It shapes it and is shaped by it; it supports the navigation of its challenges, and the exploration of its possibilities.

In the Frame: Literacy and Family

The portrait of Katie and Colin illustrates the creative and resourceful ways in which a family utilises a range of literacy practices for playing, making, and learning together. At the outset of the research, Colin didn't feel his contribution would be at all useful: he didn't see himself as someone who did any reading or writing, and didn't see some of the practices I was observing, such as gaming, as "literacy". At least, to him they were not as important or socially acceptable as the practices he says he did less often, such as reading a novel, or with less confidence, such as writing a letter. Reading and writing are imagined by Colin as things which he did not feel he "had". He associated this with his experiences at school and, three decades on, in his efforts "not to appear too thick", he still felt the acute emotional impact of believing he does not have the skills and knowledge valued by society. The ways in which literacy is seen and valued can have a dramatic effect not only on people's access to economic resources, but also, through a lack of recognition, on their sense of self-worth. However, from pursuing his interest in fishing, to researching recipes, and texting his brother, Colin talks about the ways in which reading and writing do form a crucial part of his everyday life. As their portrait demonstrates, for both Colin and Katie, family centres around a similarly wide range of engagement with texts. The family is a significant discursive space within literacy policy, education and research, and I turn now to explore some of the themes which have emerged from this, and their influence on how we understand the notion of "family literacy".

Family Literacy

Much of the research on family literacy is informed by a social practice model of literacy, highlighting the rich and diverse experiences of literacy within the home (e.g. Taylor and Dorsey-Gaines 1988; Pahl 2002; Rogers 2008; Heath 2013). This research has also recognised the way in which these practices often take place under the long-reaching shadow of dominant versions of literacy (variously described as "mandated", Comber 2012; "schooled", Street and Street 1991; or "mainstream", Heath 1983). Some of the ways in which families engage with text are in direct conflict with these dominant models (as has been explored, e.g. by Gregory and Williams 2000). This compounds further what Rebecca Rogers (2008) calls a mismatch between what is valued in terms of being a literate member of society, and the lived realities of family life.

In her study of literacy practices in one family in the USA, Rogers describes the ways in which dominant models of what it means to be literate, as well as what it means to be part of a family, can conflate into a "discursive web that holds people in place" (ibid. p. 2). For June, the mother in Rogers' study, powerful subjectivities are rooted within dominant notions of what it means to read and write, learnt at school and reinforced through the expectations of a bureaucratic system she is forced to navigate as a parent on a low income and with a child who has special educational needs. Having left school in Grade 8, June has returned to adult education to get her General Education Diploma. Her place in the family as the mother, typically responsible for the literate demands of the household, also shapes her subjectivity. Together, this means that June could be viewed as doubly deficit based on the mismatch between the way she conducts her everyday life through literacy, and the demands made upon her by dominant narratives of success in both literacy and motherhood.

Some approaches to family literacy focus on this potential mismatch, but in so doing, they can reinforce the family as the site of deficit, in need of bringing in line with dominant ways of understanding what it means to read and write in contemporary society. Gregory and Williams (2000, p. 4) describe the "myth of poverty and parental deficiency" which grew through the 1970s and 1980s, with a shift in policy discourse towards parental responsibility for children's educational success. Written narratives and story-telling were privileged in this discourse, and children were framed as "disadvantaged" if they didn't have this particular form of linguistic experience (p. 5). Research into literacies within the home has also traditionally started with school as its focus, viewing family practices in relation to how far they supported those of school (Barton and Hamilton 1998). More recently, at a policy level, focus has remained on the family as a site of support for learning that takes place in school. Involvement in school remains a key parental responsibility in policy discourse and is reflected in the way in which both formal and informal educational institutions are set up and run (e.g. Marsh 2003; Nichols et al. 2012; Smith 2018; discussed also in Chaps. 4 and 5). Little account has traditionally been given in government initiatives to what happens in non-Western homes, or to the "unofficial" literacy practices in which people engage outside formal schooling. There are echoes here, of course, of the book-gifting schemes and new philanthropy outlined in Chaps. 3 and 4, which aim to "intervene" in early literacy development by funding the supply of particular kinds of books, which support a particular cultural model of reading within the family.

Although studies of family literacy have shown support for school that is often "unwavering" (Rogers 2008, p. 2), it hasn't always been clear to parents how they can best help (Minns 1990). Schools can often seem to have little capacity, or interest in integrating home experiences into their curriculum (Livingstone and Sefton-Green 2016), and the most recent iterations of the National Curriculum in England, with its emphasis on canonical texts and the discursive practices of dominant social and cultural groups, such as formal debate, could in fact be seen as discouraging some families from doing so (Department for Education 2014).

The home is a prime site for learning, however, as a place "where personal life is regulated in the most intimate ways" (Barton and Hamilton 1998, p. 190). It is a locus from which people venture into other parts of their worlds, and to which they return, bringing with them the resources and problems they encounter in these other places. More recent research has focused on the home as the site of creative and collaborative meaning making (e.g. Pahl 2015). This is the way in which I approached my observation of literacy practices in the home of Colin and Katie. I saw much to support a broader consideration of what we understand by the term "family literacy" and I move now to explore in more depth the ways in which we can see the collaboration of Colin and Katie as a way in which they *do* family through literacy.

As the purpose of this book is to examine how framing can impact experience, I turn briefly first to the ways in which "family" itself might be understood by looking at how it has been framed as a concept in sociological literature.

The Family

"Family" is a word that is commonly used in relation to everyday lives. It often refers in particular to that part of our everyday lives which is not public, and to signify the opposite, for example, of work or school. Despite suggesting the more private aspect of our lives, "the image of family has a strong resonance in policy-making" (Hall 2016, p. 310). As policy has seen responsibility shift from the state to households, family has become "deeply rooted in how most governments convey messages of responsibility and distribute social benefits" (ibid.). The family is a central trope of neoliberal discourse, and is often a signifier of the perceived failings of those living on a low income, who are subject to the "classing gaze" (Gillies 2006, p. 283) of bureaucratic systems which measure and categorise countless aspects of their everyday lives. Alongside this, the media also regularly presents us with an image of the idealised family, often comprised of "two heterosexual parents and an unspecified number of children", engaged in activities which represent family life, consisting of enjoying time together relaxing or engaging in outdoor activities (Hall and Holdsworth 2016). Family has been the focus of prominent studies of working class lives over many years (e.g. Hoggart 1957; Young and Wilmott 2007 [1957]; Coates and Sillburn 1970; Freedman 1993; Sennett 2003). Such work has highlighted the ways in which a wider social and political context has impacted on the lived experiences of the families who are finding it hardest to make ends meet. More recently, family is a locus of concerns which have arisen due to the uncertainties brought about by globalisation and individualisation, a site for the media to locate "a host of anxieties about norms and values" (Livingstone and Sefton-Green 2016, p. 4).

As David Morgan (2011a, p. 4.3) has argued, however,

'family' is not simply just a powerful strand in ideological rhetoric but the relationships and activities that are indicated by the use of the term are important to a wide range of people going about their everyday lives throughout the world.

Families, and the ways in which we live together, may have changed, with shifts in the authority of institutions such as the church, but the fundamental place in our lives of reciprocal care and support through family remains (Valentine 2008). So does the way in which family is "done". Challenging the notion of family as having a "thing-like quality" (2011b, p. 3),

Morgan argues that family is constructed and reconstructed through actions with symbolic meanings which hold people together. These actions can be "discursive", including aspirations and memories, as well as physical and instrumental, such as the preparation and consumption of food (2011b; Fiese et al. 2006).

In her ethnographic work with families living with the impact of economic policy in Britain following the global financial crisis of 2008, Sarah Hall (2016) calls for more attention to family as a focus which offers insight into the effects of wider social and political contexts and the ways in which these are negotiated within lived realities. This echoes my own focus in this book on literacy as a lens through which we may better understand the impact of wider social, political, and cultural contexts on everyday lives. Many of the issues raised in this brief summary of the sociological literature are reflected in the experiences I heard about and observed Colin and Katie share together. As a family including a single parent in receipt of benefits, a school-age teenager embracing the digital age, and a young man with disabilities, dominant narratives readily cast them as subjects for the "gaze" of the state. Indeed, Colin could be said to have internalised a subjectivity of deficit in relation to the narrow model of literacy he feels is valued by society. That said, I saw a range of ways in which this family defies stereotypes. Their creative collaboration through a wide range of literacy practices emphasises not only the role of literacy in family, but also the importance of family to literacy. A closer look at the role of literacy in how Colin and his children "do" family offers much to challenge the narratives that frame this family, as well as others in a similar position to them.

Doing Family/Literacy: "We Help Each Other Out Like That"

As a family, Colin, Katie, and James have faced many significant changes and challenges. Since his wife's death, Colin has taken on the practical and emotional work of parenting on his own, responding to the changing needs of his son's care and those of his growing daughter. This has involved negotiating the institution of school as part of his aspirations for Katie and James to get the best out of their education. Bureaucratic institutions have also been key to him being able to support his family practically and financially. Additional pressure is placed on someone like Colin, whose confidence with reading and writing has been dented by his experience of school, by the "tightening associations between literacy skill and social viability" (Brandt 2001, p. 19). Seeing himself as someone who has struggled, and worrying about being judged by others based on his writing, exacerbates the element of surveillance and control of bureaucratic systems for Colin (Sarangi and Slembrouck 1996). There is a lot at stake: not only the physical and financial resources upon which his family rely, but also his self-worth as a provider for his family, and as a valued individual member of society (which in itself, of course, is in no small way based on his role as a father and carer).

Katie recognises the different kinds of literacy with which she engages as part of her everyday life. She showed me examples of these, and talked about many others. Her comments about school literacy also reflect an understanding that the version of reading and writing she is presented with there is only one of many versions she has at her disposal. Also evident in the portrait of their everyday literacies is Colin's problem solving attitude: whether it's finding the best fishing kit, or how to negotiate the next level of a video game, his approach is to work something out as a system and to make it work for him. Together, then, Katie and her dad make a good team when it comes to navigating the bureaucratic systems which are so crucial to their family and which have themselves been sites of rapid change in terms of the demands for literacy within society, as well as the material ways in which we are expected to engage with text (Brandt 2001).

Collaboration in accessing literacy demands, across a range of social contexts including the family, has been a theme within literacy research for some time. Sarah Padmore (1994) describes the "guiding lights" who are a feature of literacy learning, many of whom are family members. This is taken very much within a pedagogic context, with the adult often acting as a guiding light for a younger learner. Nonetheless, guiding lights "play a vital role, helping people to gain confidence and discover a sense of personal identity, or changing identity" (p. 155). Eve Gregory (2005) takes up the image of the guiding light to describe siblings teaching schooled literacy practices within multilingual homes. These children "take hold of school learning and present it as an understandable form to younger siblings during play at home" (p. 22). The idea of the guiding light reminds us that learning "is a collaborative group activity, rather than a dyadic activity between parent (usually mother) and child" (Gregory and Williams 2000, p. 11).

Brandt (2001) employs the notion of sponsors of literacy. These "are any agents, local or distant, concrete or abstract, who enable, support, teach, and model, as well as recruit, regulate, suppress, or withhold, literacy – and gain advantage from it in some way" (p. 19). For Brandt, the concept of sponsors sits within an economic model of literacy, where the pace of change in the role of literacy in our lives, and our capacity to meet this role in order to gain "access and reward", is matched by a similarly rapid increase in the ideological values placed upon literacy skills.

> Sponsors are a tangible reminder that literacy learning throughout history has always required permission, sanction, assistance, coercion, or, at minimum, contact with existing trade routes. (ibid.)

Brandt argues that sponsors of literacy are usually "more knowledgeable, and more entrenched than the sponsored" (p ibid.). We could argue that Katie has greater access to the dominant model of literacy than her father, and, through it, she provides access to the "trade route" that is represented by formal literacy within a bureaucratic process. To define her role as a sponsor of her father's literacy may not quite explain what is happening when the two work together, however.

Rogers (2008) describes literacy learning in the family context by using the apprentice model. Using examples of interaction with texts including non-fiction and research for social action, Rogers argues that Vicky, the daughter who participated in her study of literacy practices in one family, watched practice being done by a more knowledgeable other, and engaged in this practice through a guided relationship, before carrying out the practice independently. It could be argued that Colin and Katie's work together follows some aspects of this model. Alongside the practical skills learnt through apprenticeship, Rogers also argues that subjectivities are learnt within family relationships. Through conversations with Colin over time, I came to notice the way in which he had picked up on some of Katie's flexibility over text composition, her confidence in what she wanted to say, and her approach to the composition of text with a particular audience in mind.

"Literacy mediation" has also been taken up in research (Baynham 1995; Jones 2000; Thériault 2016) as a notion which "allows researchers to capture the jointly accomplished nature of much reading and writing in everyday life" (Papen 2012, p. 74). A literacy mediator is often someone positioned within the wider structures represented by the literacy demands encountered by those who need their support: they are someone who can *do* the literacies demanded of the system. Katie's knowledge of formal literacies places her in this role when she transcribes and translates her father's writing onto healthcare and welfare claim forms. A literacy mediator has a powerful role in enabling access to institutions, which are, in late modernity, increasingly represented by bureaucratic processes. Be it agricultural policy (Jones 2000), healthcare (Papen 2012), or conditions affecting youths facing precarity (Thériault 2016), the mediator can mitigate against, and challenge, the power held over individuals by institutions and their texts, allowing individuals to engage with them on their own terms (Papen 2010; Thériault 2016).

Models of interpersonal literacy support offer an interesting counter to discourses of family as a site for the reproduction of a dominant, narrow model of literacy. This support can be both practical and emotional: the guiding lights which feature in the work of Padmore (1994) and Gregory (2005) support others to read and write, sometimes in particular ways, but within the context of caring and nurturing relationships. Those who recall their guiding lights associate their support with the encouragement and fulfilment of aspirations: they will often have been role models for particular subjectivities around literacy, and not purely those of formal schooling. Observations of siblings who mediate formal schooling for their younger family members also reflect how these support the integration of formal literacies into a richly complex repertoire of literacy and language practice (Gregory 2005). Models of the sponsor (Brandt 2001) or apprentice (Rogers 2008) emphasise the ways in which the learning of literacy confers power, access, and reward. Katie's support of her father with bureaucratic and digital texts broadens the locus of this power

within the family to include the younger generation. Given their circumstances as a family, certain texts could hold significant power over them,
both practically, in terms of the resources they need, and discursively, by
defining them as in deficit because of these needs. However, when father
and daughter work together, these texts become the locus of the shared
practical and emotional work of family, and the power held over them by
texts is reduced. Katie's mediation of texts confers a degree of power upon
Colin to access the resources he needs for his family but it also takes away
the power that texts might hold over her father as someone framed by a
system which demands a specific set of skills from him. Rather than the
child being framed as a creation of the parent (as was discussed in Chaps.
3 and 4), such a view reframes the role of children in a family "doing"
everyday life together. Being able to work together in this way challenges
the power of bureaucratic texts to define the family as merely fillers-in of
forms (Taylor and Dorsey-Gaines 1988).

Interaction around formal bureaucratic texts is one way in which Katie
and Colin's literacy practices challenge narrow models of family literacy.
There is also a contingent approach to literacy learning within the home.
Rather than just being a satellite for the reinforcement of school learning,
when new demands for literacy emerge, these are often sites for innovation
(Brandt 2001, p. 8) and are another area in which Katie and Colin work
together to support each other and to share the resources they've developed as part of the work of family.

When she talks about her online activity, Katie portrays Colin as acting, in some ways, in the stereotypical father's role. Colin also describes
how he moderates and regulates her online practice (boyd 2014;
Livingstone and Sefton-Green 2016), including her entitlement to access,
which is denied unless she has done her bit around the home. However,
Colin also respects the affordance of online space to allow Katie a place to
be herself. His own nervousness around computers reflects the discourse
of the "digital native", which has readily been taken up in popular and
media discourse. As Helsper and Eynon (2010) have noted, however, this
construct is not to be taken uncritically, as access and exposure to technology are significant factors in any user's confidence, whatever age. In
much the same way as they have collaborated over physical texts, Katie
and Colin have worked together to *do* family through digital practice,

and digital practice has been a key part of the way in which they do family, reflecting Valentine's (2008) depiction of the internet as a new space for creating and exploring intimacies, knowing, loving, and caring.

The creativity of SMS—or "text"—language has been well documented (e.g. Crystal 2008; Wood et al. 2014), and father and daughter challenge the stereotypes that arose during the moral panic that has been associated with online and SMS language use by working together to make meanings they want for their own audiences. Katie's insistence on adopting the features of standard written English is challenged by her father, who realises that although this is beneficial to the official institutions with which he has to communicate, not least in the way it presents him as a person to be valued through his literate skills, the same skills are not recognised as part of who he is to his sister. Colin therefore reclaims the text composed by his daughter in order for it to mean what he wants it to mean about him to his wider family.

As well as being a source of concern over the fate of language, digital media has also been the focus of disquiet in terms of its impact on personal and family relationships. Livingstone and Sefton-Green (2016) explore the use of personal media in the families of teenagers with whom they worked. For these families, who ranged in terms of socioeconomic and cultural context, "being together in the media-rich home, is significantly a matter of choice, involving more negotiation, some conflict, and a general openness to the possibility of sharing" (p. 167). For Katie and her dad, digital devices are the currency through which domestic arrangements are upheld. As such, digital resources are a function of how contemporary family works in a practical sense. They also support the symbolic work of family, as can be seen in the lives of Katie, Colin, and James. Technology has enabled James to communicate with his family in a way in which he was unable earlier in his life. Through Skype, Katie has reunited her father with long-lost relatives, and Colin talks every night with his younger brother who works thousands of miles away. The image of the family who are in the same house—often in the same room, or at the same dining table—but who are separated by screens has become a recurring motif in discussion of contemporary family life. However, Katie, Colin, and James represent the fact that families who are physically dispersed can be connected through their screens (ibid., citing Flichy

1995). As Livingstone and Sefton-Green note, "the result is an often-mediated but still-genuine togetherness that sustains the fragile balance between individuality and commonality required in the modern 'democratic' family" (p. 167).

Reframing Family Literacy

The demands placed on individuals in relation to literacy within a knowledge society have changed dramatically in recent times, and *what* we are called upon to learn, to know, and to do has shifted considerably, as has *how* we learn, know, and do it. Such shifts are part of a wider policy context which has also seen a move towards the family as a locus of responsibility and blame, with perceived deficiencies attributed to a lack of support for officially mandated forms of literacy within the home. As we have seen in previous chapters, shifts in what is assumed and valued about everyday lives, and the literacy practices which are part of them, leave people framed as deficit and, in cases such as Colin's, often feeling that they have been left behind. As Brandt has noted,

> what people are able to do with their writing or reading in any time and place – as well as what others do to them with writing and reading – contribute to their sense of identity, normality, possibility. (2001, p. 11)

One response to this situation is reflected in the approaches to literacy described in Chaps. 3 and 4, where a redistributive model is applied to those resources and skills deemed to be of value. The family is one site where the attention of such approaches has been focused, but often this can assume that only support from outside the family, through officially mandated structures, can be of benefit.

The portrait of Colin and Katie demonstrates shared engagement with literacy in families, and the agency involved in their creative co-operation around literacy to achieve their various goals. Working together, father and daughter engage in what Rogers describes as "a delicate balance of textual encounters, institutional arrangements, and subjectivities" (2008, p. 65), negotiating contexts which shape their experiences, and the texts which are part of them. Literacy practices are central to how Colin and Katie "do" family, not only in terms of accessing economic resources but also through shared everyday experiences, such as film and games. They are important to the family in operational ways too, as evidenced by the way literacy practices are tied to the family's routines and aspirations.

Everyday literacies for Colin and Katie represent much to challenge reductive stereotypes of families in receipt of state support, as well as narrow models of what it means to read and write. For them, the family home is a space where a diverse range of literacy practices can be seen, across modes and purposes. In the next chapter, we look more closely at the home in relation to literacy when we return to Peggy's story.

Notes

1. Accelerated Reader is a scheme described by its designers as "a powerful tool for monitoring and managing independent reading practice while promoting reading for pleasure" (http://www.renlearn.co.uk/accelerated-reader/). Participating readers are assigned a graded category of books from which they are allowed to choose, and take computer quizzes after reading which generate "feedback" for the reader on their progress, and "data" which can be monitored by schools.
2. Asdf ("ass-duff") movies are short, simply drawn, comedic flash animations, originally derived from a webcomic strip, created and posted by YouTuber *TomSka* http://knowyourmeme.com/memes/asdfmovie

References

Barton, D. and Hamilton, M. (1998) *Local Literacies: Reading and Writing in One Community*. London: Routledge

Baynham, M. (1995) *Literacy Practices: Investigation literacy in social contexts*. London: Longman

boyd, d. (2014) *It's Complicated: the social lives of networked teens*. New Haven, CT: Yale University Press

Brandt, D. (2001) *Literacy in American Lives*. Cambridge: Cambridge University Press

Coates, K. and Sillburn, R. (1970) *Poverty: The Forgotten Englishmen*. Middlesex: Penguin Books

Comber, B. (2012) 'Mandated literacy assessment and the reorganisation of teachers' work: federal policy, local effects', *Critical Studies in Education*, 53 (2) 119–136

Crystal, D. (2008) *Txtng: The gr8 db8*. Oxford: Oxford University Press

Department for Education (2014) *National Curriculum for England*. https:// www.gov.uk/government/collections/national-curriculum   (accessed November 20, 2017)

Fiese, B., Foley, K.P., Spagnola, M. (2006), 'Routine and Ritual Elements in Family Mealtimes: Contexts for child well-being and family identity', *New Directions for Child and Adolescent Development*, 111, 67–89

Freedman, J. (1993) *From Cradle to Grave: The Human Face of Poverty in America*. New York: Atheneum.

Gillies, V. (2006) 'Working class mothers and school life: exploring the role of emotional capital', *Gender and Education*, 18 (3) 281–293

Green, J. (2013) *The Fault in Our Stars*. London: Penguin

Gregory, E. (2005) 'Guiding Lights: Siblings as Literacy Teachers in a Multilingual Community', in Anderson, J., Kenrick, M., Rogers, T. and Smythe, S. (eds.) *Portraits of Literacy Across Families, Communities, and Schools*. Mahwah, NJ: Lawrence Erlbaum Associates, pp. 21–40

Gregory, E. and Williams, A. (2000) *City Literacies: Learning to read across generations and cultures*. London: Routledge.

Hall, S. M. (2016) 'Everyday family experiences of the financial crisis: getting by in the recent economic recession', *Journal of Economic Geography*, 16, 305–330

Hall, S. M. and Holdsworth, C. (2016) 'Family Practices, Holiday and the Everyday', *Mobilities*, 11 (2) 284–302

Heath, S. B. (1983) *Ways with Words*. Cambridge: Cambridge University Press

Heath, S. B. (2013) *Words at Work and Play*. Cambridge: Cambridge University Press

Helsper, E. and Eynon, R. (2010) 'Digital natives: where's the evidence?', *British Education Research Journal*, 36 (3) 503–520

Hoggart, R. (1957) *The Uses of Literacy*. Middlesex: Penguin

Jones, K. (2000) 'Becoming just another alphanumeric code: farmers' encounters with the literacy and discourse practices of agricultural bureaucracy at the livestock auction', in Barton, D., Hamilton, M. and Ivanič, R. (eds.) *Situated Literacies: reading and writing in context*. London: Routledge, pp. 70–90

Livingstone, S. and Sefton-Green, J. (2016) *The Class: Living and learning in the digital age*. New York: New York University Press

Marsh, J. (2003) 'One-way traffic? Connections between Literacy Practices at Home and in the Nursery', *British Educational Research Journal*, 29 (3) 369–382

Minns, H. (1990) *Read it to me now! Learning at home and school*. Buckingham: Open University Press

Morgan, D. H. J. (2011a) 'Locating "Family Practices"', *Sociological Research Online*, 16 (4) 14

Morgan, D. H. J. (2011b) *Rethinking Family Practices*. Basingstoke: Palgrave Macmillan

Nichols, S., Rowsell, J., Nixon, H. and Rainbird, S. (2012) *Resourcing Early Learners: New Networks, New Actors*. London: Routledge

Padmore, S. (1994) 'Guiding Lights' in Hamilton, M., Barton, D. and Ivanič, R. (eds.) *Worlds of Literacy*, Clevedon: Multilingual Matters, pp. 143–156

Pahl, K. (2002) 'Ephemera, mess and miscellaneous piles: Text and practices in families', *Journal of Early Childhood Literacy*, 2 (2) 145–166

Pahl, K. (2015) *Materialising Literacies in Communities: the uses of literacy revisited*. London: Bloomsbury

Papen, U. (2010) 'Literacy Mediators, Scribes or Brokers? The Central Role of Others in Accomplishing Reading and Writing,' *Langage et Société*, 133: 63–82

Papen, U. (2012) 'Informal, Incidental and Ad Hoc: The Information-Seeking and Learning Strategies of Health Care Patients,' *Language and Education*, 26 (2) 105–119

Rogers, R. (2008) *A Critical Discourse Analysis of Family Literacy Practices: Power in and out of print*. New York: Routledge

Sarangi, S. and Slembrouck, S. (1996) *Language, Bureaucracy and Social Control*. Harlow: Longman

Sennett, R. (2003) *Respect: the formation of character in an age of inequality*. London Allen Lane

Smith, H. (2018) 'Cooking the books: what counts as literacy for young children in a public library?', *Literacy*, 52 (1) 31–38

Street, B. and Street, J. (1991) 'The Schooling of Literacy' in Barton, D. and Ivanič, R. (eds.) *Writing in the Community*. London: Sage, pp. 143–166

Taylor, D. and Dorsey-Gaines, C. (1988) *Growing Up Literate: Learning from inner-city families*. Portsmouth, NH: Heinemann

Thériault, V. (2016) 'Literacy mediation as a form of powerful literacies in community-based organisations working with young people in a situation of precarity', *Ethnography and Education*, 11 (2) 158–173

Tressell, R. (1914 [2004]) *The Ragged Trousered Philanthropists*: London: Penguin Classics

Valentine, G. (2008) 'The ties that bind: towards geographies of intimacy', *Geography Compass*, 2/6 2097–2110

Wood, C., Kemp, N. and Plester, B. (2014) *Text Messaging and Literacy: the evidence*. London: Routledge

Young, M. and Wilmott, P. (2007 [1957]) *Family and Kinship in East London*. London: Penguin

7

Material Literacies: Writing Home

Previous chapters have looked at literacy within public, community, and family life on the estate. In this chapter, the focus turns to the experience of one person, and the role of literacy practices in her local response to a national policy context. We return to the story of Peggy, whose tour of her new flat provided the starting point for the book. Moving house became the focus of our conversations during the period of the research project on everyday literacy, but I had known Peggy for a while before this. Based on interviews with Peggy, observations of her at home, and her video tour of her new flat, the portrait reflects the wider experiences, relationships, and resources she described as being part of her everyday life.

Through a focus on the everyday literacy practices Peggy experienced during the period of her response to the "bedroom tax", the chapter then goes on to illustrate what the lens of literacy can contribute to our understanding of the impact of policy on individual lives, reflecting as it does the very specific and local iterations of far wider contexts. It also allows us to see the ways in which everyday lives are shaped by these dominant forces through the narrow models of literacy which are bound up within them. Peggy's story will also be explored from the perspective offered by

© The Author(s) 2018
S. Jones, *Portraits of Everyday Literacy for Social Justice*,
https://doi.org/10.1007/978-3-319-75945-6_7

recent paradigms of literacy research which focus on the place of material and immaterial resources in everyday experience, and the ways in which these resources connect across time and space in the creative and agentive negotiation of everyday lives.

Peggy

I first met Peggy at the start of the community theatre project. She had been given the part of a woman who was reflecting back on the time when she had moved onto the estate with her young family. This character, Lilly, had a monologue in which she described her trepidation at the move from the inner city to the brand new estate on the outskirts of town, where roads were yet to be built and the houses were still to be assigned a street number. Lilly's monologue described the sight of German detainees working on building the main road through the estate as her children played in the exciting new world of steel and concrete which was emerging around them.

Peggy herself first moved to the estate as a young mother of three children. She had grown up on another estate on the other side of the city, which has a similar genesis in early twentieth-century social housing policy. She married David in 1972 and the couple had their first child, a daughter, when Peggy was 21. Two sons followed over the next two years. As newly weds with a growing young family, Peggy and David lived in various locations around the city. When their eldest child was five, they settled into the semi-detached three-bedroom house where they would live for the next three decades.

The house is built of red brick and is of the country cottage design preferred by the pre-war developers. It has a small, fenced-off front yard, entered through a gate off the street, and a garden to the rear. As part of the earlier community theatre project, I had spoken to the people who ran the Tenants and Residents' Association of this area. Peggy was aware of the flyers that came through her door advertising day trips to the coast, but otherwise did not to get involved with that particular group. She did, however, have a close circle of friends and family who lived around her. She regularly looked after her neighbours' children, and cared for an elderly next-door neighbour who died aged 95, as well as this neighbour's son who died, after a lengthy illness, not long after his mother. The area has seen some changes, one of the most significant coming with the local authority's modernisation scheme in the mid-1980s. This saw Peggy and her family moved by the local authority to another part of the city while their home was renovated. She was pleased to return after six months away; other families chose not to, however, and Peggy had lots of new neighbours.

While her children were small, Peggy stayed at home and her husband went to work at a local factory. She says:

> I'm old fashioned like that. If you've got a husband then you don't go to work while you've got kids at home. I always made sure I had the dinner on the table. It didn't matter if I hadn't – David wasn't that sort of a person! That's the way my mum did it with my dad and I like to do it that way. Have us dinner together.

As her children grew older, Peggy took up part-time work, including a twilight shift at the factory where her husband worked. She also found cleaning work which fitted in with the children's school hours, and for some time made decorated wedding and birthday cakes to order. The additional income meant that she and her husband were able to enjoy nights out together at the bingo, where they'd head off to in their new car, collecting Sandra, Peggy's sister, en route. Peggy's husband was something of a lucky charm, it would seem, and the sisters would often win when he was with them. He always gave his share of the winnings to his wife when they got home.

One of Peggy's recent jobs was as a cleaner at a local museum. Here, she studied one evening a week for a national vocational qualification in interior and exterior cleaning, learning about the right chemicals to use for various tasks, as well as practical skills such as carpet cleaning. While working as a cleaner, she became drawn to the work of the actors whose role was to engage with visitors to bring to life the historical experiences represented at the museum. She soon secured a job as a "costumed interpreter", performing to visitors including families and school children who had come to learn more about life in Victorian court rooms and prisons. This was a role Peggy particularly enjoyed, and which she undertook alongside her cleaning work and occasional work on the reception desk at the museum.

Over the time I have known Peggy, she has faced health problems which have meant that she has found it increasingly difficult to keep working in these roles. At the time of the research into everyday literacy, she was made redundant from her job at the museum. She had recently started to volunteer for a couple of afternoons a week at a charity shop near her mother's house. This was work which she found particularly enjoyable because of the variety involved, from working on the till and cashing up, to training new staff and dealing with customers' donations, including signing them up for the government's Gift Aid scheme. She also found volunteering at the shop a really good way to make new friends and to be part of social activities organised at the shop, such as a tea party for a royal wedding, where she and her colleagues set out the furniture which they had in the shop and served tea and cake to passers-by.

The shop where Peggy volunteered was run in aid of a local hospice, a cause close to Peggy's heart. After 32 years of marriage, David died following a short illness. At the time, Peggy felt she needed to be brave for the sake of her children and grandchildren, and tried hard not to show them how upset she was, but the loss of her husband has been a constant presence in Peggy's life ever since. She felt isolated by the fact that others did not know what to say to her after David's death, and so avoided her, or stopped calling by, making it even harder for Peggy to deal with the dramatic change to her life brought about by bereavement. Her involvement in the community theatre project was part of Peggy's aim to combat the loneliness she had felt since being widowed. The process of working with others, being out at rehearsals in the evenings and weekends, and making herself stand up in front of an audience helped her to regain some confidence and feel better about things. She still works hard to keep her husband's memory alive in her mind, as well as in her immediate surroundings and, over a decade on, still says goodnight to him every night before she goes to sleep.

Most of Peggy's family live no more than a short bus ride away. She spends a lot of time with her sister, who still works at the museum where Peggy had her job as a costumed interpreter. Peggy also regularly visits her mother, who is in her late 80s, and for whom she shares caring responsibilities with her siblings. Peggy's daughter is not far away, and her grandchildren visit their grandmother regularly. This is always an event which Peggy looks forward to. The children enjoy having their favourite tea made by their "Mama", and playing with the toys that she has for them. Peggy also takes great pride in showing off her infant great-grand-children. This close network of family and friends has always been a prominent feature of Peggy's life and her interaction with them is one of the main ways in which she engages with reading and writing.

Peggy's Everyday Reading and Writing

As a child, Peggy says that she "had a bit of trouble reading and writing", which resulted in her spending some of her primary education in a special school. Although, in her words, "I can read perfectly now", she feels that this lack of confidence with writing has stayed with her into her adult life.

> My handwriting starts off really nice and neat and then it goes wrong and I start to make mistakes and some words just don't look right and I end up spelling it wrong.

Despite her concerns about the technical aspects of writing, Peggy sees the purpose of writing as being for "all sorts":

> Filling forms in, writing a shopping list, writing birthday cards, writing letters to your friends. It's all sorts, isn't it?

The friends to which she refers are ones she has known since childhood, who now live in a small resort on the east coast of England. Peggy enjoys the word puzzles she finds in weekly true-life women's magazines—"the easy ones!"—and also finds the stories in there enjoyable: "whether you believe it or not is another matter!" She doesn't like reading newspapers, "because they are too depressing and don't have much good to say about people", but enjoys reading autobiographies and romantic novels. She'll often buy books that she likes the look of at the charity shop where she volunteers.

As is the case for many people, lots of the everyday reading and writing Peggy does is now digital. She has a mobile phone package with free minutes, meaning she can talk to her daughter and other family members easily. Texting is another way in which she communicates with her family, often as a way of sending short messages, such as asking her sister to pick up something for her from her trip to the shops, or to let her know her bus is about to arrive and to put the kettle on. The facility to send a text, according to Peggy, "is a good thing to have" as the short messages mean that she can easily know when someone wants her "to do something".

Peggy did once own a laptop computer, but it was stolen and she was apprehensive about getting another. At the time, Peggy's brother built computers as a hobby, and gave a PC he had been working on to his sister, which "didn't have the internet on it, just games". She used to enjoy playing these when she wanted to spend some time on her own. The machine stopped working, however, and her brother has since not been well enough to build her another. She looks forward to using the computer when she visits her sister and her mother, however.

> When I go to Sandra's I always ask if I can go on the computer and she says 'it's on ready for you, waiting', cos she knows.

At her mum's, Peggy goes on the computer for half an hour once her mum has gone to bed, and before she herself retires for the night. She enjoys games, especially "that bubbles one where you have to shoot them".

Peggy also uses the computer to interact with others through social media, especially Facebook. She sends messages to people, and responds to those of others. This way, she is able to stay in touch with former colleagues, and her friends on the coast, as well as with family and friends she sees more regularly. She "talks" to her sister Sandra on Facebook in the evenings when she can. Peggy enjoys the immediacy of this communication:

When you're chatting to them you can say 'oh, I've just done such and such' and you can have a joke with them: 'I've had a glass of wine!' If you're writing a letter, you can't talk in a letter. It's not the moment, is it?

Peggy is cautious online, but she does like to respond to posts from people she knows: "if I know who sent it, I'll click it". She also often responds to posts from her favourite celebrities, such as The Osmonds, Michael Bublé, and Cliff Richard, from charities and from public figures such as the Royal Family. By liking, sharing, or sometimes commenting on these posts, she says, she shows her support of these people and causes. In liking or sharing a Facebook post from the war veteran's charity, *Help for Heroes*, for example, Peggy is thinking about people like her own nephew, who was injured in Afghanistan.

> You're supporting them, aren't you? I do think about them. I think about all the poor kids – most of them are kids – who are being killed or wounded in their arms and their legs and it seems like they don't want to know them when they've been in and out of hospital. That's it: they've washed their hands of them. It's just not fair.

Peggy's mum enjoys using the tablet bought for her by her son to look at Facebook to see what family members have posted. She doesn't send messages, but will sometimes ask Peggy to send something brief on her behalf, such as "mum says hi". She uses the tablet to play card games and to watch YouTube videos of babies or animals, which make her laugh.

The computer is used for collaborative purposes in each family home. For example, during one visit where I met Peggy at her sister Sandra's house, she was in the process of arranging a trip for herself and her granddaughter to go and see her son in the north of England. This involved researching times and fares for public transport, as well as finding somewhere to stay that was within budget. At one point, Sandra was showing Peggy how to search the website Trip Advisor for a bed and breakfast, while Peggy's daughter, Dawn, was speaking to her on the phone having found out coach times and fares. Peggy was writing all of this down on a notepad that was beside the computer.

As we saw in Chap. 6, the rapidity of change seen in recent decades in the ways in which we read and write has meant that skillsets have needed to quickly adapt. Not all of these skills come through formal learning, and much relies on the "intuitive" nature of technology, or on learning from peers, and is often centred on what we need to know. Peggy is aware of what she can do on the computer, and this often revolves around things she wants to, or has to do in her everyday life. She knows too where she can get support to learn those things that she is yet to know.

Soon after she was made redundant, Peggy was signed up by her local job centre to attend a computer course, where the focus was on writing letters and formatting CVs. Given her health, however, finding work was going to be difficult for Peggy at the time. Accessing the support she needed during this period meant navigating the welfare systems that were part of the reform which characterised the Conservative-led coalition government that had recently come into power. The texts which constituted the enactment of these systems became a key part of everyday life for Peggy, who had to undergo a Work Capability Assessment to judge her "fitness to work". The result of this was that she was deemed "fit to work", and the disability benefit which provided a core element of her income was cut as a result.

Unfair outcomes of Work Capability Assessments have been the focus of much attention since the introduction of harsh welfare reforms in the UK. This includes high-profile legal challenges, and a ruling that the assessment originally in place was in breach of equality law because of its discrimination against people with mental health conditions (see, e.g. Bingham 2013). Some highly publicised accounts have described the tragic consequences which have followed sometimes gravely ill and profoundly disabled people being deemed fit for work (e.g. Butler 2015; Centre for Welfare Reform 2015). The bureaucracy of the process at its most labyrinthine and cruelly impersonal was depicted in the award-winning film *I, Daniel Blake*, directed by Ken Loach (2016), and I have written about this in more detail elsewhere (Jones 2017). According to the website of the Department for Work and Pensions, the process of appealing a decision such as the one received by Peggy involves first of all asking for a "mandatory reconsideration", which must be done within a month of the decision being made. To ask for mandatory reconsideration, a claimant must write to the address given on their decision letter, explaining why they disagree, and including supporting evidence. A "mandatory reconsideration notice" is then issued, telling the claimant whether their decision has been changed. If this has not resolved the problem, then an applicant may appeal to Her Majesty's Courts and Tribunal Service, again within one month (Department for Work and Pensions 2017). The complexity of the process, not least in its terminology and bureaucracy, is feared to be discouraging for many vulnerable claimants (Social Security Advisory Committee 2016).

Peggy was extremely worried about the decision to reduce her disability benefit. She wasn't sure how she was going to make ends meet, and her anxieties compounded her health problems. However, Peggy had the support of her daughter and her doctor and she lodged an appeal. Her appeal was eventually successful and her income was restored several weeks after the initial decision. At the same time as she was undergoing the Work Capability Assessment and appeal, another new government policy also directly affected Peggy as a recipient of Housing Benefit. As she told me on one visit:

> In April, they'll charge you for the two bedrooms that you're not using – it's called a 'bedroom tax' – and I said to [my daughter] 'I can't afford to live here'.

So Peggy began the process of looking for a new home. Again, this was a process in which texts played a central part. As I observed Peggy adjusting to this forced change in her circumstances, I also saw the way in which she drew on a range of material resources from her everyday life in order to make and share meanings.

Moving House

The process of moving house began with Peggy having to engage with the bureaucratic systems set up by the Housing Association that managed the social housing on the estate on behalf of the local council. During her marriage, Peggy always used to do the household paperwork:

It never used to bother me but I think since I've been on my own I seem to worry more. When David was around it weren't so bad because I'd got support there but since I've been on my own I seem to worry about things more.

More recently, her daughter has helped with these domestic responsibilities, including arranging the installation of a water meter to save some money on utility bills. Arranging a move was also something that Peggy's daughter helped her with. Peggy's description of the process highlights the texts that were central to shaping the experience, and the systems of which they are a part:

> To move, I'd have to fill in a form for the council and then start bidding. Which would be a problem. You have to either look in the paper or you'd go on the computer but when you haven't got a computer it's a bit awkward.

> Usually on a Monday they put what's going in the paper and you have to bid and if someone has a higher bid that you, like if they have more need than you, then they get it. [...] I couldn't go in a bungalow because even though I have got disabilities, they don't class it as urgent.

> I've filled in the form. [My daughter] did it for me. I've sent it in – or I think I've sent it anyway – and I've just got to wait for my bidding number to come and it hasn't come yet.

During this wait, and as the move grew closer, our conversation turned to Peggy's preparations, both practical and emotional:

> I'm a bit unsure about moving because it's the memories in the house. Me and David and the kids growing up and all that.

She shared one such memory of the house she was leaving:

> The proudest moment [in this house] was when we brought my first grandson home from the hospital and I took him out of the car and I brought him into the house and said 'this is Mama's bedroom, and this is Uncle

Andrew's bedroom, and this is yours and mummy's bedroom'. I took him all round the house and showed him every room in the house. And then we used to have him at weekends and me and David used to have him on us own here and it was like having us own babies again. It was lovely. He's twenty now. I'll never forget that day.

Even before she'd heard about where she was to move to, Peggy started to prepare by sorting her possessions. This became a way through which Peggy began to manage the physical and emotional process of moving home. She gave away lots of the books she had read, blankets that she would have no use for in a smaller flat, some of her electrical items, and some of her ornaments. She was adamant, however, that some things would go with her to her new home:

I've been very harsh with myself [...] but there are some things I'll never part with even though I ain't got room to put them.

Amongst these things were the most special of her salt and pepper pot collection, which had been growing since she and David bought the first one on holiday when they were engaged. The little teddy bear, which was the last thing bought for her by her husband, was also something which Peggy would "never, ever part with" (see Fig. 7.1).

Practical help with the move came from friends and family, including an online order placed by Peggy's brother for a new fridge and washing machine. Emotional support was also provided in response to Peggy's Facebook posts where she expressed her anxieties about the move as it approached, and her gratitude for the support she was getting. Moving day itself was marked by a post in which Peggy looked ahead with some trepidation. This was tempered, however, with a pragmatic sense of hope.

The last time I visited Peggy in her old house, she told me how she imagined her new home:

I'm going to sit outside in the garden and I'm going to buy myself one of those folding chairs and have a little fold up table so I can bring it inside at night. So I'll sit there and read a book and watch the world go by.

Fig. 7.1 Taken from her video tour, Peggy shows the teddy bought for her by her husband

Peggy's New Flat

Soon after she moved and was settled in to her new flat, Peggy invited me to come and have a look around. She was pleased with the way the move had gone, including the help she'd had from her family. Work was already underway to set up the new flat in a way she was happy with. Over the next visits, Peggy agreed to do a video tour of her flat where she filmed what was important to her, narrating a description and explanation of particular items, what they meant to her, and why.

Viewing Peggy's flat through her video tour shows how moving and settling into new accommodation has focused Peggy's mind on what things mean: what they mean to her, and what she would like them to mean about her. Although the move and her future in the new flat is something Peggy will live entirely on her own, David's presence is evident throughout her new home, in photographs and other mementoes of their life together. His loss is also strongly felt in each room. On the windowsill in her bathroom is his ornamental shaving mug, decorated with an image of a steam train. By her bedside, Peggy keeps a framed verse cross-stitched for her by her daughter; the verse was one which featured in a condolence card received by Peggy after losing her husband, and which she found especially comforting. Elsewhere in her living room, Peggy has a glass bowl, which was given to her by a friend, "so that I had something for myself, to remember him by".

As we saw at the start of the book, Peggy's glass display cabinet is where she keeps her "special things", including items of china featuring Queen Elizabeth II bought for her by her mother, and a champagne flute bought for her by her granddaughters on the occasion of her 60th birthday. The tiny teddy bear sits in a teacup in this cabinet, "on show".

Peggy's video tour also focused on her collection of Cliff Richard memorabilia. This includes cups, a teapot, and a limited edition plate, which is accompanied by a certificate of authenticity, tucked behind it on the windowsill.

> I'm a Cliff Richard fan. I like my Cliff Richard. These were stuck in my bedroom when I lived in [my old house] because nobody wanted them out, now I've got a chance to get them out.

Her tour highlights the importance of family to Peggy. Not only are they featured visually in the photographs which adorn each surface, but also in the tokens of their love for her which are on display. Peggy recalls with pride what was given to her, by whom and why.

Like many people, Peggy displays items on her fridge door, stuck on with fridge magnets. The magnets themselves are also important items. They include souvenirs from Cliff Richard concerts she has attended, holidays she has enjoyed, or places visited by friends and family (see Fig. 7.2). On her fridge is an A4 piece paper, on which is a message drawn in brightly coloured lettering by her seven-year-old granddaughter when she was recently visiting: "Mama I Love You". Alongside this sits a postcard sent by Peggy's sister from a recent holiday in the Canary Islands. At the top corner of the fridge door, on a piece of brown cardboard which looks as if it's been torn from the corner of some food packaging, is a handwritten reminder of an appointment at the dentist.

The objects Peggy has chosen to bring with her from the house she shared with her family for three decades are reminders that her home was

Fig. 7.2   Peggy's fridge

a space that was actively and collaboratively constructed across time. Similarly, the items through which Peggy has begun to establish her new home are more than just a curation of silent artefacts displayed on shelves and in cabinets; they contribute to the creation of a space through the making and sharing of meanings. Some objects represent those memories of the past which have constituted her as a wife, sister, daughter, mother, grandmother, and friend. However, the same objects are also key resources in her negotiation of her present, and her future in this new space where she lives alone. Recent paradigms of literacy have allowed us to explore the ways in which such meanings are constituted through a range of modes, across time and space, and through resources which are both material and immaterial.

In the next section of the chapter, I examine how the lens of literacy adds to our understanding of Peggy "writing home". Her story demonstrates the impact on everyday lives of recent policy contexts, and of being able to trace the role of narrow models of literacy within the enactment of these policies. That is, of course, an important aspect of what a focus on literacy can offer to challenge the threats to social justice posed by wider contexts, not least in its implication in fair access to economic resources. Taking a view of literacy as drawing on the material and immaterial, and as constituted by the complex interaction of local and global contexts, also allows us to identify the ways in which narrow models fail to recognise the realities of everyday lives, such as the impact of forcing people like Peggy out of their homes. Framing literacies from this broader perspective recognises the creative, agentive, and dynamic negotiation of everyday life that is evident in Peggy's story.

In the Frame: Literacy and the Stuff of Life

In our discussion of reading and writing, Peggy shared many examples of an instrumental model of literacy and of practices which fail to recognise the everyday realities of people's lives. These can be seen both in her past educational experiences and in the current bureaucratic systems she navigates as a claimant of welfare support. Like Colin, whose experience we saw in Chap. 6, Peggy's lack of confidence in the technical aspects of literacy stems from her experience of school, where a reductive view of reading and writing left a lifelong belief in herself as deficient. This subjectivity is framed by a narrow model of literacy which has frozen Peggy in time, regardless of the ways in which she has engaged with reading and writing in her later life. Her attendance at computer classes tied to her welfare claims also frames her as someone whose worth to others comes from her ability to manage the layout of word processed documents.

Perhaps one of the most acute examples of the disempowering effect of dominant practices on individuals already in challenging circumstances comes in Peggy's description of the system she had to navigate to facilitate her house move. This was a move she felt she had no choice but to make, to avoid cuts to her income which would leave her struggling to afford her rent. For someone without her own computer, the online system was difficult and time-consuming to use, as described in relation to the local library in Chap. 4. Peggy's experience is a further illustration that a purely redistributive model of literacy and social justice, focused only on access to physical resources and skills, does not always recognise other realities in people's lives and that it often compounds rather than alleviates the impact of inequalities.

Peggy's description of the process of applying for a house move shows how she is deprived of power. Her repeated use of phrases such as "you have to", "I've got to" show her to be the subject of this process, rather than an active agent within it. Not having her own computer means that she is even less able to be in control. The stripping of the individual from this search for a home is also emphasised by the way in which Peggy is waiting for a number by which her case will be identified. Peggy's description also shows how time is shaping the experience as something else which she cannot control. She knew that the new policy would mean she would lose income from April. She describes a weekly cycle of checking in the paper, or online, of bidding and of waiting. She is waiting for decisions to be made for her, and about her, based on how her needs are classified.

Compton-Lilly's (2017) work on time in literacy research highlights the way in which instrumental models of literacy often assume time as a neutral resource. In schooling, for example, literacy activities, and what is deemed as success within these, are shaped by often arbitrary timing of tasks, lessons, terms, or school years. At the hands of a system in which she has little control, Peggy faces at least uncertainty and worry, and at worst humiliation and a threat to her means to get by. The way in which the system, constructed by the bureaucracies within it, is measured through their own process of time makes them anything but neutral.

As well as reflecting the link between literacy and time, Peggy's experience as a result of the "bedroom tax" also reflects how the literacy practices which are part of her everyday life at the very local level of her own home also connect across space to far wider, global contexts. This is a theme that has been reflected across recent literacy research. The next part of the chapter looks at some of the debates about the local and global in relation to literacy, considering what this has meant to our understanding of literacy and its potential as a lens through which we might develop our understanding of everyday experiences.

The Local and the Global in Literacy Research

A social practice model of literacy, as discussed in Chaps. 5 and 6, fore-grounds context within any analysis of literacy practice. With its strong link to ethnographic traditions, the social practice paradigm is full of examples of rich and detailed attention to very specific local circum-stances and to everyday lives, experiences, and practices. Focusing on everyday examples of local practice holds powerful potential to shed light on wider contexts, as it does in Peggy's story.

In their critique of what they saw as the "limits of the local", Brandt and Clinton (2002) warn of the danger of offering accounts of local practice without consideration of the relationship between this practice and wider contexts. This includes ignoring the potential of literacy in everyday lives to inform our understanding of the impact of wider hegemonic structures upon experience as well as the agency of individuals and communities in negotiating these structures at a local level. They call for us to:

> see the ways that literacy arises out of local, particular, situated human interactions while also seeing how it also regularly arrives from other places – infiltrating, disjointing, and displacing local life. (p. 344)

For Brandt and Clinton, literacy is an agent in processes which they call the "localizing moves" and "globalizing connects" (p. 351) of everyday life. They argue that literacy research needs to take "a perspective that can begin to expose the ways that 'local literates' are recruited into distant campaigns through reading and writing" (ibid., p. 348).

Street (2003a, b) has argued that the concept of *literacy practice* already assumes the location of any interaction with text within a wider social, cultural, and political context. However, he also challenges the notion "that distant literacies come into local contexts with their force and mean-ing intact" (Street 2012, p. 19). Since its inception, the social practice model has acknowledged the ways in which literacy "often functions restrictively and hegemonically in societies to implement social controls and maintain social hierarchies" (Reder and Davila 2005, p. 172). Addressing the issue of local/global influences on literacy, Street offers the notion of hybridity (2003b, p. 80). He contends that:

the result of local-global encounters around literacy is always a new hybrid rather than a single essentialised version of either. It is these hybrid literacy practices that NLS[1] [New Literacy Studies] focuses upon rather than either romanticising the local or conceding the dominant privileging of the supposed 'global'.

Reder and Davila (2005) also extend the debate to question the ways in which the boundaries of the local and global are defined. They argue for the consideration of "multiple contexts, each of which has its own time and space margins" (p. 180). Such "polycontextual" practice includes that which is locally bounded in time and space and exists in an "immediate" context. However, they argue that "a typical realisation of the use of writing" also involves the mediation of distant or remote social interactions, situated within

> much broader space and time boundaries, expanded by the durable and portable material properties of writing as used in culturally and historically shaped literacy practices. (ibid.)

An illustrative example here might be Peggy's Facebook posts in response to the *Help for Heroes* charity. These reflect her local engagement with global issues of war and its impact on men and women who have served in the British armed forces. The ideology of this cause includes the notion of sacrifice made by individuals in serving their country, and the duty of its supporters to "help" those to whom they are indebted as a result of their sacrifice. In their very name, the charity frames those affected by their service in the armed forces as "heroes". It draws on icons of the battlefield in its logo, where the initial *H* is represented by two soldiers carrying a stretcher on which a third soldier is lying. The campaign therefore aims to bring to public consciousness the ongoing difficulties faced by those affected, physically and mentally, in the line of military duty on a global stage. Peggy's response on Facebook is shaped not least by her very local concern for her nephew and the other young men she knows who have been affected by their experiences of war in Afghanistan. Liking and sharing the Help the Heroes page she finds on her Facebook timeline is a public act of allegiance with their cause. The construction of wounded service women and men as "heroes" is compounded by the frustration felt by Peggy and others about the ways in which their friends and family members have been treated since their return from the front line: they are doubly presented as heroes for their service to their country, and by those who recognise the lack of power they experience at the hands of authority. There is a small, local act of power, therefore, in clicking on an online link to join a wider voice of protest, acting on a personal, offline family connection, demonstrating "the threads and traces of other times and places that play out in any literacy event, particularly those involving digital media" (Burnett et al. 2014, p. 92). Wider issues of power can also be seen, of course, if we argue that the construction of the "hero" by such charities plays into the hands of government in glorifying wars and reinforcing the "othering" of those affected by such conflicts in the countries in which they take place.

The characterisation of literacy practice as "hybrid" or "polycontextual" accounts for multiple influences upon it. Importantly, it also avoids the over-simplified dichotomy of local and global. Blackburn and Clark (2007, p. 9) argue that "examination of the relationship between the local and the global warrants more than determining which side trumps the other". A focus on the local/global must also interrogate the processes which can lead to some practices becoming hegemonic and highlight the impact of hegemonies on already marginalised individuals and communities. They must also attend to the issues of power which are central to the macro- and micro-level interactions between local and global that exist within everyday literacy practice (Collins and Blot 2003). The story of Peggy's response to wider contexts through her own very local practice allows us not only to identify local practice and its links to global forces, but also to examine this relationship and the role played by literacy within it. Her entanglement in the bureaucracy of welfare claims and housing allocation shows her everyday life as constituted by participation in what Compton-Lilly (2017, p. 7) calls the "intersecting trajectories" of macro and micro systems. Compton-Lilly argues that understanding of this complex intersection of forces requires analysis that "recognises people as agential while also attending to existing structures and potential limits" (p. 8).

Kathleen Stewart's work on "ordinary affects" is also helpful here. These are "the many little *some*things worth noting in the direct composition of the ordinary" (2007, p. 48, emphasis in the original). For Stewart, "ordinary affects highlight the question of the intimate impacts of forces in circulation" (ibid., p. 40):

> Ideologies happen. Power snaps into place. Structures grow entrenched. Identities take place. Ways of knowing become habitual at a drop of a hat. But it's ordinary affects that give things the quality of a *some*thing to inhabit and animate. (ibid., p. 15)

Peggy's response to moving home illustrates well how a focus on everyday literacies, in particular how these are manifested in things that seem to be ordinary, allows insight into the impact of wider forces while also recognising agency and creativity in responses to these contexts. In Peggy's case, one of the main sites for this negotiation of the local and global is what is happening to her home. Sociological literature has highlighted how the home itself is symbolic of this interaction between local and global, the personal and political. This makes a focus on the literacy practices which are part of "writing home" for Peggy even more pertinent to any exploration of the issues raised by her story. Through a focus on how we understand "home", therefore, and by focusing on Peggy moving house, I now move on to explore recent paradigms of literacy which have drawn upon material anthropology and which challenge the possibility of fixing literacy as a narrowly defined set of skills which occurs in defined time and space.

Literacy at Home

A focus on literacy in the home offers lots to challenge narrow models of what it means to make and share meaning. Kate Pahl (2015) reminds us that home literacies, such as those she documents in her work with families and communities in the north of England, represent a disruption to the instrumental models of literacy embodied by school curricula, which are held still by externally imposed standards and values. Homes, as described by Pahl (p. 53), are "places of stories". Such stories are shaped around events, relationships, and objects, retold over time and across generations. Home literacy practice tends to be unplanned and linked to the flow of activities within the space of the home. This often involves intergenerational collaboration in the construction of texts which draw upon multiple modes and senses. Texts might be arranged and rearranged in different places and at different times. The ephemeral products of children's craft sessions, for example, may be tidied away. Texts may also be endowed with value through their shifting relationship to time and space within the home. The drawings on Peggy's fridge, for example, made as a gift from her visiting granddaughter, are positioned "on show" as a marker of the value placed on family in Peggy's home. The verse from a sympathy card that was cross-stitched by Peggy's daughter, and now sits framed by Peggy's bedside, emphasises how "the apprehending of experience and inscribing of that experience into textual forms is located within the rhythms of family life" (p. 54). The cross-stitched verse also illustrates the way in which literacies in a home bring together a range of practices which inscribe meaning. The verse was originally published in a mass-produced card, chosen and sent from a friend at the time of David's death. Its sentiment has been captured by Dawn in her hand-stitched work, the value of it enriched by its association with its original source of comfort, as well as the time and love she has invested in it. During the house move, this was an object that was preserved by Peggy as one of her "special things", and given pride of place by her bedside. The story of Peggy's move shows how the meaning of home comes through a series of material and immaterial interactions. The stories of these interactions are embodied by us and are told and retold through our "stuff" (Miller 2010).

In many ways, home literacy practices are reflective of a common understanding of what "home" represents: a highly personal space constituted by "emotional and material geographies" (Sims et al. 2009). Mary Douglas (1991, p. 290) has described home as "the realisation of ideas" related to people's lives, captured in time and space. Home is associated with intimacy, familiarity, and comfort; being "at home" is suggestive of belonging, confidence, and security. However, home is also a powerful signifier in political and ideological discourse. This is reflected, for example, in historical, gendered associations between a woman's role in maintaining the physical and spiritual cleanliness of home and her own morally framed femininity (Pink 2004). Shelley Mallet's (2004) critical review of the concept of home outlines how a particular ideology of home is also seen in the aspiration of home ownership which is a feature in many capitalist economies. This harks back to the home as a source of status and security (as is suggested, for example, by the phrase "an Englishman's home is his castle"). The shift from state to family in neoliberal politics, discussed in Chap. 6, positions the home as the locus of care and responsibility. The emphasis on private over public seen in neoliberalism is also reflected in the way that home has associations as distinct from public space; it is a space "removed from public scrutiny and surveillance" (p. 71).

Although its definition is broad and reflective of wider political debates, the idea of home has particularly resonant associations in Peggy's story, not least in its emotionally charged associations. Douglas argues (1991, p. 289) "having a shelter is not having a home, nor is having a house, nor is home the same as household". However, this does not seem to have been reflected in the policy that led to Peggy having to move home. The idea of home as a safe place, and one where we are safe from public scrutiny and in which our value to society is played out (through ownership, or efficient running of the home) does not appear to apply to those who find they need to claim housing benefit in order to be able to pay their rent. The "bedroom tax" in particular emphasises that the space within the home is not their own but can be deemed by others to be "spare". This policy has led to very public scrutiny of how space is allocated and used within social housing, with punitive results, despite claims of this being in the name of "fairness" (see Chap. 3).

The symbolic resonance of the "bedroom tax" comes in no small part as a result of the way it challenged a sense of home as a safe space away from public scrutiny, and of those in receipt of housing benefit being entitled to the same rights to the physical and emotional security of a stable place to call home. Sims and her colleagues (2009) recount the responses of people who have been removed from their homes in crises, in their case by flooding. Although people often change the place where they live several times over the course of their life, continuity is also something which is significant to providing emotional wellbeing and disruption to this continuity is stressful. In their research, Sims et al. found families who had faced the loss of their homes gained comfort by re-creating aspects of everyday life in non-familiar places through the use of familiar items. In a similar way, Peggy has faced the difficult process of having to move home, and although she had time to respond over the weeks she was waiting, her familiar objects became a resource in the physical and emotional navigation of the move.

The active process of home *making*, seen in Peggy's story, emphasises the association of home as a journey (Mallett 2004). For Peggy, "writing home" is an active process. As she waited to hear about where she was to move, and in the process of setting up in her new place, through her engagement with her material possessions, and the immaterial associations they hold, across space and time, Peggy can be seen to be authoring herself into the space of her new flat. To illustrate, let's take Peggy's Cliff Richard memorabilia. These, she says, were packed away in her former home because "nobody wanted them out". Although she had lived on her own in the house for a few years, this suggests that it still had associations of being a family home, oriented to the compromise required by the collective demands of different generations living within it. The memorabilia had been bought for her over many Christmases and birthdays by friends and family, who fondly understood Cliff to be one of Peggy's "ruling passions" (Barton and Hamilton 1998). This fandom has stretched back to her teenage years, before she had met her husband, and remains as strong as ever. At a secret birthday party organised for Peggy by her sister, the cake arranged by the family even featured an edible Cliff. Individual items of Cliff merchandise represent different points both of his career and of Peggy's memories as a fan. The plate she has on display, for example, commemorates "Forty years of Cliff Richard". Owning this plate also represents Peggy's 40 years of being a proud Cliff Richard fan. Other items have specific memories related to experiences she has shared with family members, such as the Cliff fridge magnet which was bought at one of his concerts at the local arena. Pointing out the fridge magnet, Peggy remembers with a smile how dizzy she felt in one of the highest seats right at the back of the arena, and how she had to keep hold of her sister's arm throughout as she thought she would fall (see Fig. 7.3). This small object, then, represents a lifetime's fandom lived at a distance from its object, as well as a very specific and embodied experience shared with her sister. Along with the rest of Peggy's collection, they represent the

Fig. 7.3   Peggy's fridge magnet collection

gathering together of experiences across a lifetime, but are presented in this new space as an active choice about what Peggy wishes to say about what's important to her, how she wishes to be seen, and how she sees her future as a single occupant of a flat in the next stage of her life.

In her new home, making the choice to have her Cliff Richard stuff "on show" reflects the role of material objects in Peggy's authoring of herself into this space. In her ethnography of domestic practices, Sarah Pink has noted how "visual home decoration is interlinked with the construction of the self in the present through selective biographical representations of the past and projections of an imagined future" (2004, p. 64). Peggy's emphasis on these objects being newly "on show" emphasises "the visual as a means of self-expression" (ibid.).

This emphasises the ways in which meanings are not only made across time and space but also across modes. The notion of "artifactual literacies" proposed by Pahl and Rowsell (2010) draws together the ways in which objects hold within them the power to make and communicate meanings that work across many modes and senses. This reminds us of the embodied nature of meanings, and how they are connected to identities, which, for Pahl and Rowsell, "ride on a sea of stuff and of experiences" (p. 8). This can be seen in Peggy's tour of her home and in her active choice of objects within it. Describing his ethnographic research of material objects in people's living rooms in one London street, material anthropologist Daniel Miller (2008, p. 2) says that "every object in that room is equally a form by which they have chosen to express themselves". The emotional significance of objects is evident in Peggy's tour of her flat, emphasising the power of the affective in how Peggy chooses to make and express meanings. This is a more prominent feature of her commentary than their functional and aesthetic roles. She describes the use of the rose bowl bought by a friend, for example, as being to remember David, rather than to hold flowers, and she gives this as the reason why it is on display in her new flat.

The rose bowl, and the tiny teddy in the teacup, are examples of what Miller (2010) calls the matter of life and death. Objects such as these, and the way in which Peggy has used them over the course of her move, illustrate the "résumé effect" of home (2010, p. 149). Her relationship to objects is infused with her relationship to the people in her life. The process of moving and setting up her new home has involved Peggy in a series of choices of what to take with her and what to have on display. Equally, these choices have included what *not* to take and what to discard.

Choices made to keep things or to discard them all reflect the place of those objects within our relationships to other people. The loss of a loved one is a sad aspect of life that we will all share, but to which we each respond differently. For many, the process of dealing with the lost person's things is part of coming to terms with dealing with bereavement. We face choices throughout our lives, about keeping things, choices which are based on "the economy of relationships [...] to persons or periods and events in [the] past" (p. 148). This is balanced throughout by the spaces and relationships we occupy in the present. It might also be tempered by the durability of objects themselves. A piece of art made by a small child at nursery may not endure as long as an ornament made of glass, for example, which itself is more fragile than a piece of furniture. The choices Peggy has made in moving to her one-bedroom flat as a single woman in her 60s reflect the ways in which her relationships with others have shaped and been shaped by her role as a wife, mother, grandmother, sister, and friend.

The process of authoring herself into her new home was also partly negotiated before the move. Louise Crewe discusses the way in which value and significance "may emerge through practices of discard, loss and remembering as well as through more conventional processes of production and purchase" (2011, p. 28). This emphasises the ways in which the value of objects is held in the context of space and time: "it is not merely 'things', but things in motion that illuminate their human and social context and in turn their value" (p. 34). Choices made about particular things, and their relationship to memories across time and space, are evocative of bell hooks' description of the "struggle of memory against forgetting" (1990, p. 147). Choosing to discard, to keep hold of, and to display memories as part of writing her new home is not just an act of nostalgia for Peggy, of preserving a past or reinforcing a situation of loss enforced upon her, but an active process of "remembering that serves to illuminate and transform the present" (ibid.). Through this process, she is able to celebrate what is important to her, what she wants to communicate about herself, and how.

Everyday Literacy Practices: Something to Write Home About

The title of this chapter refers to several ways in which we can understand Peggy's experience, the role of literacy practices within her everyday life, and how this relates to socially just ways of framing literacy. "Writing home" brings together two of the key areas of focus in the book: the practice of literacy and the home as perhaps the most characteristic space of the "everyday". As already discussed in Chap. 5, space can be understood as constructed through the actions, interactions, and values of those who use it. As she "writes home", Peggy's literacy practices are a means by which she actively constructs her home as a space in which—and through which—she makes and explores meaning.

Peggy's story challenges the notion of everyday practice as banal and mundane. Far from "nothing to write home about", the experience of home cannot be reduced to that which characterises it in the kinds of discourse that have shaped and justified policies such as the "bedroom tax", the policy which forced Peggy, and many others like her, out of their homes. Peggy's everyday practice suggests that there is much to reveal about the challenges faced by individuals and families enduring the brunt of this policy, as well as other equally harsh reforms which have emerged under the guise of "austerity". There is much to reveal also about the agency with which they approach their circumstances.

Everyday literacies, including material objects, disrupt the values, practices, rhythms of schooled and other official literacies (Pahl 2015). The process of writing home, for Peggy, tells us a lot about the agentive and creative work that is involved when we engage with our environment to make meanings, emphasising the power of individuals in deciding what is important, what they want to say, how they see themselves and are seen by others. Peggy's move is a powerful metaphor for how this way of looking at literacy resists attempts to hold it still and define it, and how we use literacy as part of our everyday lives.

A focus on literacy in Peggy's everyday life shows the impact of austerity policies on her as an individual, on her access to resources, on how her experiences are neither valued nor recognised, and how little voice she has within the system. A focus on the material within everyday literacy practices also broadens the way a person such as Peggy is framed within the discourse of austerity that has affected her so directly. As Miller (2010, pp. 2–3) has argued in relation to the power of attention to material objects and their meanings in everyday life:

> surely if we can learn to listen to these things we have access to an authentic other voice [...] that which some people have themselves crafted as patiently as any artist, as an outward expression of themselves.

As has been shown in the preceding chapters, the narrow framing of individuals, families, and communities has a direct impact on the policies which shape their experiences. Such policies are enacted through an equally narrowly defined model of literacy and its role in everyday lives. Looking at literacy differently allows us to see the impact of this framing but also to begin the process of reframing. Seeing literacy not as something that people have, but as something people *do*, means that, rather than being passively in deficit, those who bear the brunt of policy reform, and the discourse that has shaped it, are framed as actively engaged in their response to this context, in the making of meanings, and of homes, families, and communities.

Notes

1. *New Literacy Studies* refers to perspectives on literacy which draw upon a social practice model, as outlined in Chap. 5. The NLS considers literacy to be best understood within the social and cultural contexts in which it takes place, and represented by a diverse range of communicative practice, not confined to print-based text.

References

Barton, D. and Hamilton, M. (1998) *Local Literacies: Reading and Writing in One Community.* London: Routledge

Bingham, J. (2013) 'Judges rule back-to-work assessments 'unfair' to mentally ill', http://www.telegraph.co.uk/news/health/news/10074192/Judges-rule-back-to-work-assessments-unfair-to-mentally-ill.html (accessed November 20, 2017)

Blackburn, M. V. and Clark, C. T. (2007) 'Bridging the Local/ Global Divide: Theorizing Connections Between Global Issues and Local Action', in Blackburn, M.V. and Clark, C.T. (eds.) *Literacy Research for Political and Social Change.* New York: Peter Lang, pp. 9–27

Brandt, D. and Clinton, K. (2002) 'Limits of the Local: Expanding Perspectives on Literacy as a Social Practice', *Journal of Literacy Research,* 34, 337–356

Burnett, C., Merchant, G., Pahl, K. and Rowsell, J. (2014) 'The (im)materiality of literacy: the significance of subjectivity to new literacies research', *Discourse: Studies in the Cultural Politics of Education,* 35 (1) 90–103

Butler, P. (2015) 'Thousands have died after being found fit for work, DWP figures show', Guardian, August 28 2017, https://www.theguardian.com/society/2015/aug/27/thousands-died-after-fit-for-work-assessment-dwp-figures (accessed August 27, 2017)

Centre for Welfare Reform (2015) 'Work Capability Assessment: deaths and suicides', available at https://www.scribd.com/document/262851896/Work-Capability-Assessment-deaths-and-*suicides*#download&from_embed (accessed August 26, 2017)

Collins, J. and Blot, R. (2003) *Literacy and Literacies: Texts, power and identity*. Cambridge: Cambridge University Press

Compton-Lilly, C. (2017) *Reading Students' Lives: Literacy learning across time*. New York: Routledge

Crewe, L. (2011) 'Life Itemised: lists, loss, unexpected significance, and the enduring geographies of discard', *Environment and Planning D: Society and Space*, 29, 27–46

Douglas, M. (1991) 'The Idea of a Home: A Kind of Space', *Social Research*, 58 (1) 287–307

Department for Work and Pensions (2017) 'Appeal to the Social Security and Child Support Tribunal' https://www.gov.uk/social-security-child-support-tribunal/before-you-appeal, (accessed August 27, 2017)

hooks, b. (1990) *Yearning: race, gender, and cultural politics*. Cambridge, MA: South End Press

Jones, S. (2017) '"Words of wisdom": Text, Voice and Justice in *I, Daniel Blake*', *Changing English*, 24 (4) 372–385

Loach, K. (dir.) (2016) *I, Daniel Blake*. UK: Sixteen Films

Mallett, S. (2004) 'Understanding home: a critical review of the literature', *Sociological Review*, 52 (1) 62–89

Miller, D. (2008) *The Comfort of Things*. Cambridge: Polity Press

Miller, D. (2010) *Stuff*. Cambridge: Polity Press

Pahl, K. (2015) *Materialising Literacies in Communities: the uses of literacy revisited*. London: Bloomsbury

Pahl, K. and Rowsell, J. (2010) *Artifactual Literacies: Every object tells a story*. New York: Teachers College Press

Pink, S. (2004) *Home Truths: Gender, domestic objects and everyday life*. Oxford: Berg

Reder, S. and Davila, E. (2005) 'Context and literacy practices', *Annual Review of Applied Linguistics*, 25, 170–187

Sims, R., Medd, W., Mort, M. and Twigger-Ross, C. (2009) 'When a "Home" Becomes a "House": care and caring in the flood recovery process', *Space and Culture*, 12, 303–316

Social Security Advisory Committee (2016) 'Decision Making and Mandatory Reconsideration: a study by the Social Security Advisory Committee Occasional Paper No. 18', https://www.gov.uk/government/uploads/system/ uploads/attachment_data/file/538836/decision-making-and-mandatory-reconsideration-ssac-op18.pdf#page=22 (accessed November 20, 2017)

Stewart, K. (2007) *Ordinary Affects*. Durham and London: Duke University Press

Street, B. (2003a) 'The limits of the local – "autonomous" or "disembedding"?', *International Journal of Learning*, 10

Street, B. (2003b) 'What's "new" in New Literacy Studies? Critical approaches to literacy in theory and practice', *Current Issues in Comparative Education*, 5 (2) 77–91

Street, B. (2012) 'Contexts for literacy work: New Literacy Studies, multimodality, and the "local and the global", in Tett, L., Hamilton, M. and Crowther, J. (eds.) *More Powerful Literacies*. Leicester: NIACE, pp. 31–58

8

Reframing Literacy for Social Justice

Throughout this book, I have illustrated the ways in which the lens of literacy is useful in illuminating the relationship between wider social, political, and economic contexts and everyday lives. The portraits have shown how literacy itself can also be implicated in the threat posed by these wider contexts. Through the portraits of Terry, Carol, Katie, Colin, and Peggy, we have seen how focusing on the diversity of meaning-making practices in people's lives offers an alternative to the narrowly framed discourses of deficit that are used to justify punitive policy, and which compound the challenge for families and communities already facing economic, social, and cultural marginalisation. In this final chapter, I revisit the framework for justice offered by Nancy Fraser, and argue that a focus on literacy is central both to understanding and to challenging injustice.

My aim in creating the portraits of everyday lives on the estate was to illustrate the richness of the residents' responses to the circumstances they face, and the ways in which they navigate these. I have focused on particular experiences, but this emphasis on specific situations and people is by no means intended to suggest that the problem of the cycle of mutually reinforcing deficit discourses and punitive policy is limited to the

© The Author(s) 2018
S. Jones, *Portraits of Everyday Literacy for Social Justice*,
https://doi.org/10.1007/978-3-319-75945-6_8

time and place of the research that has informed this book, or to the people who have participated in it. I believe, and I will argue in this chapter, that the documenting and sharing of experiences through portraits like the ones I have presented in this book is of urgent relevance to making the case for social justice. I believe that understanding literacy in a broad and multifaceted way is not just a goal or a desirable outcome of wider social change but is also central to the process of working towards that change. The reasons why social change is vitally important should never be far from our attention.

The portraits in this book have presented the everyday experiences of individuals, families, and communities living in one part of a city in the Midlands of England. The work of Graham and his team of library staff is, of course, reflected in local libraries across other towns and cities. Tony and Carol are amongst the many people, across many different communities, who support others and try to make a difference to their lives. In homes across the UK and further afield, parents and their children, like Colin and Katie, work together to navigate experiences, to make and share meanings. And as we continue to see in the media reporting across jurisdictions enduring the "sweeping and ruinous legacy" (O'Hara 2015, p. xx) of the politics of "austerity", individuals like Peggy are forced to respond, on a very local level, to the global forces that shape everyday lives. In these portraits we have seen the centrality of literacy to the negotiations and practices of everyday life.

The research in this book draws on observations of everyday lives in a particular place but also at a particular time in terms of socioeconomic policy. This is a time when the gap between the richest and poorest has grown to its widest for several generations (Dorling 2015; Savage 2015) and the impact of policy reform is hitting the most vulnerable the hardest. During the time of my research with families on the estate, national data were already showing "the magnitude of poverty and privation" experienced across the UK: this included 1.5 million children living in homes that were not properly heated and four million children and adults who were not being properly fed (O'Hara 2015, p. 47, citing the 2013 Economic and Social Research Council report, Impoverishment of the UK). As O'Hara goes on to point out, these statistics were captured at a time before the impact of welfare reforms enforced by subsequent governments was felt with the force we have come to know in recent years. Over that time, as I continued to work with Peggy, Colin, Katie, Terry, and Carol, and during the course of writing this book about their experiences, there has been a consistent flow of media reports about families and individuals who are facing acute hardship, and the choice between heating and eating has become a grim idiom for the cost of "austerity", and the fact that it is being paid by those least able to afford it (Ryan 2016). In the UK, we have seen increased reliance on food banks, a stark rise in homelessness, a toll of early deaths attributed to the impact of welfare reform, and concerns expressed by the United Nations Committee on Economic, Social and Cultural Rights about breaches to international human rights obligations as a result of policies made in the name of "austerity" (Mortimer 2016). At the time of writing this, several years after politicians first claimed that "we're all in this together" (e.g. Osborne 2012), a review of welfare and tax reform conducted by the Equalities and Human Rights Commission warns of worse to come as the impact of changes in the most recent parliament is absorbed over the coming years. The report states that "in cash terms, those in the bottom half of income distribution lose more than those in the top 10 per cent" (Portes and Reid 2017, p. 3). Amongst the groups most adversely affected by cuts are Black and Minority Ethnic families, lone parents, and homes where one or more residents have a disability (a group that will have lost nearly twice as much of their income if that person is a child).

The starkest of indications that the costs of austerity politics are being met by families and communities in the most vulnerable of circumstances came in the early hours of June 14th, 2017, as flames engulfed Grenfell Tower, a 24-storey block of flats in North Kensington, London, trapping many of its residents in their homes. Seventy-one people are known to have died in the fire, including 18 children, many of whom died along with their parents and siblings. Over 70 people were injured. The tower block was home to a diverse community, many of whom were social housing tenants. Residents came from a wide range of cultural and professional backgrounds. Soon after the devastating fire, it became evident that several contributing factors could have been avoided and lives saved. Deregulated building safety standards meant that the warnings of fire safety experts had been ignored: warnings about the materials used in the recent refurbishment of the tower, and the lack of basic safety measures such as sprinklers. Residents of Grenfell Tower had, over at least four years preceding the fire, regularly voiced their concerns about fire safety in a blog. With such warnings and concerns unheeded, however, the refurbishment, including the fitting of lower-cost, highly flammable external cladding, led to catastrophic undermining of the building's structure.

The tragedy is an acute symbol of how socioeconomic and cultural injustices are entwined, and the impact of this injustice on equal participation in society. I write this not long after this disaster happened. As you read, other injustices will be happening which illustrate what is really being valued about people and their everyday lives. This is evident when we look at the ways in which knowledge and the dominant means of communication are controlled to deny the fair distribution of resources, to refuse to recognise lived realities, and to frame whole communities as abject. How we view literacy, including its role in the pursuit of social justice, is therefore central to a continued challenge to injustice. This places those working in the field of literacy at the heart of this challenge.

The Lens of Literacy

The portraits presented in this book illustrate in several ways what the lens of literacy offers in relation to social justice. The first aim of the book has been to argue, through the portraits and the discussion which results from each, that literacy shouldn't be viewed as a neutrally applied *solution* to issues raised by policy. Before we can arrive at solutions, a focus on everyday interaction with and through texts of all kinds should also be a lens through which we gain a deeper understanding of *what the issues are*, and the complex imbrication of factors that shapes them. Viewed through the lens of literacy, there are examples in each portrait of the ways in which the politics of "austerity" has compounded injustice, and the impact of this on the experiences of individuals, families, and communities.

A focus on literacy also illustrates the limitations of what may well be well-intentioned connections between literacy and social justice. As we have seen in the portraits, efforts to remedy inequalities in some cases compounded, rather than reduced, the injustice experienced by people who are already marginalised. The portraits show how a narrow model of what it means to read and right is part of the system which enacts policy. This has practical as well as symbolic implications for the ways in which individuals, families, and communities experience everyday life.

The lens of literacy also provides a wider perspective, allowing us to consider the different ways in which people's everyday lives are the result of interactions between local and global contexts. Through a focus on their everyday literacy practices, we have seen how the experiences of Peggy and the other participants are both shaped by these contexts, and how they use them to shape their experiences in creative, resourceful, and agentive ways.

These insights challenge the dominant discourses that frame places such as the estate, and those living in them, as problems that need to be solved. In the context of the broader understanding of injustice and its impact that this allows, it is helpful to return to Nancy Fraser's points about injustice and the three-dimensional framework she proposes. This framework, originally discussed in Chap. 1, has underpinned the thinking in this book: in each chapter I have tried to show how work in the different fields of literacy research has, over many decades, offered illustrations of what is at stake in each of the dimensions Fraser identifies—redistribution, recognition, and representation. I'll briefly revisit these dimensions here.

Redistribution

A focus on literacy in everyday lives has shown the challenge of accessing resources for those bearing the brunt of the politics of "austerity". Online welfare systems pose problems for those who do not own their own computer, or who have little experience in using one. Having to use the computer at the library incurs costs in terms of hourly use, as well as transport and the time involved. Complex bureaucratic systems also need to be navigated by families such as Colin's in order to access vital resources to support those with disabilities. During the time when she had to appeal the ruling regarding her disability benefit, in order to reinstate the income upon which she relied to get by, Peggy faced an arduous and arcane process bound by complex language. Literacy is therefore tied up in the enactment of policy in ways which make it more difficult to access resources.

Links between literacy and social justice can be well-intentioned with aims to facilitate fairer distribution of resources. Free computer classes at the library are an example, and the ways in which people go on to make use of online resources in their everyday lives demonstrate that this is an important aspect of equality of resource distribution. Policy solutions, including the tying of welfare claims to computer classes, for example, are also an attempt to remedy a perceived deficit in the skills needed to get by within the system.

However, these, and the systems of which they are a part, are too often premised upon narrow models of literacy and driven by a moral impetus which frames the preferred subjectivities of neoliberal societies and the practices identified as being needed to be a part of those societies. We have seen how this cultural injustice adds to the negative impact of socio-economic injustice.

Recognition

The knowledge economy ties literacy into a redistributive model of justice, making it central to how people now access resources. The change in society over recent years has meant that expectations about engaging with text have changed too. The portraits in this book have illustrated the wide repertoire of communicative resources drawn upon as part of everyday lives. However, a lack of recognition of these, and the creativity, agency, and resourcefulness they represent, risks leaving the cultural practices of parts of our society ignored. Without consideration of the complexity of everyday lives, policies such as the bedroom tax result in the physical and emotional upheaval experienced by Peggy. The subjectivities shaped by the values of a knowledge economy leave many framed as in deficit because their knowledges, skills, and experience do not appear to match dominant practices.

As we have seen in the portraits, when people's lives are already inextricably tied to policy systems, this represents a lot of knowledge and experience that is not valued (Eubanks 2012). Rogers (2008, p. 144) notes that the absence of literacy or literacy competence is not the issue; rather, she argues, we need to actively question "the assumption that more literacy is better literacy". Cultural injustice results not only from this mismatch between dominant and vernacular practices but also in the way that subjectivities are shaped by dominant discourses and how people come to see themselves as a result (Hayes et al. 2017). Colin's lifelong view of himself as a poor reader and writer, and the strategies he uses so as not to appear "too thick", is an example of this. Examples in the portraits also illustrate the danger of this resulting in a feeling of powerlessness, and of being unable to participate as freely as others.

Representation

Fraser argues that "justice requires social arrangements that permit all (adult) members of society to interact with one another as peers" (2003, p. 36). The bureaucratic systems which impact upon the lives of Peggy and Colin, for example, are based on information sharing, rather than on communication and collaboration. Participants are not equally positioned within this process, and both Colin and Peggy articulated the demands placed upon them to engage effectively with systems which ultimately controlled whether or not they had the means to get by. Computer classes which focus on formatting CVs, or the proliferation of form filling involved in navigating the result of the bedroom tax, involve literacy practices which emphasise "what" and not "what if?". Such systems rely on a narrow mode of communicating, and the complexity of everyday experience is not always recognised. We have seen how a narrow model of what it means to read and write is also reflective of a far wider discourse which reduces the complexity of lived experience to media-friendly epithets. The reducing of everyday lives that is seen in this discourse not only has a negative impact on people's access to resources, but also affects the extent to which people's voices are heard.

Taken together, the portraits and perspectives from literacy research presented in the chapters of this book also emphasise the interrelatedness of the three dimensions of justice presented by Fraser, and the fact that social justice can only be achieved through consideration and action which relates to all three. The notion of capital is illustrative of this. Approaches to literacy in policy and practice are often premised upon more equitable access to economic and cultural resources. As we saw in Chap. 4, however, the notion of capital also raises the issue of recognition, and who gets to decide what resources are important not only to get by in society, but also to get on. The bedroom tax emphasises both socio-economic and cultural injustices through its lack of recognition of the realities faced by those affected. The disempowering bureaucratic systems in which such policies are entrenched also lead to the lack of representation experienced by Peggy, who is rendered voiceless by a system which does not value what she stands to lose as a result of this policy.

Literacy is about communication. It plays an important part in explorations of the ways in which we see ourselves, and how we see, and want to be seen by, each other, our friends, families, communities, and the wider world. This can be in different ways and about different things. The portraits presented in this book illustrate how the three dimensions of justice compromise this ability to be heard. But as the novelist Arundhati Roy (2004) has said: "there's really no such thing as the 'voiceless'. There are only the deliberately silenced, or the preferably unheard". The frame is a significant part of the process that makes this silencing happen. It can also be an important part of how the silencing is challenged.

The Power of the Frame: Reading, Writing, and What Counts

A second key theme of this book is the significance of the frame to social justice, and the importance of *how we look at literacy*. The frame, for Fraser (2010), is about active inclusion and exclusion from the processes that allow people to be seen and heard on an equal footing. The discourses outlined in Chap. 3, and the enactment of policies that result from these, are part of this process of framing and, as I've already out-lined, the lens of literacy is a useful tool for illuminating the impact of this.

Drawing attention to the framing of literacy is an important aspect of the relationship between literacy and social justice, and of what research can do in this field. This means not only foregrounding negative implications, but also highlighting what alternative frames might contribute to our understanding. As a process which enables the recognition and representation of different perspectives, presenting a broader view of literacy practices can itself be a part of Fraser's three-dimensional framework of justice. The framing of the book, as portraits of everyday literacy *for* social justice, also aims to contribute to social justice in other important ways.

Firstly, the *portrait*, as a means of exploring and presenting these broader perspectives, represents a challenge to the dominant discourses of deficit which have been described in this book, and the "facile enquiry" that feeds them. These discourses are premised upon the "relentless scrutiny of failure" (Lawrence-Lightfoot and Hoffmann Davis 1997, pp. 8–9) and both grow out of, and result in, cynicism that frames issues as problems to be fixed and that attributes blame to the victimised. In each portrait in this book, the lens of literacy shows how people are framed and their subjectivities defined by this cynical negativity. Moral judgements are made about people and their role in society. These are used to justify policies that deem them not important enough to have vital resources made easily accessible. Knowledge itself is a resource that is withheld within bureaucratic systems. The homes that people have worked hard to build, and the lives that were built within them, cease to be officially valued. *How* literacy research is conducted and presented therefore also needs to work for social justice by championing the diverse literacies of everyday lives.

One way in which literacy research has done this is in its emphasis on the *everyday*, situating literacy practice in the context in which it takes place. The understanding of literacy as a plural concept is also important in challenging the dominance of the idea that there is just one way of reading and writing. As was explored in Chaps. 5, 6, and 7, research within the social paradigm of literacy has also challenged the notion that literacy is something people *have* (or not). Rather, the social practice paradigm views literacy as something people *do*, and Chaps. 5 and 6 have illustrated how it is something that people do together in the collaborative negotiation and construction of experiences. This has links with sociological interpretations of two areas commonly linked within discussion of literacy and social justice: family and community. Both of these can also be viewed as things that people *do*, not on their own in a fixed time or place, but collaboratively, across time and space. This challenges reductive notions of places like the estate as in deficit, or in need of being "fixed" by external policy makers. Family, community and home are all constituted through collective action, and examples in the book show how literacy practices are an important feature of this action.

An orientation in research towards looking at how literacy is *done* has profound implications. The portrait, with its focus on the active identification and presentation of "what is good here?" (Lawrence-Lightfoot and Hoffman Davis 1997, p. 9), reframes the dominant representations which shape public and policy discourse. It offers an asset-based perspective on the creativity and resourcefulness with which people engage with aspects of their everyday lives, including their navigation of the challenges they face. Portraits are based not on the "documentation of pathology" (ibid.) but on listening and sharing experiences, of working *with* participants. Unlike large quantitative studies, which cannot engage closely with the specific, locally produced, and often unintended consequences of literacy in its social context, portraits based on ethnographic study engage with the day-to-day experiences of people with little power. Through noticing and describing what is often hidden, the description of these experiences disrupts dominant ways of understanding and presenting everyday lives.

The examples we have seen of families and communities working together through literacy practices, engaging with a range of texts in creative, collaborative, and agentive ways, illustrate how participation is inherently social, with people "actively involved in some co-operative endeavour" (Olson 2008, p. 25). The portraits of Katie and Colin, Terry and Carol, and Peggy each show worlds being made through interaction, and texts of all kinds being central to the construction of family, community, and—literally in the case of Peggy—home. The meanings made in the examples featured in each portrait emerge from the specific "simultaneity of stories-so-far" (Massey 2005, p. 12). This challenges the possibility of holding still any one version of a place, community, family, individual, or indeed literacy, as the only version that can exist.

The work of many in the field of literacy studies in presenting different ways of looking at literacy has allowed broader understanding of how it is part of everyday lives, and a wider range of perspectives from which this may be understood. As I've said, this has the potential to contribute to social justice through increased recognition and representation for diverse voices and experiences. However, at a time when increasingly narrow models continue to threaten social justice in the complex ways we have seen in this book, *what* we research, and arguing for the importance of this, remains vital. Alongside this, *how* we present the stories that emerge from research must continue to be a priority in the challenge to injustice and in work for social change.

So far in this chapter, I've explored two of the book's aims through Fraser's three-dimensional framework for justice. The first is the role of literacy as a lens for understanding the impact of injustices, including the implications when a narrow model of literacy is part of the way in which policies are enacted. The second is the importance of the frame to any discussion of injustice: this is focused on how we *see* literacy, and includes the implications for *what* we research in relation to literacy, as well as *how* we conduct and present that research. In the next part of the chapter, I move on to explore a further challenge posed by Fraser, and what this means for how we understand the notion of literacy *for* social justice.

How Literacy Can Count

Exposing the frame is an important part of the tradition of literacy research. As we have seen in earlier chapters, this includes highlighting the injustice of marginalising practices and subjectivities which do not fit with mandated forms; challenging the hegemony of schooled literacy, and pointing out the effects of this on voice and inclusion across diverse communities; and describing the impact on everyday lives of narrow models and pernicious discourses of deficit.

However, the history of literacy studies explored in this book also emphasises the role of *presenting alternatives* to the dominant frame. This has been recognised as a valuable contribution to social justice that can be made by literacy research and education, where pedagogies allow space for diverse voices and experiences, and support for the development of subjectivities that can challenge the status quo (e.g. Hamilton 2014; Duckworth 2014; Comber 2016; Freire and Macedo 1987).

The challenge, however, lies in the ways in which literacy research has been taken up in wider practice, and how this influences, and is part of, wider social change. Traditional links between literacy and social justice have often positioned so-called "low" literacy as being a cause of poverty, rather than the other way round. This has led to approaches to literacy research and education which have sought merely to address the perceived symptoms without consideration of the wider structural problems that have a negative impact on people's experience of everyday life.

Graff (1979) describes the "literacy myth", whereby support for traditional curricula is based on the possibility of alternative voices being included. Many others have gone on to draw on the notion of the literacy myth to describe the challenge for transformative literacy education (e.g. Lambirth 2011). Elsa Auerbach (2005), in her case for a "pedagogy of not-literacy", discusses the paradox of the literacy myth, and how approaches to pedagogy reflect this. She argues that pedagogic approaches which aim to challenge inequalities and oppression by using these as a vehicle or context for analysis only go some way towards organising for change if the structural frameworks from which such struggles emanate are not also examined, or are not the focus of challenge. As such, she argues, "the antidote to problems of inequity and oppression is organizing for change through concerted political action, rather than educational interventions per se" (p. 365). Gutierrez et al. (2009) call for "re-mediating" literacy: this involves moving away from pedagogic approaches which attempt to counter perceived deficits of students from non-dominant communities, to approaches which emphasise the role of literacy in how we mediate cultural practice, and reconcile differences.

Although they may well challenge a dominant frame, approaches to literacy and inequalities which leave intact the workings of the framing process therefore do little to change the wider social context. They are examples of what Fraser calls "affirmative remedies": these are "aimed at correcting inequitable outcomes of social arrangements without disturbing the underlying framework that generates them" (1997, p. 23). The "pedagogisation of literacy" (Street and Street 1991, p. 143), which promotes a narrow model of literacy that reflects dominant school discourse, is a feature not only of education, but also of literacy research (Baynham 2004). Here, literacy is the goal, however arrived at. This approach is inherently limited if it does not address the means by which the problems it aims to address are framed. Street (2004) has called on research in literacy to do more than merely offer an account of alternative practices, which echoes this idea of the literacy myth. We need to do more than get different literacies accepted; we need to challenge the foundational discourses that marginalise in the first place (Street and Street 1991). This links to Street's identification of the key struggle in the debate on literacy and inequality being over "the power to name and define" (2011, p. 580). As Rogers (2008, p. 156) has argued, "because of the power of discourse in constraining individuals' destinies […] a liberating education must include a reflexive awareness of discursive environments". What Fraser calls "the deep grammar of frame-setting" (2010, p. 23) is located within these discursive environments, as we have seen in earlier chapters. What she terms *transformative* justice involves disruption to this "grammar".

This means more than challenging the dominance of one frame over another. Dichotomies are common in many discursive environments, not least in the field of literacy studies. Discussion in previous chapters has illustrated some of these, including local/global, policy/practice, ideological/autonomous, and everyday/institutional. However, overall, the preceding chapters have argued for plurality, rather than essentialism, in how we see literacy and its role in social justice. Chapters 5 and 7 have, in particular, challenged the possibility of holding still one meaning, given the way in which meanings are collectively constructed, drawing on multiple resources across time and space. This is another reason why Fraser's model of justice can be helpful to discussion about literacy, as it explicitly argues that justice involves addressing issues across different categories, as well as attention to the process of how these issues are framed. It questions the positioning of literacy as the solution in and of itself, and asks us to consider how literacy works within a wider ideological context.

In her work on the demonisation of the working class, Tyler (2013) argues that the question is not whether demonisation stands up to scrutiny by challenging its limitations and offering alternatives, but to understand "how the representation of self and other – which sustains hierarchy, consensus, conflict – are formed and how it might be transformed" (p. 170). In a similar vein, in relation to literacy education, Auerbach (2005) argues that our attention should be on the bigger picture in which it is located:

> I want to turn the question of how globalization shapes literacy education on its head and ask instead: How can literacy education contribute to shaping and resisting the dominant forces of globalization? (p. 366)

A transformative approach to literacy and social justice, then, means more than the replacement of the existing dominant frame with the dominance of another that fails to attend to the structures of power that underpin the ways in which we use literacy in everyday lives.

There has been recognition within social policy that targets inequality that complex problems require complex solutions and that multifaceted issues require flexible and multifaceted approaches (e.g. the "Christie Commission" on the Future Delivery of Public Services, Scottish Parliament 2011). Work at Strathclyde University (Ellis et al. 2017) has emphasised the interrelated factors that shape literacy learning, providing a framework that acknowledges that evidence from across home, school, and social, cultural, and cognitive factors must be drawn upon by teachers in their decision-making.

As Fraser points out, "any remedy will produce its own exclusions" (Nash and Bell 2007, p. 79), and disputes about framing are a permanent part of a political landscape. This means that, firstly, we need spaces and institutions where questions of justice can be democratically debated and addressed. Literacy research can, and should, have a central place in these debates. It also reminds us that debates about literacy are part of wider debates about society. Auerbach (2005) recognises that "the struggles in which literacy education is embedded (as opposed to literacy itself) are the forces that change" (2005, p. 369). Using Fraser's three-dimensional framework for justice to explore literacy in everyday lives positions this work as political. It reminds us that any focus on transforming literacy research and education is part of a struggle for wider social change.

References

Auerbach, E. (2005) 'Connecting the Local and the Global: A pedagogy of Not-Literacy', in Anderson, J., Kendrick, M., Rogers, T. and Smythe, S. (eds.) *Portraits of Literacy across Families, Communities and Schools: Intersections and tensions*, Mahwah, New Jersey: Lawrence Erlbaum Associates, pp. 363–379

Baynham, M. (2004) 'Ethnographies of Literacy: Introduction', *Language and Education*, 18 (4) 285–290

Comber, B. (2016) *Literacy, Place and the Pedagogies of Possibility*. Oxon and New York: Routledge

Dorling, D. (2015) *Inequality and the 1%*. London: Verso

Duckworth, V. (2014) *Learning Trajectories, Violence and Empowerment amongst Adult Basic Skills Learners*. London: Routledge

Ellis, S., Thomson, J. and Carey, J. (2017) 'Generating Data, Generating Knowledge: Professional Identity and the Strathclyde Literacy Clinic', in Ng, C. and Bartlett, B. (eds.) *Improving Reading Engagement in the 21st Century*. Singapore: Springer, pp. 255–268

Eubanks, V. (2012) *Digital Dead End: Fighting for social justice in the information age*. Cambridge MA: MIT Press

Fraser, N. (1997) *Justice Interruptus: Critical reflections on the 'postsocialist' condition*. New York: Routledge

Fraser, N. (2003) 'Social justice in the age of identity politics', in Fraser, N. and Honneth, A. *Redistribution or recognition? A political-philosophical exchange*. London: Verso, pp. 7–109

Fraser, N. (2010) *Scales of Justice: Reimagining Political Space in a Globalizing World*. New York: Columbia University Press

Freire, P. and Macedo, D. (1987) *Literacy: Reading the Word and the World*. New York: Bergin and Garvey

Graff, H. (1979) *The Literacy Myth*. New York: Academic Press

Gutiérrez, K., Morales, Z,. and Martinez, D. (2009) 'Re-mediating Literacy: Culture, Difference, and Learning for students from non-dominant communities', *Review of Research in Education*, 33, 212–245

Hamilton, M. (2014) 'Global, regional and local influences on adult literacy policy in England', *Globalisation, Society and Education,* 12 (1) 110–126

Hayes, D., Hattam, R., Comber, B., Kerkham, L., Lupton, R. and Thomson, P. (2017) *Literacy, Leading and Learning: beyond pedagogies of poverty.* London: Routledge

Lambirth, A. (2011) *Literacy on the Left: Reform and revolution.* London: Bloomsbury

Lawrence-Lightfoot, S. and Hoffmann Davis, J. (1997) *The Art and Science of Portraiture.* San Francisco: Jossey-Bass Books

Massey, D. (2005) *For Space.* London: Sage

Mortimer, C. (2016) 'Government austerity policy a breach of international human rights, says UN Report', *The Independent,* 29 June, http://www.independent.co.uk/news/uk/politics/austerity-government-policy-conservatives-poor-food-banks-inequality-un-a7110066.html (accessed November 20, 2017)

Nash, K. and Bell, V. (2007) 'The Politics of Framing: an interview with Nancy Fraser', *Theory, Culture and Society,* 24 (4) 73–86

Olson, K. (2008) 'Participatory Parity' in Olson, K. (ed.) *Adding Insult to Injury: Nancy Fraser debates her critics.* London: Verso, pp. 246–272

O'Hara, M. (2015) *Austerity Bites: A journey to the sharp end of cuts in the UK.* Bristol: Polity Press

Osborne, G. (2012) Speech to Conservative Party Conference, http://www.newstatesman.com/blogs/politics/2012/10/george-osbornes-speech-conservative-conference-full-text (accessed March 3, 2017)

Portes, J. and Reid, H. (2017) 'Distributional results for the impact of tax and welfare reform between 2010–17, modelled in the 2021/22 tax year, *Equalities and Human Rights Commission Research Report,* https://www.equalityhumanrights.com/sites/default/files/impact-of-tax-and-welfare-reforms-2010-2017-interim-report_0.pdf (accessed November 20, 2017)

Rogers, R. (2008) *A Critical Discourse Analysis of Family Literacy Practices: Power in and out of print.* New York: Routledge

Roy, A. (2004) 'Peace and the new corporate liberation theology', *Sydney Peace Prize Lecture,* http://sydney.edu.au/news/84.html?newsstoryid=279 (accessed November 20, 2017)

Ryan, F. (2016) 'Eating v heating: this is what destitution looks like', *The Guardian,* https://www.theguardian.com/commentisfree/2016/may/05/decent-toilet-roll-kids-delighted-hope-for-food (accessed November 20, 2017)

Savage, M. (2015) *Social Class in the 21st Century*. London: Pelican Books

Scottish Parliament (2011) 'Commission on the Future Delivery of Public Services' http://www.gov.scot/resource/doc/352649/0118638.pdf (accessed November 22, 2017)

Street, B. (2004) 'Futures of the Ethnography of Literacy?', *Language and Education*, 18 (4) 326–330

Street, B. (2011) 'Literacy inequalities in theory and practice: The power to name and define', *International Journal of Educational Development*, 31, 580–586

Street, B. and Street, J. (1991) 'The Schooling of Literacy' in Barton, D. and Ivanič, R. (eds.) *Writing in the Community*. London: Sage, pp. 143–166

Tyler, I. (2013) *Revolting Subjects: Social abjection and resistance in neoliberal Britain*. London: Zed Books

References

Ade-Ojo, G. and Duckworth, V. (2015) *Adult Literacy Policy and Practice: From intrinsic values to instrumentalism.* London: Palgrave Macmillan

Auerbach, E. (2005) 'Connecting the Local and the Global: A pedagogy of Not-Literacy', in Anderson, J., Kendrick, M., Rogers, T. and Smythe, S. (eds.) *Portraits of Literacy across Families, Communities and Schools: Intersections and tensions,* Mahwah, New Jersey: Lawrence Erlbaum Associates, pp. 363–379

Atkinson, T. (2012) 'Beyond disempowering counts: Mapping a fruitful future for adult literacies', in Tett, L., Hamilton, M. and Crowther, J. (eds.) *More Powerful Literacies.* Leicester: NIACE, pp. 75–88

Baker-Bell, A. (2013) '"I Never Really Knew the History behind African American Language": Critical Language Pedagogy in an Advanced Placement English Language Arts Class,' *Equity & Excellence in Education,* 46 (3) 355–370

Bailey, M., Harrison, C. and Brooks, G. (2002) The 'Boots Books for Babies' project: Impact on library registrations and book loans', *Journal of Early Childhood Literacy,* 2 (1) 45–63

Ball, S. (2006) *Education Policy and Social Class.* London: Routledge

Ball, S. (2013) *The Education Debate* (Second Edition). Bristol: Polity Press

Bartlett, L. (2008) 'Literacy's verb: exploring what literacy is and what literacy does', *International Journal of Educational Development,* 28, 737–753

© The Author(s) 2018
S. Jones, *Portraits of Everyday Literacy for Social Justice,*
https://doi.org/10.1007/978-3-319-75945-6

Barton, D. (1994) *Literacy: An introduction to the ecology of written language.* Oxford: Blackwell

Barton, D. and Hamilton, M. (1998) *Local Literacies: Reading and Writing in One Community.* London: Routledge

Barton, D. and Hamilton, M. (2000) 'Literacy Practices' in Barton, D., Hamilton, M. and Ivanič, R. (eds.) *Situated Literacies: reading and writing in context.* London: Routledge, pp. 7–15

Barton, D., Hamilton, M. and Ivanič, R. (eds.) (2000) *Situated Literacies: reading and writing in context.* London: Routledge

Baumberg, B., Bell, K. and Gaffney, D. (2012) *Benefits Stigma in Britain.* University of Kent/Elizabeth Finn Care

Baynham, M. (1995) *Literacy Practices: Investigation literacy in social contexts.* London: Longman

Baynham, M. (2004) 'Ethnographies of Literacy: Introduction', *Language and Education,* 18 (4) 285–290

Behar, R. (1996) *The Vulnerable Observer.* Boston: Beacon Press

Berthould, E. and Elderkin, S. (2013) *The Novel Cure.* London: Canongate

Besnier, N. (1993) 'Literacy and Feelings: the encoding of affect in Nukulaelae letters', in Street, B. (ed.) *Cross-cultural Approaches to Literacy,* Cambridge: Cambridge University Press, pp. 62–86

Bingham, J. (2013) 'Judges rule back-to-work assessments 'unfair' to mentally ill', http://www.telegraph.co.uk/news/health/news/10074192/Judges-rule-back-to-work-assessments-unfair-to-mentally-ill.html (accessed November 20, 2017)

Bourdieu, H. (1977) *Outline of a Theory of Practice.* Cambridge: Cambridge University Press

Bourdieu, H. (1984) *Distinction.* London: Routledge

Blackburn, M. V. and Clark, C. T. (2007) 'Bridging the Local/ Global Divide: Theorizing Connections Between Global Issues and Local Action', in Blackburn, M.V. and Clark, C.T. (eds.) *Literacy Research for Political and Social Change.* New York: Peter Lang, pp. 9–27

Boughton, B. (2016) 'Popular Education and Mass Literacy: beyond "New Literacy Studies"', in Yasukawa, K. and Black, S. (eds.) *Beyond Economic Interests: Critical perspectives on adult literacy and numeracy in a globalized world.* Rotterdam: Sense Publishers

boyd, d. (2014) *It's Complicated: The social lives of networked teens.* New Haven, CT: Yale University Press

Brandt, D. and Clinton, K. (2002) 'Limits of the Local: Expanding Perspectives on Literacy as a Social Practice', *Journal of Literacy Research,* 34, 337–356

Brandt, D. (2001) *Literacy in American Lives.* Cambridge: Cambridge University Press

Brandt, D. (2015) *The Rise of Writing: Redefining mass literacy.* Cambridge: Cambridge University Press

Burnett, C., Merchant, G., Pahl, K. and Rowsell, J. (2014) 'The (im)materiality of literacy: the significance of subjectivity to new literacies research', *Discourse: Studies in the Cultural Politics of Education*, 35 (1) 90–103

Butler, P. (2015) 'Thousands have died after being found fit for work, DWP figures show', Guardian, August 28 2017, https://www.theguardian.com/society/2015/aug/27/thousands-died-after-fit-for-work-assessment-dwp-figures (accessed August 27 2017)

Bynner, J. (2014) *The impact of adult literacy and numeracy based on the 1970 British Cohort Study.* London: Centre for Longitudinal Studies

Centre for Literacy (2012) 'Literacy Learning and Poverty Using IALS data on Earnings', *Canadian Literacy and Learning Network*

Centre for Welfare Reform (2015) 'Work Capability Assessment: deaths and suicides', available at https://www.scribd.com/document/262851896/Work-Capability-Assessment-deaths-and-*suicides*#download&from_embed (accessed August 26, 2017)

Channel 4 (2014) *Benefits Street*, Love Productions/ Rebel Uncut

Clarke, J. and Newman, J. (2012) 'The alchemy of austerity', *Critical Social Policy*, 32 (2) 299–319

Clifford, J. (1986) 'Introduction: Partial Truths', in Clifford, J. and Marcus, G.E. (eds.) *Writing Culture: The poetics and politics of ethnography.* London: University of California Press, pp. 1–26

Coates, K. and Sillburn, R. (1970) *Poverty: The Forgotten Englishmen.* Middlesex: Penguin Books

Collins, J. and Blot, R. (2003) *Literacy and Literacies: Texts, power and identity.* Cambridge: Cambridge University Press

Comber, B. (2012) 'Mandated literacy assessment and the reorganisation of teachers' work: federal policy, local effects', *Critical Studies in Education*, 53 (2) 119–136

Comber, B. (2014) 'Literacy, poverty and schooling: what matters in young people's education?', *Literacy*, 48 (3) 115–123

Comber, B. (2016) *Literacy, Place and the Pedagogies of Possibility.* Oxon and New York: Routledge

Compton-Lilly, C. (2017) *Reading Students' Lives: Literacy learning across time.* New York: Routledge

Corcoran, M. (2002) 'Place attachment and community sentiment in marginalized neighbourhoods: A European case study', *Canadian Journal of Urban Research*, 11 (1) 47–67

Cresswell, T. (2004) *Place: a short introduction*. Oxford: Blackwell

Crewe, L. (2011) 'Life Itemised: lists, loss, unexpected significance, and the enduring geographies of discard', *Environment and Planning D: Society and Space*, 29, 27–46

Crystal, D. (2008) *Txtng: The gr8 db8*. Oxford: Oxford University Press

Dean, J. and Hastings, A. (2000) *Challenging Images: Housing estates, stigma and regeneration*. Bristol: Policy Press

De Benedictis, S., Allen, K. and Jensen, T. (2017) 'Portraying Poverty: The economics and ethics of factual welfare television', *Cultural Sociology*, 11 (3) 337–358

De Certeau, M. (1984) *The Practice of Everyday Life*. London: University of California Press

Douglas, M. (1991) 'The Idea of a Home: A Kind of Space', *Social Research*, 58 (1) 287–307

Department for Work and Pensions (2013) 'Simplifying the welfare system and making sure work pays', https://www.gov.uk/government/policies/simplifying-the-welfare-system-and-making-sure-work-pays/supporting-pages/making-sure-housing-support-is-fair-and-affordable (accessed June 4, 2013)

Department for Work and Pensions (2017) 'Appeal to the Social Security and Child Support Tribunal' https://www.gov.uk/social-security-child-support-tribunal/before-you-appeal, (accessed August 27, 2017)

Department for Education (2014) *National Curriculum for England*. https://www.gov.uk/government/collections/national-curriculum   (accessed November 20, 2017)

Dorling, D. (2015) *Inequality and the 1%*. London: Verso

Dowrick, C., Billington, J., Robinson, J., Hamer, A. and Williams, C. (2012) 'Get into Reading as an intervention for common mental health problems: exploring catalysts for change', *Medical Humanities*, 38, 15–20

Duckworth, V. (2014) *Learning Trajectories, Violence and Empowerment amongst Adult Basic Skills Learners*. London: Routledge

Duncan, S. (2012) *Reading Circles, Novels and Adult Reading Development*. London: Bloomsbury

Eakle, J. (2007) 'Literacy Spaces of a Christian Faith-Based School', *Reading Research Quarterly*, 42 (4) 472–510

Ellis, S., Thomson, J. and Carey, J. (2017) 'Generating Data, Generating Knowledge: Professional Identity and the Strathclyde Literacy Clinic', in Ng,

C. and Bartlett, B. (eds.) *Improving Reading Engagement in the 21st Century.* Singapore: Springer, pp. 255–268

Eubanks, V. (2012) *Digital Dead End: Fighting for social justice in the information age.* Cambridge MA: MIT Press

Featherstone, J. (1989) 'To Make the Spirit Whole', *Harvard Educational Review*, 59 (3) 367–378

Field, F. (2010) *The Foundation Years: preventing poor children becoming poor adults.* London HM Government

Field, J. (2008) *Social Capital.* Second edition. Abingdon: Routledge

Fiese, B., Foley, K.P., Spagnola, M. (2006), 'Routine and Ritual Elements in Family Mealtimes: Contexts for child well-being and family identity', *New Directions for Child and Adolescent Development*, 111, 67–89

Fraser, N. (1997) *Justice Interruptus: Critical reflections on the 'postsocialist' condition.* New York: Routledge

Fraser, N. (2003a) 'Distorted beyond all recognition: a rejoinder to Axel Honneth', in Fraser, N. and Honneth, A., *Redistribution or recognition? A political-philosophical exchange.* London: Verso, pp. 198–236

Fraser, N. (2003b) 'Social justice in the age of identity politics', in Fraser, N. and Honneth, A. *Redistribution or recognition? A political-philosophical exchange.* London: Verso, pp. 7–109

Fraser, N. (2010) *Scales of Justice: Reimagining Political Space in a Globalizing World.* New York: Columbia University Press

Fraser, N. and Honneth, A. (2003) 'Introduction: Redistribution or Recognition?', in Fraser, N. and Honneth, A., *Redistribution or recognition? A political-philosophical exchange.* London: Verso

Freedman, J. (1993) *From Cradle to Grave: The Human Face of Poverty in America.* New York: Atheneum

Freire, P. and Macedo, D. (1987) *Literacy: Reading the word and the world.* New York: Bergin and Garvey

Fuller, D. and Rehberg Sedo, D. (2013) *Reading Beyond the Book: The social practices of contemporary literary culture.* Abingdon: Routledge

Gardiner, M. (2009) 'Book Review: *Everyday Life: Theories and Practices from Surrealism to the Present*, Michael Sheringham', *Space and Culture*, 12, 283–389

Garthwaite, K. (2011) 'The language of shirkers and scroungers?' Talking about illness and disability and coalition welfare reform', *Disability and Society*, 26 (3) 369–372

Garthwaite, K. (2016) *Hunger Pains. Life inside foodbank Britain.* Bristol: Policy Press

Geertz, C. (1973) *The Interpretation of Cultures*. New York: Basic Books

Gillies, V. (2006) 'Working class mothers and school life: exploring the role of emotional capital', *Gender and Education*, 18 (3) 281–293

Graff, H. (1979) *The Literacy Myth*. New York: Academic Press

Green, J. (2013) *The Fault in Our Stars*. London: Penguin

Gregory, E. (2005) 'Guiding Lights: Siblings as Literacy Teachers in a Multilingual Community', in Anderson, J., Kenrick, M., Rogers, T. and Smythe, S. (eds.) *Portraits of Literacy Across Families, Communities, and Schools*. Mahwah, NJ: Lawrence Erlbaum Associates, pp. 21–40

Gregory, E. and Williams, A. (2000) *City Literacies: Learning to read across generations and cultures*. London: Routledge

Gregory, E., Long, S. and Volk, D. (2004) *Many Pathways to Literacy: Young children learning with siblings, grandparents and communities*. London: RoutledgeFalmer

Gutiérrez, K., Morales, Z,. and Martinez, D. (2009) 'Re-mediating Literacy: Culture, Difference, and Learning for students from non-dominant communities', *Review of Research in Education*, 33, 212–245

Haddad, M. (2012) *The Perfect Storm: Economic stagnation, the rising cost of living, public spending cuts, and the impact of UK poverty*. Oxford: Oxfam GB

Hall, C. and Thomson, P. (2010) 'Grounded literacies: the power of listening to, telling and performing community stories', *Literacy*, 44 (2) 69–75

Hall, C. and Jones, S. (2016) 'Making Sense in the City: Dolly Parton, early reading and educational policy making', *Literacy*, 50 (1) 40–48

Hall, S. M. (2016) 'Everyday family experiences of the financial crisis: getting by in the recent economic recession', *Journal of Economic Geography*, 16, 305–330

Hall, S. M. and Holdsworth, C. (2016) 'Family Practices, Holiday and the Everyday', *Mobilities*, 11 (2) 284–302

Hall, S., McIntosh, K., Neitzert, E., Pottinger, K.S., Stephenson, M-A., Reed, H. and Taylor, L. (2017) *Intersecting Inequalities: The impact of austerity on Black and Minority Ethnic Women in the UK*, Report by the Women's Budget Group and Runnymede Trust with RECLAIM and Coventry Women's Voices.

Hamilton, M. (2012) *Literacy and the Politics of Representation*. Oxon: Routledge

Hamilton, M. (2014) 'Global, regional and local influences on adult literacy policy in England', *Globalisation, Society and Education*, 12 (1) 110–126

Hamilton, M. and Pitt, K. (2011) 'Changing Policy Discourses: constructing literacy inequalities', *International Journal of Education Development*, 31, 596–605

Hamilton, M. and Tett, L. (2012) 'More powerful literacies: The policy context', in Tett, L., Hamilton, M. and Crowther, J. (eds.) *More Powerful Literacies*. Leicester: NIACE, pp. 31–58

Hamilton, M., Tett, L. and Crowther, J. (2012) 'More powerful literacies: An introduction' in Tett, L., Hamilton, M. and Crowther, J. (eds.) *More Powerful Literacies*. Leicester: NIACE, pp. 1–12

Hammersley, M. and Atkinson, P. (1995) *Ethnography: Principles in practice* (Second Edition). London: Routledge

Hanley, L. (2012) *Estates: An intimate history* (New Edition). London: Granta

Hansard (2013) http://www.publications.parliament.uk/pa/cm201314/cmhansrd/cm130626/debtext/130626-0001.htm#13062665000002 (accessed January 13, 2014)

Hartley, J. (2001) *Reading Groups*. Oxford: Oxford University Press

Hayes, D., Hattam, R., Comber, B., Kerkham, L., Lupton, R. and Thomson, P. (2017) *Literacy, Leading and Learning: beyond pedagogies of poverty*. London: Routledge

Heath, S. B. (1983) *Ways with Words*. Cambridge: Cambridge University Press

Heath, S. B. (2013) *Words at Work and Play*. Cambridge: Cambridge University Press

Helsper, E. and Eynon, R. (2010) 'Digital natives: where's the evidence?', *British Education Research Journal*, 36 (3) 503–520

Hills, J. (2015) *Good Times, Bad Times: The welfare myth of them and us*. Bristol: Polity Press

Hoggart, R. (1957) *The Uses of Literacy*. Middlesex: Penguin

hooks, b. (1990) *Yearning: race, gender, and cultural politics*. Cambridge, MA: South End Press

Hubbard, G., Backett-Milburn, K. and Kemner, D. (2001) 'Working with emotion: issues for the researcher in fieldwork and teamwork', *Social Research Methodology*, 4 (2) 119–137

Janes, H. and Kermani, H. (2001) 'Caregivers' story reading to young children in family literacy programs: pleasure or punishment?', *Journal of Adolescent and Adult Literacy*, 44 (5) 458–466

Jones, K. (2000) 'Becoming just another alphanumeric code: farmers' encounters with the literacy and discourse practices of agricultural bureaucracy at the livestock auction', in Barton, D., Hamilton, M. and Ivanič, R. (eds.) *Situated Literacies: reading and writing in context*. London: Routledge, pp. 70–90

Jones, S. (2006a) 'One body and two heads: Girls exploring their bicultural identities through text', *English in Education*, 40 (2) 5–21

Jones, S. (2006b). 'A Tale of Two Literacies: Girls growing up biculturally literate in two UK communities', in Hickey, T. (ed.) *Language Learning and Literacy*, Dublin: RAI, pp. 99–113

Jones, S. (2007) 'Land of "My 9": Welsh-English Bilingual Girls Creating Spaces to Explore Identity', *Changing English*, 14 (1) 39–50

Jones, S. (2009) 'Bilingual Identities in Two UK Communities: A Study of the languages and literacies of Welsh and British-Asian Girls', unpublished PhD thesis, University of Nottingham, available at: http://eprints.nottingham. ac.uk/10836/1/Susan_Jones_Bilingual_Identities.pdf

Jones, S. (2014) '"How people read and write and they don't even notice": Everyday lives and literacies on a Midlands council estate', *Literacy*, 48 (2) 59–65

Jones, S. (2016) 'Constricting or constructing everyday lives? Literacies and inequality' in Parry, B., Burnett, C. and Merchant, G (eds.) *Literacy, Media and Technology: Past, Present and Future*. London: Bloomsbury, pp. 63–77

Jones, S. (2017) '"Words of wisdom": Text, Voice and Justice in I, Daniel Blake', *Changing English*, 24 (4) 372–385

Jones, S., Hall, C., Thomson, P., Barrett, A. & Hanby, J. (2013) 'Representing the 'forgotten estate': participatory theatre, place and community identity', *Discourse: Studies in the Cultural Politics of Education*, 34 (1) 118–131

Jones, S. and Chapman, K. (2017) 'Telling stories: engaging critical literacy through urban legends in an English secondary school', *English Teaching, Practice and Critique,* 16 (1) 85–96

Jones, S. and Harvey, K. (2016) 'He should have put them in the freezer': creating and connecting through shared reading', *Journal of Arts and Communities*, 7 (3) 153–166

Jones, S. and McIntyre, (2014) 'It's not what it looks like. I'm Santa': connecting community through film', *Changing English*, 21 (4) 322–33

Jordan, A. B. (2006) 'Make yourself at home: the social construction of research roles in family studies', *Qualitative Research*, 6 (2) 169–185

Kellett, M. and Dar, A. (2007) *Children researching links between poverty and literacy*. York: Joseph Rowntree Foundation

Kendrick, M., Rogers, T., Smythe, S. and Anderson, J. (2005) 'Portraits of Literacy Across Families, Communities, and Schools: An introduction', in Anderson, J., Kendrick, M., Rogers, T. and Smythe, S. (eds.) *Portraits of Literacy across Families, Communities and Schools: Intersections and tensions*, Mahwah, New Jersey: Lawrence Erlbaum Associates, pp. 1–17

Kenner, C. and Ruby, M. (2012) *Interconnecting Worlds: Teacher partnerships for bilingual learning*. Stoke-on-Trent: Trentham Books

Lambirth, A. (2011) *Literacy on the Left: Reform and revolution*. London: Bloomsbury

Lankshear, C. (1997) *Changing Literacies*. Milton Keynes: Open University Press

Lankshear, K. and Knobel, M. (2011) *New Literacies: Everyday practices and social learning* (Third Edition). Maidenhead: McGraw Hill/OUP

Lawrence-Lightfoot, S. and Hoffmann Davis, J. (1997) *The Art and Science of Portraiture*. San Francisco: Jossey-Bass Books

Leander, K. and Sheehy, M. (2004) 'Introduction' in Leander, K. and Sheehy, M. (eds.) *Spatializing Literacy Research*. New York: Peter Lang

Leckie, G. J. and Hopkins, J. (2002) 'The public place of central libraries: findings from Toronto and Vancouver', *Library Quarterly*, 72 (3) 326–372

Lefebvre, H. (1991) *Critique of Everyday Life: Volume 1*. London: Verso

Lefebvre, H. (1996) 'Seen from the window', in *Writings on Cities*, Eleonore Kofman and Elizabeth Lebas (trans and ed.), Oxford: Blackwell, pp. 219–27

Lippard, L. (1997) *The Lure of the Local*. New York: The New Press

Lister, R. (2004) *Poverty*. Cambridge: Polity Press

Livingstone, S. and Sefton-Green, J. (2016) *The Class: Living and learning in the digital age*. New York: New York University Press

Loach, K. (dir.) (2016) *I, Daniel Blake*. UK: Sixteen Films

Long, E. (2003) *Book Groups: Women and the uses of reading in everyday life*. Chicago: University of Chicago Press

Longden, E., Davis, P., Billington, J., Lampropoulou, S., Farrington, G., Magee, F., Walsh, E., and Corcoran, R. (2015) 'Shared Reading: assessing the intrinsic value of a literature-based health intervention', *Medical Humanities*, 41 (2) 113–20

Luke, A. (2012) 'Critical literacy: Foundational notes', *Theory into Practice*, 51 (1) 4–11

Lytra, V., Volk, D. and Gregory, E. (eds.) (2016) *Navigating Languages, Literacies and Identities: Religion in young lives*. New York and Abingdon: Routledge

MacGillivray, L., Ardell, A. and Curwen, M. (2010) 'Libraries, churches, and schools: the literate lives of mothers and children in a homeless shelter', *Urban Education*, 45 (2) 221–245

Maddox, B. (2007) 'What can ethnographic studies tell us about the consequences of literacy?', *Comparative Education*, 43 (2) 253–271

Mallett, S. (2004) 'Understanding home: a critical review of the literature', *Sociological Review*, 52 (1) 62–89

Manguel, A. (2006) *The Library at Night*. New Haven: Yale University Press

Marsh, J. (2003) 'One-way traffic? Connections between Literacy Practices at Home and in the Nursery', *British Educational Research Journal*, 29 (3) 369–382

Massey, D. (2005) *For Space*. London: Sage

Matthews, C. (2015) *Homes and Places: A history of Nottingham's council houses*. Nottingham: Nottingham City Homes

McCoy, E. (2013) 'Lost for words: Poor literacy, the hidden issue in Child Poverty', London: National Literacy Trust

McKenzie, L. (2015) *Getting By: Estates, class and culture in austerity Britain*. Bristol: Policy Press

McIntyre, J. and Jones, S. (2014) 'Possibility in Impossibility? Working with beginning teachers of English in times of change', *English in Education*, 41 (1) 26–40

Moran, J. (2005a) *Reading the Everyday*. Abingdon: Routledge

Miller, D. (2008) *The Comfort of Things*. Cambridge: Polity Press

Miller, D. (2010) *Stuff*. Cambridge: Polity Press

Minns, H. (1990) *Read it to me now! Learning at home and school*. Buckingham: Open University Press

Moje, E. (2004) 'Powerful Spaces: Tracing the Out-of-School Literacy Spaces of Latino/a Youth', in Leander, K. and Sheehy, M. (eds.) *Spatializing Literacy Research and Practice*. New York: Peter Lang, pp. 15–38

Moll, L.C., Amanti, C., Neff, D. and Gonzalez, N. (1992) 'Funds of Knowledge for teaching: using a qualitative approach to connect homes and classrooms', *Theory into Practice*, XXXI (2) 132–141

Mooney, G. and Hancock, L. (2010) 'Poverty Porn and the Broken Society', *Variant*, 39/40 http://www.variant.org.uk/39_40texts/povertp39_40.html (accessed September 28, 2016)

Moran, J. (2005b) *Reading the Everyday*. Oxon: Routledge

Morgan, D. H. J. (2011a) 'Locating "Family Practices"', *Sociological Research Online*, 16 (4) 14

Morgan, D. H. J. (2011b) *Rethinking Family Practices*. Basingstoke: Palgrave Macmillan

Mortimer, C. (2016) 'Government austerity policy a breach of international human rights, says UN Report', *The Independent*, 29 June, http://www.independent.co.uk/news/uk/politics/austerity-government-policy-conservatives-poor-food-banks-inequality-un-a7110066.html (accessed 20 November, 2017)

Nabi, R., Rogers, A. and Street, B. (2009) *Hidden Literacies: Ethnographic studies of literacy and numeracy practices in Pakistan*. Bury St Edmunds: Uppingham Press

Nabokov, V. (1980) *Lectures on Literature*. New York, USA: Harcourt Brace

Nash, K. and Bell, V. (2007) 'The Politics of Framing: an interview with Nancy Fraser', *Theory, Culture and Society*, 24 (4) 73–86

Neuman, S. and Celano, D. (2001) 'Access to print in low-income and middle-income communities: An ecological study of four neighbourhoods', *Reading Research Quarterly*, 35 (1) 8–26

Neuman, S. and Celano, D. (2006) 'The knowledge gap: implications of leveling the playing field for low-income and middle-income children', *Reading Research Quarterly*, 41 (2) 176–201

Neuman, S. and Celano, D. (2012) *Giving Our Children a Fighting Chance: Poverty, literacy and the development of information capital*. New York: Teachers College Press

Nichols, S. (2011) 'Young children's literacy in the activity space of the library', *Journal of Early Childhood Literacy*, 11 (2) 164–189

Nichols, S., Rowsell, J., Nixon, H. and Rainbird, S. (2012) *Resourcing Early Learners: new networks, new actors*. London: Routledge

Nikulin, D. (2010) *Dialectic and Dialogue*. Stanford: Stanford University Press

Olson, K. (2008) 'Participatory Parity' in Olson, K. (ed.) *Adding Insult to Injury: Nancy Fraser debates her critics*. London: Verso, pp. 246–272

Office for National Statistics (n.d) http://www.neighbourhood.statistics.gov.uk (accessed November 19, 2017)

Office for National Statistics (2016) 'Persistent poverty in the UK and EU: 2014', https://www.ons.gov.uk/peoplepopulationandcommunity/personalandhouseholdfinances/incomeandwealth/articles/persistentpovertyintheukandeu/2014 (accessed November 19, 2017)

O'Hara, M. (2015) *Austerity Bites: A journey to the sharp end of cuts in the UK*. Bristol: Polity Press

Osborne, G. (2012) Speech to Conservative Party Conference, http://www.newstatesman.com/blogs/politics/2012/10/george-osbornes-speechconservative-conference-full-text (accessed March 3, 2017)

Padmore, S. (1994) 'Guiding Lights' in Hamilton, M., Barton, D. and Ivanič, R. (eds.) *Worlds of Literacy*, Clevedon: Multilingual Matters, pp. 143–156

Page, D. (2000) *Communities in the balance: the reality of social exclusion on housing estates*. York: Joseph Rowntree Foundation

Pahl, K. (2002) 'Ephemera, mess and miscellaneous piles: Text and practices in families', *Journal of Early Childhood Literacy*, 2 (2) 145–166

Pahl, K. (2007) 'Timescales and ethnography: understanding a child's meaning making across three sites, a home, a classroom, and a family literacy class', *Ethnography and Education*, 2 (2) 175–190

Pahl, K. (2015) *Materialising Literacies in Communities: the uses of literacy revisited*. London: Bloomsbury

Pahl, K. and Allan C. (2011) 'I don't know what literacy is: Uncovering hidden literacies in a community library using ecological and participatory methodologies with children', *Journal of Early Childhood Literacy,* 11 (2) 190–213

Pahl, K. and Rowsell, J. (eds.) (2006) *Travel Notes from the New Literacy Studies: Instances of practice*. Clevedon: Multilingual Matters

Pahl, K. and Rowsell, J. (2010) *Artifactual Literacies: Every object tells a story*. New York: Teachers College Press

Papen, U. (2010) 'Literacy Mediators, Scribes or Brokers? The Central Role of Others in Accomplishing Reading and Writing,' *Langage et Société*, 133: 63–82

Papen, U. (2012) 'Informal, Incidental and Ad Hoc: The Information-Seeking and Learning Strategies of Health Care Patients,' *Language and Education,* 26 (2) 105–119

Peers, C. (2011) 'The Australian Early Development Index: reshaping family-child relationships in early childhood education', *Contemporary Issues in Early Childhood*, 12 (2) 134–147

Peplow, D., Swann, J, Trimarco, P., and Whiteley, S. (2016) *The Discourse of Reading Groups: Integrating cognitive and sociocultural perspectives*. Abingdon: Routledge

Pickering, M. (2001) *Stereotyping*. Basingstoke: Palgrave

Pink, S. (2004) *Home Truths: Gender, domestic objects and everyday life*. Oxford: Berg

Pink, S (2007) 'Walking with Video', *Visual Studies*, 22 (3) 240–252

Pink, S. (2012) *Situating Everyday Life*. London: Sage

Portes, J. and Reid, H. (2017) 'Distributional results for the impact of tax and welfare reform between 2010–17, modelled in the 2021/22 tax year, *Equalities and Human Rights Commission Research Report*, https://www.equalityhuman-rights.com/sites/default/files/impact-of-tax-and-welfare-reforms-2010-2017-interim-report_0.pdf (accessed November 20, 2017)

Purcell-Gates, V. (1995) *Other People's Words: the cycle of low literacy*. Cambridge, MA: Harvard University Press

Putnam, R. (2000) *Bowling Alone: The collapse and revival of American community*. New York: Simon and Schuster

Rackley, E. (2014) 'Scripture-Based Discourses of Latter-Day Saint and Methodist Youths', *Reading Research Quarterly*, 49 (4) 417–435

Rackley, E. (2016) 'Religious Youth's Motivations for Reading Complex, Religious Texts', *Teachers College Record*, 118 (11) 1–50

Rappaport, J. (2000) 'Community Narratives: Tales of Terror and Joy', *American Journal of Community Psychology*, 28 (1) 1–24

Rayward, W. B. and Jenkins, C. (2007) 'Libraries in Times of War, Revolution, and Social Change', *Library Trends*, 55 (3) 361–369

Reder, S. and Davila, E. (2005) 'Context and literacy practices', *Annual Review of Applied Linguistics*, 25, 170–187

Relph, E. (1976) *Place and placelessness*. London: Pion

Robinson-Pant, A. (2008) 'Why Literacy Matters': Exploring a policy perspective on literacies, identities and social change', *Journal of Development Studies*, 44 (6) 779–796

Robinson-Pant, A. (2010) 'Changing discourses: literacy development in Nepal', *Journal of Educational Development*, 30, 136–144

Rogers, R. (2008) *A Critical Discourse Analysis of Family Literacy Practices: Power in and out of print*. New York: Routledge

Rosowsky, A. (2017) 'The role of Muslim devotional practices in the reversal of language shift', *Journal of Multilingual and Multicultural Development*, 38 (1) 79–93

Roy, A. (2004) 'Peace and the new corporate liberation theology', *Sydney Peace Prize Lecture*, http://sydney.edu.au/news/84.html?newsstoryid=279 (accessed November 20, 2017)

Ryan, F. (2016) 'Eating v heating: this is what destitution looks like', *The Guardian*, https://www.theguardian.com/commentisfree/2016/may/05/decent-toilet-roll-kids-delighted-hope-for-food (accessed November 20, 2017)

Sarangi, S. and Slembrouck, S. (1996) *Language, Bureaucracy and Social Control*. Harlow: Longman

Savage, M. (2015) *Social Class in the 21st Century*. London: Pelican Books

Savage, M., Warde, A. and Devine, F. (2005) 'Capitals, assets, and resources: some critical issues', *The British Journal of Sociology*, 56 (1) 31–47

Saxena, M. (1994) 'Literacies among Punjabis in Southall' in Barton, D. and Ivanič, R. (eds.) *Worlds of Literacy*. Clevedon: Multilingual Matters, pp. 195–214

Scottish Parliament (2011) 'Commission on the Future Delivery of Public Services' http://www.gov.scot/resource/doc/352649/0118638.pdf (accessed November 22, 2017)

Seabrook, J. (2013) *Pauperland: Poverty and the poor in Britain*. London: Hurst

Sennett, R. (2003) *Respect: the formation of character in an age of inequality*. London Allen Lane

Sennett, R. (2012) *Together: the rituals, pleasures and politics of co-operation*. London: Penguin

Sheehy, M. and Leander, K. (2004) 'Introduction' in Leander, K. and Sheehy, M. (eds.) *Spatializing Literacy Research and Practice*. New York: Peter Lang, pp. 1–14

Sheffield Hallam University (2012) *Evaluation of Bookstart England: review of resources*. Centre for Education and Inclusion Research

Shields, R. (1991) *Places on the Margins: Alternative geographies of modernity*. London: Routledge

Sieghart, W. (2014) *Independent Library Report*. Department for Culture, Media and Sport

Sims, R., Medd, W., Mort, M. and Twigger-Ross, C. (2009) 'When a "Home" Becomes a "House": care and caring in the flood recovery process', *Space and Culture*, 12, 303–316

Smith, D. and Schryer, C. (2008) 'On Documentary Society' in Bazerman, C. (ed.) *Handbook of Research on Writing*. New York: Lawrence Erlbaum Associates, pp. 113–128

Smith, H. (2018) 'Cooking the books: what counts as literacy for young children in a public library?', *Literacy*, 52 (1) 31–38

Social Security Advisory Committee (2016) 'Decision Making and Mandatory Reconsideration: a study by the Social Security Advisory Committee Occasional Paper No. 18', https://www.gov.uk/government/uploads/system/uploads/attachment_data/file/538836/decision-making-and-mandatory-reconsideration-ssac-op18.pdf#page=22 (accessed November 20, 2017)

Soja, E. (2004) 'Preface', in Leander, K. and Sheehy, M. (eds.) *Spatializing Literacy Research*. New York: Peter Lang, pp. ix-xv

Stanovich, K. (1986) 'Matthew Effects in Reading: Some consequences of individual differences in the acquisition of literacy', *Reading Research Quarterly*, 21 (4) 360–406

Stanley, L. and Wise, S. (1993) *Breaking Out Again: Feminist Ontology and Epistemology*. New Edition. London: Routledge

Stewart, K. (2007) *Ordinary Affects*. Durham and London: Duke University Press

Street, B. (1984) *Literacy in Theory and Practice*. Cambridge: Cambridge University Press

Street, B. (1993) *Cross Cultural approaches to literacy*. Cambridge. Cambridge University Press

Street, B. (1995) *Social Literacies: Critical approaches to literacy in development, ethnography and education*. Harlow: Pearson Education

Street, B. (2003a) 'The limits of the local – "autonomous" or "disembedding"?', *International Journal of Learning*, 10

Street, B. (2003b) 'What's "new" in New Literacy Studies? Critical approaches to literacy in theory and practice', *Current Issues in Comparative Education*, 5 (2) 77–91

Street, B. (2004) 'Futures of the Ethnography of Literacy?', *Language and Education*, 18 (4) 326–330

Street, B. (2011) 'Literacy inequalities in theory and practice: The power to name and define', *International Journal of Educational Development*, 31, 580–586

Street, B. (2012) 'Contexts for literacy work: New Literacy Studies, multimodality, and the "local and the global", in Tett, L., Hamilton, M. and Crowther, J. (eds.) *More Powerful Literacies*. Leicester: NIACE, pp. 31–58

Street, B. and Street, J. (1991) 'The Schooling of Literacy' in Barton, D. and Ivanič, R. (eds.) *Writing in the Community*. London: Sage, pp. 143–166

Studdert, D. (2005) *Conceptualising Community: Beyond the state and the individual*. Basingstoke: Palgrave Macmillan

Studdert, D. (2016) 'Sociality and a proposed analytic for investigating communal being-ness', *The Sociological Review*, 64, 622–638

Swann, J. and Allington, D. (2009) 'Reading groups and the language of literary texts: a case study in social reading', *Language and Literature*, 18 (3) 247–264

Taylor, D. and Dorsey-Gaines, C. (1988) *Growing Up Literate: Learning from inner-city families*. Portsmouth, NH: Heinemann

Taylor, D. (1996) *Toxic Literacies: Exposing the injustice of bureaucratic texts*. Portsmouth, NH: Heinemann

Taylor, D. (1998) *Family Literacy: Young children learn to read and write* (Second edition). Portsmouth, NH: Heinemann

Thériault, V. (2016) 'Literacy mediation as a form of powerful literacies in community-based organisations working with young people in a situation of precarity', *Ethnography and Education*, 11 (2) 158–173

Thomson, P. Barrett, A,. Hall, C., Hanby, J., and Jones, S. (2014) 'Arts in the community as a place-making event', in Fleming, M., Bresler, L. and O'Toole, J. (eds.) *The Routledge International Handbook of Arts and Education* London: Routledge

Toynbee, P. (2003) *Hard Work: Life in low-pay Britain*. London: Bloomsbury

Tressell, R. (1914 [2004]) *The Ragged Trousered Philanthropists*: London: Penguin Classics

Trussell Trust (2017) https://www.trusselltrust.org/news-and-blog/latest-stats/ (accessed September 28, 2017)

Tuan, Y-F. (1977) *Space and Place: The perspective of experience.* Minneapolis, MN: University of Minnesota Press

Tyler, I. (2013) *Revolting Subjects: Social abjection and resistance in neoliberal Britain.* London: Zed Books

Valentine, G. (2008) 'The ties that bind: towards geographies of intimacy', *Geography Compass,* 2/6 2097–2110

Viseu, A., Clement, A; Aspinall, J. and Kennedy, T. (2006) 'The interplay of public and private spaces in internet access', *Information, Communication and Society,* 9 (5) 633–656

Volk, D. (2008) 'Julializ and Bible Readings in the United States', in Gregory, E. (ed.) *Learning to Read in a New Language: Making sense of words and worlds.* London: Sage. pp. 30–34

Wainwright, E. and Marandet, E. (2013) 'Family learning and the socio-spatial practice of 'supportive' power', *British Journal of Sociology of Education,* 34 (4) 504–524

Ward, A. and Wason-Ellam, L. (2005) 'Reading beyond school: Literacies in a neighbourhood library', *Canadian Journal of Education,* 28 (1/2) 92–108

Wegerif, R. (2013) *Dialogic: Education for the Internet Age.* Oxon: Routledge

Williams, R. (1988) *Keywords: a vocabulary of culture and society.* London: HarperCollins

Wilkinson, R. and Pickett, K. (2010) *The Spirit Level: Why Equality is Better for Everyone.* London: Penguin

Willis, P. (2000) *The Ethnographic Imagination.* Cambridge: Polity Press

Wills, J. (2016) '(Re)Locating community in relationships: questions for public policy', *The Sociological Review,* 64, 639–656

Wood, C., Kemp, N. and Plester, B. (2014) *Text Messaging and Literacy: the evidence.* London: Routledge

Young, M. and Wilmott, P. (2007 [1957]) *Family and Kinship in East London.* London: Penguin

Zeldin, T. (1998) *Conversation: how talk can change your life.* London: The Harvill Press

Zubair, S. (2001) 'Literacies, Gender and Power in Rural Pakistan', in Street, B. V. (ed.) *Literacy and Development: Ethnographic perspectives.* London: Routledge, pp. 188–204

Index

© The Author(s) 2018
S. Jones, *Portraits of Everyday Literacy for Social Justice*,
https://doi.org/10.1007/978-3-319-75945-6